THE LAST PAGAN

THE LAST PAGAN

JULIAN THE APOSTATE

AND THE DEATH OF THE ANCIENT WORLD

Adrian Murdoch

Inner Traditions
Rochester, Vermont

>>> <<<

To my parents

Inner Traditions
One Park Street
Rochester, Vermont 05767
www.InnerTraditions.com

Copyright © 2003, 2005, 2008 by Adrian Murdoch

Originally published in the United Kingdom in 2003 by Sutton Publishing Limited
First U.S. edition published in 2008 by Inner Traditions

Library of Congress Cataloging-in-Publication Data
Murdoch, Adrian.
  The last pagan : Julian the Apostate and the death of the ancient world / Adrian Murdoch. — 1st U.S. ed.
      p. cm.
  Originally published: Stroud, Gloucestershire : Sutton Pub., 2003.
  Includes bibliographical references and index.
  ISBN: 978-1-59477-226-9 (pbk.)
  1. Julian, Emperor of Rome, 331-363. 2. Rome—History—Julian, 361-363.
  3. Rome—Religion. 4. Emperors—Rome—Biography. I. Title.
  DG317.M87 2008
  937'.08092—dc22
  [B]

                                                          2008000587

Printed and bound in the United States

10

Text design and layout by Virginia Scott Bowman
This book was typeset in Sabon with Trajan Pro and Gil Sans as display typefaces.

Extracts from Collected Poems by C. P. Cavafy translated by Edmund Keeley and Philip Sherrard and published by Hogarth Press. Used by permission of the Estate of C. P. Cavafy and The Random House Group Limited.

To send correspondence to the author of this book, mail a first-class letter to the author c/o Inner Traditions • Bear & Company, One Park Street, Rochester, VT 05767, and we will forward the communication.

CONTENTS

LIST OF PLATES AND MAPS

MAPS

1. The Roman world in the fourth century AD
2. Gaul and the Rhine frontier at the time of Julian
3. Julian's campaign against Shapur

PLATES

1. Statue of the Emperor Julian in the Louvre. (AKG London/Erich Lessing)
2. Colossal head of Constantine the Great in the Museo dei Conservatori in Rome. (Bridgeman Art Library)
3A. Aqueduct in Antioch. (AKG London/Erich Lessing)
3B. Sassanid bas-relief showing Mithras and Shapur facing Ahura-Mazda, standing on a fallen Julian. From Taq-i Bustan, Iran. (Bridgeman Art Library)
4. Detail of Julian from Simone Martini's *St. Martin's Renunciation of Arms*. (AKG London)
5. Antonio Verrio's illustrations of Julian's *The Caesars* on the King's Staircase at Hampton Court Palace. (Historic Royal Palaces)
6. The east-facing doorway arch of Shapur's palace at Ctesiphon. (Giraudon/Bridgeman Art Library)

ACKNOWLEDGMENTS

The Last Pagan could not have been written without the help of a number of people. First and foremost, I would like to thank my tutors at The Queen's College, Oxford, especially Dr. Sam Barnish for introducing me to the late Roman world. Thomas Williams encouraged me to write about Julian. His insights into the classical mind have been an inspiration and a delight for many years. I cannot begin to thank Kamal Mehta enough for her insightful comments on the final manuscript. I have benefited hugely from the help of Ilona Gymer, Dr. Malcolm Read, David Derrick, Dr. John Kelt, Renny Hutchison, and John Hatfield. Christopher Feeney and his colleagues at Sutton Publishing have been unfailingly helpful, as have the staff of Glasgow University Library. I would like to thank my wife, Susy, for her forbearance while I was writing this book. She read the first draft of every chapter, discussed every historical point of contention, and has lived with Julian for too long. Finally, I must thank my father, without whose constant help and advice I could never have finished *The Last Pagan*. All mistakes, of course, remain my own.

A Note on Names

Trying to achieve any kind of consistency of names when writing about the ancient world is a near impossibility. To use only ancient names rapidly becomes an exercise in pedantry. While most people would be comfortable reading Lutetia for Paris, it seems hardly sensible to use Londinium and Ancyra for London and Ankara respectively. On the other hand if you use only modern names—Antakya rather than Antioch and Taq-i-Kesra rather than Ctesiphon—you risk losing the reader. A further problem arises the further East that you travel, especially where history meets transliteration. Consider the Syrian city of Manbij, the town that Julian will have known as Hierapolis. At various times in its long history it has been known as Bambyce, Mabug, Mabbog, Bumbuj, Membij, and Membej. The best you can hope for is a compromise. The rule I have followed is that where there is a known and familiar anglicized version of a city name, I have tried to use that: so we have Cologne, Milan, and Aleppo rather than Köln, Milano, or Haleb. In all other cases I have referred to towns by the names I believe will be understood by the greatest number of people.

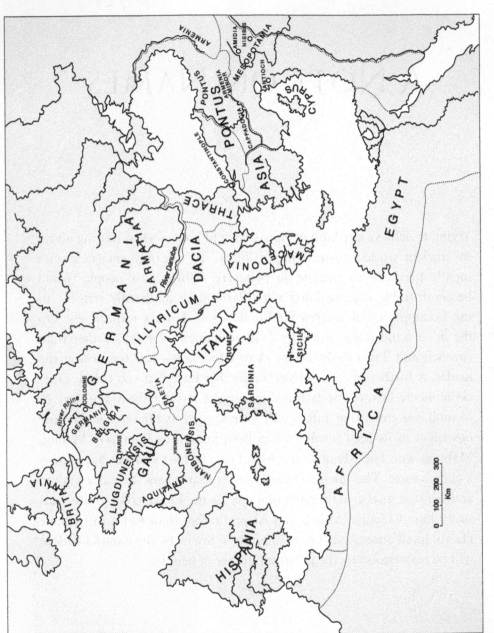

Map 1. The Roman world in the fourth century AD

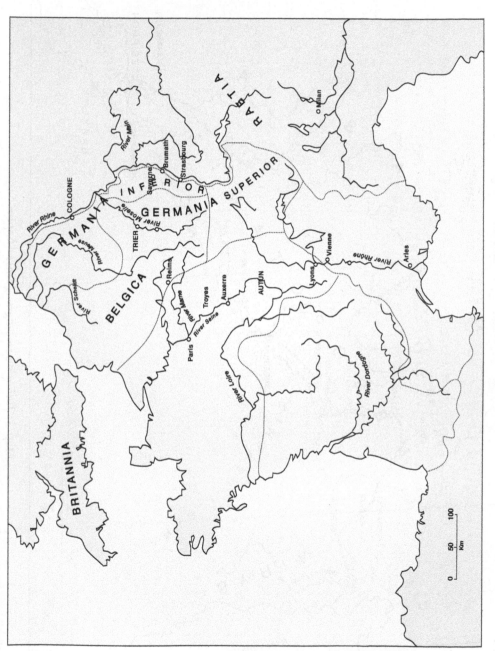

Map 2. Gaul and the Rhine frontier at the time of Julian

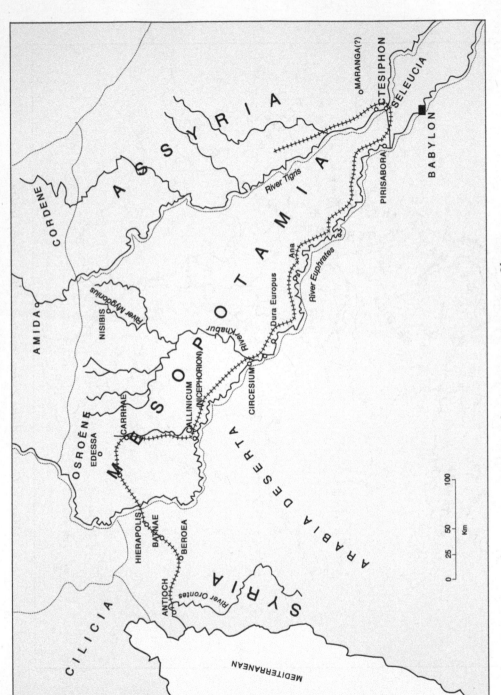

Map 3. Julian's campaign against Shapur

INTRODUCTION

THE BRITTLE GLASS

> I shall die as my fathers died, and sleep as they sleep,
>> even so.
> For the glass of the years is brittle wherein we gaze for
>> a span;
> A little soul for a little bears up this corpse which is
>> man.
> So long I endure, no longer; and laugh not again,
>> neither weep.
> For there is no God found stronger than death; and
>> death is a sleep.

ALGERNON CHARLES SWINBURNE,

HYMN TO PROSERPINE

 At around midnight a man died in a tent roughly fifty-three miles north of the capital of what is now Iraq. It was the end of June, AD 363, and with him paganism died.

A month after his thirty-first birthday, Flavius Claudius Julianus, better known as Julian the Apostate, had been ruler of the Roman Empire

1

for less than two years. He was dark haired, of average height for the era—around 5 foot 4 inches—and with a trim build. Underneath his hair, which he tended to wear combed down onto his forehead like all the members of his family, he had penetrating eyes, heavy eyebrows, a straight nose, and a rather large mouth with a pendulous lower lip that was hidden behind the bristly beard he wore trimmed to a point, like those you can see of the ancient Greek philosophers in the Louvre or the British Museum. It was a deliberate affectation, a sign of his deep love of Hellenic culture and passionate hatred of the Galileans, as he dubbed Christians. Many mocked him and called him a goat behind his back.

He had been wounded in battle, three months into a campaign in the East against the Persian Empire and its king, Shapur II. Although the Roman army had been advancing slowly in readiness for battle, Julian, who had gone on ahead to reconnoiter, had received word that the rear-guard had been ambushed from behind. As he rode back to lend moral support to those in the rear, he was summoned by the news that the van, which he had just left, had been similarly attacked. Before he could restore the position, a troop of Parthian cuirassiers attacked the center and breached its left wing. The soldiers broke ranks in confusion—just as Alexander the Great's had in India six centuries previously—at the sight, smell, and noise of elephants.

But the center held and the enemy was beaten off. Julian charged at the Persians to encourage his soldiers to pursue the now routed army. It was a foolhardy move. He had forgotten his breastplate and was armed only with a shield—some say that he was confident in his victory but more plausibly he had rushed out without time to put on his armor, or perhaps had disregarded it because of the heat of the Mesopotamian summer. There was blood everywhere, and dying and screaming men. The confusion was made worse because as the battle raged, a violent dust storm had arisen that reduced visibility so much that reports say that the sky and the sun were totally concealed by the clouds.

Nonetheless Julian continued his attack, shouting and waving his arms. In his enthusiasm and in the heat of the battle, he had only one attendant. The rest of the emperor's escort of guards had been scattered in the mêlée.

A horseman appeared through the dust charging at full gallop. He rode up and aimed his cavalry lance directly at the emperor. It found its mark. The spear grazed Julian's arm, pierced his ribs, and ended up in the lower part of his liver. It was a double-bladed spear, so sharp that as Julian tried to pull it out he cut the fingers of his right hand to the bone.

In pain he fell from his horse. Although now weak from loss of blood, Julian tried to conceal what had occurred from his soldiers. He remounted straightaway and gave some orders, calling out to everyone he met not to be afraid about his wound for it was not fatal. He then lost consciousness. Men rushed to the spot and the emperor was carried to the camp and laid out on his lion skin and straw bed where he received medical attention.

Four people were with Julian as he died: his doctor and confidant Oribasius; a friend from his tours of duty in Gaul, Salutius Secundus, prefect of the East; and two philosophers Maximus and Priscus. On his deathbed he asked after Anatolius, his minister of finance. Aware that he was about to die, the emperor had wanted to appoint him executor of his will. When told that he had fallen in battle, the emperor spent time mourning him.

In his last hours, Julian engaged his friends in a philosophic dialogue about the nature of the soul. Aware that they were in enemy territory, harried on all sides, and about to be without a leader, they kept interrupting him and begged him to appoint a successor. Julian had decided to leave that decision to the army, his men—many of whom had followed him faithfully all the way from Gaul. Suddenly the wound in his side gaped wide and the veins in his throat swelled up and obstructed his breath. He asked for, and drank, some cold water. Then at around midnight, Julian lost consciousness and passed away peacefully.

The rule of few Roman emperors had been quite so eagerly anticipated as Julian's. When the new emperor entered Constantinople, the capital of the Roman Empire, on December 11, 361, he was met by the classical equivalent of a ticker-tape parade. His popularity is hardly surprising; Julian was young, quick-witted, and had a proven track record in the two areas most citizens cared about—on the battlefield and in reducing taxes. He was also popular with the soldiery and despite his obvious adherence to pagan religion; there was little trace of sectarianism about him.

As emperor, Julian ruled for only eighteen months, yet his reign is a beacon of light in the later Roman Empire and the story of Julian's life and death has survived vividly. Along with Constantine, he is arguably the only late Roman emperor of whom most people have heard. How did this happen?

First, Julian was different. The previous century had been a time of upheaval and a series of violent and forgettable soldier emperors sat on the throne. As often as not they were soon murdered by the men who had put them there in the first place. An intellectual was a curiosity and a novelty.

The battle that Julian picked—Christianity—was fought by the era's greatest and most articulate thinkers. When the emperor Constantine accepted Christianity as the religion of the Roman Empire in 313, he let loose a philosophy that was to pervade every aspect of political, social, cultural, and, of course, religious life right up to modern times. But that is all with the benefit of hindsight. Christianity did not become the official winner until seventeen years after Julian's death. When Julian took the purple, the battle against Christianity was by no means over. The Christians were not a unified organization, splintered as they were into numerous groups; indeed, much of the empire was still pagan.

At a time when neither pagan nor Christian ideologies reigned supreme, the state of your soul was arguably the single most important issue of the day. Few were short of opinions on the last Roman emperor to oppose Christianity—seen most trenchantly in the way that he is still best known as the "Apostate," the one who renounced Christianity—and it is of little surprise that both pagan and Christian apologists comment extensively on his reign, in Latin, Greek, Syriac, Arabic, and Armenian. For most writers then, as now, Julian is either monster or saint. He was just as Napoleon was to the Italian poet Manzoni: "an object of undying hatred and incomparable love."

When news of his death broke, one of the emperor's closest friends wailed: "Gone is the glory of good. The company of the wicked and the licentious is uplifted. . . . Now the broad path, the great doors lie wide open for the doers of evil to attack the just. The walls are down."[1] At the same time, a former fellow student from the university in Athens trumpeted the death of "the dragon, the apostate, the great mind, the Assyrian, the public and private enemy of all in common, him that has madly raged and threatened much upon earth, and that has spoken and mediated much unrighteousness against Heaven."[2] It is a cry that is as exultant as it is pitiless.

As a result of the passion that he generated, Julian's reign is one of the best-illuminated periods in antiquity. It is comparable to, and arguably much better served than, the latter days of the Roman republic and the early empire. But even more intriguing, a huge range of Julian's own writings has survived, more so than of any other Roman ruler. For Julius Caesar we have the self-serving propaganda of *The Civil War* and *Conquest of Gaul* of which one modern editor dryly notes: "des Mémoires ne sont pas des *Confessions.*" For the philosopher emperor Marcus Aurelius we have his stoic *Meditations,* which tell us a great deal about his thoughts on philosophy but very little about the man himself. But in Julian's vast array of extant writings—which run to over 700 pages—we have more than sixty letters, both public and private, speeches, philosophical and religious thoughts, even a satire.

What all of this material does is to make Julian emerge from history a vital, engaging, flesh and blood man. It is too easy to pigeonhole many of the other great Roman leaders, from Julius Caesar, the consummate politician and Trajan, the workaholic soldier, to Constantine, the cynical opportunist. But the wealth of contemporary material gives us Julian warts and all. He can be kind, thoughtful, funny, and whimsical. He can also be petulant, childish, bad-tempered, and even sulky.

But we do not just remember Julian because he is a three-dimensional character. A mystique developed around the emperor because of the mythic nature of his demise, something that continues to intrigue. Julian has in many ways become a figure of far greater potency in death than he ever was alive. Who was that mysterious cavalryman? The Persian king offered a reward for Julian's killer, yet it was never claimed. Within a few years various suggestions had been made which range from the plausible to the utterly fanciful. They emerged almost at once and make Julian's death the classical equivalent of the JFK assassination—the cavalryman became a fourth-century spearman on the grassy knoll. Even contemporaries admitted as much. "One and the same story is not told by all, but different accounts are reported and made up by different people—both of those present at the battle and those not present,"[3] wrote one former friend.

For many pagans, Julian's death had parallels with that of his spiritual mentor Alexander the Great—indeed he had not wholly discouraged those comparisons during his lifetime—at its most basic level with the war in Asia Minor itself. One historian writing only fifty years or so after the emperor's death, suggested that Julian believed that he was possessed of Alexander's soul.[4]

But Julian never did comprehensively defeat the Persian king and he never did conquer Asia, and this is a complementary part of the attraction. Julian failed, quite magnificently and irredeemably. The romantic failure has always been attractive in Western thought and not only did few of Julian's innovations survive his death, many were starting to unravel even before he died. Just as when reading Shakespeare's *Hamlet*, Goethe's *Sorrows of Young Werther*, or Pushkin's *Eugene Onegin*, the reader of any biography of the emperor knows that Julian is doomed from the beginning. He stops being an emperor and starts being a tragic hero.

The dark portent of Julian's death is brought into sharp relief because, unlike literature, there are so few moments in history that can be regarded as definitive watersheds. Take the fall of the Roman Empire as an example. When did it finally collapse? Was it on August 24, 410, when Rome was sacked by Alaric the Visigoth? Was it on September 4, 476, when the last of the Western Roman emperors, the thirteen-year-old Romulus Augustulus, was deposed by barbarians and sent off to live in peace and obscurity with his relatives near Naples? Or was it on May 29, 1453, when Constantine XI, the final Byzantine emperor, died on the ramparts of Byzantium clutching a picture of the Virgin Mary to his chest as the Turks sacked the city?

In a way all of them are right. But with the death of Julian we have something different. To all intents and purposes we can say that paganism died as a credible political and social force in the last days of June 363.

As soon as the man becomes myth, he becomes depersonalized.

It was in his role as an opponent of Christianity that Julian not only became best known, but known at all. As such he was lumped together with all the other opponents of the Church. When, in the aftermath of the murder of Thomas Beckett in 1170, a French archbishop wrote to the pope to complain about Henry II, he refers to the actions of the English king as exhibiting the "wickedness of Nero, the perfidiousness of Julian and even the sacrilegious treachery of Judas."

The emperor became a touchstone for man's relationship with God and the Church throughout history. In the unwavering Christian societies from the Middle Ages to the seventeenth century it was a black-and-white affair. One of the biographers of Charlemagne refers to Julian simply as "hateful in the eyes of God,"[5] while John Milton in his pamphlet on the freedom of the press written in 1644 called the emperor "the subtlest enemy to our faith."

As society's relationship with God began to change during the Enlightenment, so too Julian's position shifted in the popular mind. The emperor's apostasy fitted Voltaire's idea of abstract deism as well as his anti-clericalism. The author of *Candide* famously dismissed a contemporary biography of the emperor by the Abbé de la Bleterie with: "above all you must be dispassionate and that is not something that ever applies to a priest." It is not hard to imagine Julian saying the same thing. The Roman emperor was being reborn as a creature of the Enlightenment and began to stand for the liberation of man. Most influentially of all, Edward Gibbon made Julian the hero of the *Decline and Fall of the Roman Empire*.

But by the end of the nineteenth century it was the emperor's paganism that was celebrated by the later Victorian poets like Swinburne and writers like Thomas Hardy, only for him to suffer again in the twentieth century. The brilliant modern Greek poet, Constantine Cavafy, who wrote a cycle of nine poems about Julian, thought that the emperor was "a bore and perhaps the only thing he tolerated in him was the fact that his was a lost cause"[6] while Gore Vidal's 1964 novel *Julian* brings us almost full circle, presenting an overly exuberant young philosopher king.

If all of this shape-shifting seems confusing to the reader, it presents even more problems for the biographer. The difficulty with trying to disentangle Julian the man from Julian the myth is that almost too much has survived. Nonetheless, it is possible to strip away the many veneers of bias and distortion and see the man, his motivations, and the world in which he lived.

There are always going to be difficulties in understanding a man who stood on the boundary of the classical and medieval world, particularly in a society that has become distanced from the day-to-day practice of religion. But these challenges can be overcome and it is possible to make the connection across the centuries. After all, the idea of divine voices, visions, and revelations in the contemporary framework of our understanding would appear no more odd to Julian than our speaking of the subconscious would to him.

It is unfair that Julian is still known to us primarily for attributed and spurious dying words. That tradition has the wounded and dying emperor filling his hand with blood, flinging it into the air and crying: "Thou hast conquered, O Galilean!" But then the history, as ever, was written by the winning side. Whether the Galilean actually won or not, it is perfectly possible to go beyond an entry in the *Oxford Dictionary of Quotations* and look not just at Julian's death but, beyond that, to his life, to see how he was a product of his time. It was a narrow—one might even say lucky—victory for the Galilean, and Julian might just as easily have entered the history books as Julian the Philosopher rather than as Julian the Apostate.

1
RETURN OF THE GODS

> *See they return; ah, see the tentative*
> *Movements, and the slow feet,*
> *The trouble in the pace and the uncertain*
> *Wavering!*
>
> EZRA POUND, *THE RETURN*

When the emperor Diocletian retired to his palace on the Dalmatian Coast to tend his cabbages in May 305 Julian's family spent a great deal of the next fifty years developing ingenious ways to kill each other.

The background of the family was not that of pampered nobility; they were hard, grim fighters. Julian's grandfather was an Illyrian soldier called Flavius Constantius, generally identified by his nickname "Chlorus"—best translated by the Scots expression "peely-wally" though normally rendered "green-faced" or simply "pale." Constantius Chlorus had risen through the ranks to become first Caesar—deputy emperor—and then eventually Augustus. En route he had picked up Helena. Far better known now than her partner, she famously, at the age of eighty, went on a pilgrimage to the Holy Land, where legend has

9

it that she discovered the True Cross. Another tradition, one explored by Evelyn Waugh in his fictionalized biography of her, portrays Helena as British, a prototype Essex girl. That legend has her as the daughter of Coel of Caercovin, the Old King Cole of the nursery rhyme. Rather more prosaically, she seems to have been the daughter of an innkeeper, from Bithynia, in the northeast of what is now Turkey.

It was Helena's son, born on February 27, 272, in modern Nis in Serbia, who was to become the next emperor even though Constantius Chlorus was later forced to put her aside in favor of the more politically appropriate daughter of his boss. The man who has become known as Constantine the Great became the only emperor to be hailed as such in Britain, close to the spot where his bronze statue stands today by the south door of York Minster, on the death of his father on July 26, 306. Constantine was thirty-three.

The six years it took for Constantine to consolidate his position are a confusing blur of conflicts, culminating in the decisive battle of Milvian Bridge, just north of Rome. Warring factions, each with as much of a right to the throne as the other, tried to get the upper hand in the West. But when Constantine entered the city in triumph after the battle in October 312 and addressed the Senate, he had won.

Constantine was now emperor of the West. The East had suffered a similarly bloody power struggle, but by February of the following year, Constantine's counterpart Licinius (dismissed by Julian as a "miserable old man"[1]) was effectively sole Augustus in the East. An *entente* only patchily *cordiale* was drawn up in Milan, one of the empire's unofficial capitals. The two agreed to rule together and, as a sign of good faith, Licinius married Constantine's sister. The partnership stumbled along for another eleven years until verbal conflicts became physical. Licinius was captured in battle in September 324 and, after a short period under house arrest, was executed. Constantine was now sole emperor—the first time the empire had seen this in forty years.

He was to remain in power for the next thirteen years. Those years were a time of welcome stability and consolidation as the empire breathed a sigh of relief. Most obviously this was seen economically. The introduction of a new gold coin, the *solidus,* helped to alleviate the inflation that had plagued the reign of previous emperors.

Of course it is for his Christianity that Constantine is best known. His conversion is traditionally dated to the eve of the battle of Milvian Bridge. One legend, propagated by the man he had hired as tutor to his son, has it that the emperor was commanded in a dream that his soldiers write the sign of Christ—the first two letters of his name in Greek—on their shields.[2] The more Hollywood version that emerged twenty-five years after the event (beautifully depicted by Raphael in the Vatican Museum) has Constantine seeing a cross in the sky at midday bearing the words "By this sign you will be the victor."[3]

Julian, on the other hand, was later to ascribe Constantine's conversion to guilt. The emperor was responsible for a series of murders that occurred in 326—among them that of his twenty-one-year-old bastard son Crispus and of his first wife Fausta.[4] The details surrounding these gruesome deaths are difficult to discern, made even more so as they are tinged by rumors of a sexual relationship between the two, but appear to have their origin in a dynastic dispute. It seems that Fausta had accused Crispus, the golden boy of the empire and therefore a threat to any of Constantine's other children, of treason. When the truth emerged, only after the execution of his son, Fausta was suffocated in the sauna.

In his satirical fantasy *The Caesars,* written thirty-five years after the deaths and long enough for rumor to have become fact, Julian portrays Constantine as a sensualist in every sense. In a viciously funny passage, when asked to pick a god, Constantine runs first to Pleasure who leads him to Dissolution and finally to Jesus who offers to wash away his sins.[5]

The realities of the depth and timings of Constantine's conversion to Christianity are much more complex issues. It was a conversion only in the sense that the empire was now more open to other ideas and not a Christian one in a sense that would be understood today. But Constantine's belief that Christianity was a good thing for the Roman Empire, and the disappearance of religious persecution with his Edict of Toleration in 313, was the breach in the wall of centuries of intolerance.

Despite the momentous symbolism of this move, it is crucial to remember that paganism did not disappear overnight. Pagan gods appeared on coins until quite late in Constantine's reign and for all the program of church building that the emperor instituted (most famously

St. Peter's in Rome and the Church of the Holy Sepulchre in Jerusalem),
he continued to allow temples to be dedicated to him. There was no
mass conversion and as yet there was no unified Catholic Church—
one of the prerequisites of a Christian empire. Indeed, what marks this
period is confusion, as Christianity tried simultaneously to develop
both a theology and a structure. All that had really changed was the
empire's attitude.

But Constantine's crowning glory was the new capital of the
empire, Constantinople, the city that for eleven centuries carried his
name. Constantine picked the ancient town of Byzantium, founded by
Greek emigrants from one of Athens' neighbors in Greece, to celebrate
the emperor's victory over his opponents. It had been consecrated on
November 8, 324, and dedicated less than six years later, on May 11,
330, just in time for Constantine's jubilee. The relocation of the capital from Italy to the ancient Greek city of Byzantium—like Rome it
was built on seven hills and divided into fourteen districts—was one
of the most significant events of the later Roman Empire. Some said
that Constantine had moved the capital out of pique at Rome's calcified
republican and pagan elite. It was certainly noted that the new capital
had a Greek name—the *polis*, or city of Constantine—not a Latin one,
and had an overriding Christian atmosphere. More plausibly, however,
it was a move born out of more prosaic, economic, and logistical reasons. As the centers of the empire moved eastward, Rome increasingly
appeared an anachronism and, more damning, both a monetary liability
and a political irrelevance. In the West it had already been superseded
by centers in Milan and Trier.

The new site was ideal for a capital—a triangular peninsula that
dominated the land route from Europe to Asia and the sea route from
the Black Sea to the Mediterranean. The strip of water off the peninsula's northern coast known as the Golden Horn made a perfect natural
harbor, while the city was protected to the south by the Sea of Marmara
with the landward side comparatively short and easy to defend. From
a logistical point of view, the city was better positioned than Rome,
too. The two fronts that consistently gave the empire the most head-
aches—the Danube frontier and Sassanid Persia to the east—were easily
accessible. Soon Byzantium had become Constantinople, but the locals

preferred to call it simply *stan polin* or "the city," which provides the roots for the name of the modern city of Istanbul.

It was here, two years later, in the middle of May 332[6] that a son was born to Constantine's half-brother, Julius Constantius. Julius and his brother had suffered in their youth at the hands of Constantine's mother. The willful Helena had never accepted the fact that her relationship had been broken up for the good of the state. She took revenge on her husband's children and made sure that they were kept out of the public eye and, at various times, under house arrest. It was not until after her death in 328 that Constantine relented and the emperor's half-brother found himself back in Constantinople, in a luxurious palace with many of the glamorous trappings of power, if not the actual thing itself. Here he met his second wife, Basilina.

The young Flavius Claudius Julianus, the couple's only child, was born in the world's newest capital, nephew to the emperor, and very much part of the dynasty. His mother, daughter of a noble family from Bithynia, had died soon after giving birth to him but there is no reason to suppose that Julian's first few years were anything other than happy. He lived in the heart of the new capital with his father and spent a great deal of time with his maternal grandmother on her estate on the southern shore of the Sea of Marmara. Many years later Julian was to write an intensely evocative letter describing his happy summers there.

> My grandmother gave me a small estate of four fields just a few miles from the Sea of Marmara and I am giving you this as an offering to your great affection for me. It is too small either to bring a man any great wealth or to make him seem rich, but it is a present that cannot fail to please you, at least a little. . . . It is just over two miles from the sea so no trader or sailor disturbs the place with chatter and cheek. Yet it is not completely deprived of the favors of Nereus [a sea god] because it has a constant supply of fish so fresh that they are still gasping. And if you walk up onto a sort of hill away from the house, you will see the sea, the Propontis, the islands and Constantinople. Nor will you have to stand on seaweed and brambles, or be annoyed by the rubbish that is always thrown out on beaches and sands, which is so very unpleasant and unmentionable.

No, you will stand on the smilax, thyme, and fragrant grasses. It is extremely peaceful to lie down there and gaze into some book and then while resting one's eyes it is very agreeable to look at the ships and the sea.[7]

If the family had seemed bloody up to now, no one could have predicted the carnage that resulted in the struggle for supremacy in the months after Constantine's death on May 22, 337, in a barn just outside Nicomedia. By September 9, when the emperor's three sons—Constantine II, Constantius II, and Constans—were officially declared emperors by the army, all of the males who could have posed a credible challenge to the throne had been eliminated.

A chronology of these four confusing and event-filled months is almost impossible to establish—the only two firm dates are the ones mentioned above. Nonetheless it was probably in mid- to late August that eight family members were killed, including Julian's father and the elder of his two half-brothers, as well as some other senior figures who might have supported them. In true mythic form, the only survivors of this massacre were Julian and his other half-brother Gallus—the former was thought to be too young to be any real threat and the latter was ill. The general view was that nature would achieve what the sword had failed to do. There was obviously little opportunity to play on family feelings even though Gallus was Constantius's brother-in-law (the emperor had married his sister). The boys' survival is most likely down to the intervention and protection offered by Eusebius of Nicomedia. He was a bishop—indeed, had baptized Constantine—but what made him an appropriate guardian was not his religious credentials but that he was related to Julian's mother and one of the few male relatives alive.

There is little doubt that the massacre was, if not engineered by Constantius, Constantine's favorite son and now emperor of the East, then not stopped by him. There would be enough circumstantial evidence to convict him today and the action was not out of character. On several other occasions, Constantius was to have no qualms about putting to death those suspected of treason on the most slender of evidence. Julian certainly always blamed his cousin and was later to write of him: "Our fathers were brothers, sons of the same father. And close relations as we were, how this most humane emperor treated us. He put to death six of our cousins, my father who was his uncle, another of our uncles on my father's side and my eldest brother, without trial."[8] It is hard to point the finger at any other suspect: Constantius had a motive, he was in Constantinople at the time and, most incriminating of all, he was the main beneficiary.

If the character of Julian has suffered at the hands of Christian bias, in many ways Constantius has suffered worse. Now aged thirty, he was born in Sirmium, Sremska Mitrovica in Serbia, on August 17, 317. Although he was a dull, rather uncharismatic emperor, most interpretations have seen him as at best an incompetent, at worst a paranoid monster. The most pleasant that Julian could come up with was that his rule was no different from that of Constantine,[9] a sentiment that can be taken many ways, as he undoubtedly intended. The jaundiced view of soldier and historian Ammianus Marcellinus is the most voluble, but neither pagan nor Christian writers had much time for Constantius. To the former he was the murderer of Julian's family; to the latter he was a supporter of Arianism. And however lukewarm his adherence to that Christian spin-off may have been, he was still a meddling heretic. One went as far as calling him the Antichrist.[10]

What was he really like? Physically Constantius was unprepossessing. He had blond hair with dark coloring, frog-like eyes and short and bowed legs. He was not intellectually gifted, one of the reasons he hid behind the pomp and ritual of the court. An out-and-out monster he might not have been, but there was a nasty and sneaky aspect to his personality.

Several of the more subtle analyses of his character comment that Constantius was much better at fighting civil wars than actual wars. The emperor had more need of experience in the former than the latter, but this does not fully explain away the fact that he was not above using any means necessary to protect his position. On at least two occasions he sent fake letters to people to draw them to the capital and their deaths.

It is a sign of his inadequacy that if his reign has a characteristic it is that he was easily swayed. More than any other emperor of the period, Constantius was overly influenced in his decisions by the people who surrounded him; the courtiers and the eunuchs who made up the court. Julian was later to refer to "the wild beasts that surrounded him and cast their evil eyes on all men,"[11] while a bishop more elegantly, but no less harshly, wrote: "I find that he does not possess common understanding, but that his mind is solely regulated by the suggestions of others and that he has no mind of his own at all."[12]

With all potential rivals out of the way, Constantine's three sons now had the empire to themselves. As with other triumvirates throughout history, soon there were only two. Constantine II was killed trying to invade his brother Constans's lands two and a half years later, in March 340, and again the empire found itself split between East and West. In the meantime, however, neither Constantius nor the politics of the next years had much impact on the boys. Young Julian was taken off by his mother's family to Nicomedia, while his brother ended up studying near Ephesus, probably on the land of his paternal grandmother. It is worth wondering how much the five-year-old Julian was aware of what was happening around him. He was still surrounded by luxury, but many of the people who had been most familiar to him had been taken away. Was there a code of silence to protect him? It is impossible to guess; yet it would be melodramatic to say that Julian was completely starved of affection. He was an orphan, that is true, but he spent much time with his grandmother and he developed a close relationship with his uncle, his mother's brother Julianus, which was to last until the end of his life.

It was here, at Nicomedia, that Julian's education began. The future emperor was first taught by a Gothic eunuch called Mardonius who had been the tutor of Julian's own mother and the boy was brought up reading the classics of Greek literature: Homer, Hesiod, the Greek playwrights, both tragedians and comedians, and the philosophers. Mardonius was an inspiration and the two soon became close.[13]

It does not require a vast amount of psychological analysis to understand the depth of the relationship that grew up between the two. Mardonius was probably one of the few people not to have treated the young boy like an unexploded bomb. The link with his mother and her family gave him a connection to his own family that he never had the chance to make in person. Julian himself gives a great deal of insight into those early years. Much later, while emperor and staying in Antioch, he describes how his tutor made him look at the ground as he walked to school and forbade him to go to the theater. "While I was still a mere boy my tutor would often say to me: 'Never let the crowd of your play-mates who flock to the theaters lead you into the mistake of craving such spectacles as these. Do you have a passion for horse races? There is one in Homer, very cleverly described. Take the book and study it,'" he writes with studied irony.[14]

If his upbringing sounds strict to modern ears, the time with Mardonius was a time of peace and idyll. Two years later, when Eusebius was promoted bishop of Constantinople, Julian went too and moved back to the capital. But by the time he was nine, Julian had come to understand what being of the house of Constantine meant. However young the boy might have been, he was still a son of Julius Constantius and always a potential focus for rebellion. His presence in the capital was considered too much of an accident waiting to happen and after the death of the bishop, there was no one to speak up for them. Julian and Gallus were unceremoniously shipped off to Macellum—an imperial estate, yet for all that a secluded gilded cage, in central Turkey in 342. The palace itself was just north of Hisarcik, in the shadow of the daunt-ing Mount Erciyas, the Mount Argaeus of antiquity, for most of the year covered with snow. The peculiarly lunar quality of the landscape of Cappadocia can have done little to alleviate the sense of banishment under which Julian must have suffered.[15]

Although Mardonius had come with Julian to Constantinople, he did not follow to Macellum. Few details have survived about the boys' time there and it is tempting to read too much into the facts that we do have. Julian's own description is wretched: "We lived as though on the estate of a stranger and we were watched as though we were in some Persian garrison. No stranger came to see us and none of our old friends were allowed to visit us. We lived shut off from every liberal study and from all free speech in a glittering servitude, sharing the exercises of our own slaves as though they were friends. No one our age ever came near us or was allowed to do so."[16]

Even allowing for some exaggeration it appears to have been a miserable time—cut off from all contact his own age except his brother.

Despite the rapidity with which boys then became men, it is worth questioning what the ten-year-old Julian and the sixteen-year-old Gallus had in common, especially as they were to all intents and purposes strangers. The differences between them were heightened not only by their dissimilar temperament and interests, but more simply by their looks: Julian's dark hair contrasting with Gallus's blond coloring. An uneasy awareness of why he was imprisoned must have affected the already bookish young man, exacerbated by the fact that eunuchs from court kept a close watch on their every move—even their attendance at church—and by what can presumably have been the lack of discussion about the violent events of the summer of 337. Julian was not taken in by Constantius's protestations of innocence. "They kept telling us and tried to convince us that Constantius had acted in this way partly because he was deceived and partly because he gave into the violence and tumult of an undisciplined and mutinous army," was his skeptical comment several years later.[17]

While the emperor's biographers played down the years in Macellum giving us few insights into life there, Julian himself mentions that he was saved by books—almost the only things not rationed by Constantius. "Through philosophy, the gods caused me to remain untouched by my situation and unharmed," he wrote.[18] We know the kinds of books that Julian read. Many years later George, bishop of Caesarea who was nominally supervising Julian's education in Macellum, was promoted to bishop of Alexandria. There he was lynched by an angry mob and Julian wrote two letters asking local officials for his library. The first one was written to the prefect of Egypt two months into his reign and just after Julian had heard about the lynching.

> Some men have a passion for horses, others for birds, others again for wild beasts; but I, from childhood have been infused with a passionate longing to acquire books. It would therefore be absurd if I should suffer these to be appropriated by men, whose inordinate desire for wealth gold alone cannot satiate, and who unscrupulously design to steal these as well. Grant me therefore this personal favor, that all of the books which belonged to George be looked out. In his house there were many on philosophy, many on rhetoric

and many as well on the teachings of the impious Galileans. These latterly I should wish to be utterly annihilated but for fear that along with them more useful works may be destroyed by mistake; let all these also be looked for with the greatest care. Let George's secretary take charge of this search for you and if he hunts for them faithfully, let him know that he will obtain his freedom as a reward, but that if he is in any way dishonest in the business, he will be tortured. And I know what books George had, many of them, at any rate if not all; for he lent me some of them to copy when I was in Cappadocia and these he received back.[19]

The secretary obviously did not apply himself to this task as rapidly as the emperor had intended and five months later Julian wrote to him directly.[20] Presumably the request was complied with.

Even though he was now emperor and clearly had more interest in the pagan volumes to be shipped to him, as a member of a family, which had led the conversion of the empire and surrounded as he was by bishops, of course his literary diet at that point would have been predominantly Christian. Julian was probably baptized in these years and became a reader in the church—it was his job to read lessons during the Eucharist.

Two anecdotes have survived which have a ring of truth about them. The first is a vignette of Julian practicing debating with his brother. He always took the position of the pagan because, he said, he wanted to "practice the weaker argument."[21] Even though his apostasy lay somewhat in the future, it is easy to see the quick-minded and quick-tongued Julian trying to outmaneuver his brother. The second, which has survived in a number of sources, tells how both Julian and Gallus decided to rebuild the church to St. Mamas.[22] In itself this was not an extraordinary move. The idea of philanthropy from noble families was well known. Julian's mother, a committed Christian throughout her life, left money to dedicate a church in Ephesus after her death. Symbolically (though not too surprisingly in what is, after all, an area notorious for earthquakes) the part built by Julian fell down, while that of Gallus remained standing.

A more immediately significant event that occurred in those six years is Constantius's visit. A precise date is difficult to give, but the first quarter of 347 is likely as Constantius was in the region, passing through on his way to the eastern front. The pomp and circumstance of the imperial court arriving must have impressed and terrified the fourteen-year-old Julian. Up until now, the man who had massacred his family and the boy who was to become emperor had never met face-to-face. We do not know what happened—Julian did not write about it—but the question must be asked of why Constantius came. It is easy to interpret this as guilt on the part of Constantius—wanting to face the boys whose father he had killed—but this is unlikely. It is far more likely that the emperor had had no need, no interest, and no desire to see them until then. And even more damning to Julian's hagiographers, it is unlikely that he was the purpose of the visit—the boy was simply not important enough. It makes much more sense that the emperor wanted to see Gallus, not Julian, as a potential resource.

This explanation is lent weight by the events of the following year. In 348 the cage was unlocked and the two brothers were separated again. Gallus, now twenty-two, after a brief stay in his lands in Ephesus, was given the Hobson's choice of court. The open politicking of Constantius's circle must have come as a shock after the quiet of Macellum. For Julian, on the other hand, it must have seemed a time of comparative freedom as long as he steered well clear of anything to do with politics. He was given his grandmother's estate (she had died during his incarceration), and so found himself, aged sixteen, with an assured income and the freedom to continue studying.

He was soon back in the schools of Constantinople and studying under Nicocles the Spartan and Hecebolius, an interesting pair, the first a pagan and one of the best-known grammarians of the age, the second a Christian. The former is usually credited with a greater influence on the young man, giving him advanced lessons on Homer, while Hecebolius, who taught Julian rhetoric, is often seen as a little second rate.

It is difficult to assess the influence of Julian's tutors at this period primarily because the young man found himself caught in the middle of some extraordinarily vicious academic rivalry, which can be seen most clearly in the way that Hecebolius has been portrayed. To be fair, he did not help his case. Although he was by no means unique in this period in changing religious sides as frequently as the empire changed rulers, Hecebolius's rather melodramatic cry of "Trample on me, for

I am as salt that has lost its savor,"[23] as he prostrated himself before the church doors after Julian's death won him few plaudits. Acidly, a colleague remarked that he worshipped the purple, not God.[24]

A charming, if clumsy, piece of juvenilia dates to this period, the first of Julian's writings to have survived. A poem to an organ, it was composed as he was leaving the Church of the Holy Apostles where his uncle was buried.

> *How strange! A growth of most unusual reeds I see*
> *Sprung wild up from a field of brass so suddenly!*
> *The winds that make them sway, no earthly zephyrs chase,*
> *But rather breezes from a bull-hide cave set free.*
> *By way of well-bored pipes they reach the reedy base,*
> *Whilst one of noble mien, with dext'rous fingering*
> *Handles the keys, which send word to the deepest wells,*
> *Pressing them lightly, and the melody then swells.*[25]

Julian was again on the move that winter—this time back to Nicomedia. It seems likely that Constantius was having second thoughts about a male relative in the capital when events were heating up elsewhere and he was in Syria. At any rate, for the first time Julian came under the influence of Libanius, self-professed pagan, rampant intellectual snob, and chronic hypochondriac. Born in 314, the proud Antiochene philosopher embodies the spirit of the pagan empire, fighting what he did not realize was the fruitless battle against Christianity. More importantly, this pagan Prufrock, who measured out his life in coffee spoons, was an obsessive chronicler and over 1,500 of his letters survive as well as numerous orations. Although the deliberate archaisms and affectations of Libanius's prose are occasionally jarring to modern tastes, he is a peerless source for the period not only as a friend and supporter of Julian but also for his observations on his times.

Both Hecebolius and Nicocles had had massive professional disagreements with Libanius and the Antiochene was expelled from the capital.[26] Although relations with Nicocles were eventually restored, Libanius continued to refer to Hecebolius as an "incompetent" and "a good-for-nothing."[27] In turn, Hecebolius had forbidden Julian from attending Libanius's lectures. To Julian's credit he adhered to the letter if not the spirit of his tutor's ban—perhaps wary of courting any kind of controversy by attending the lecture of such an open pagan—and although he did not turn up in person, he did hire another student to take notes of Libanius's lectures for him.

The year 351 marked a significant turning point for the surviving heirs of Constantine. It was the year in which Constantius, after the murder of his remaining brother Constans, found himself sole ruler of the empire. A fifty-year-old former commander of two of Rome's crack legions in the West from northeastern Gaul called Magnus Magnentius had declared himself Augustus in the early hours of January 18, 350.[28] The so-called after-dinner emperor[29] had had himself proclaimed during a dinner party for a colleague's son. Magnentius had left the room to relieve himself and had returned, theatrically, wearing the purple, at which point he was proclaimed emperor. By the end of the month, Constantius's brother Constans had been murdered. Magnentius's assassins dragged the deeply unpopular emperor of the West—he was arrogant, greedy, impulsive, and a predatory homosexual to boot[30]—from the temple in which he had sought refuge (in the small town of what is now Elne in the Pyrenees[31]) and killed him. Constantius, faced with difficulties in the East, did not find out until the end of the year. The threats that were being made against Constantius were not from his own flesh and blood, but from outsiders.

This changed the dynamic of power. The situation also highlights the problems of communication in the ancient world. It was apparent that trying to cope with issues in the West when it could take six months for dispatches to reach him was ludicrous. Constantius needed to head west to deal with this new upstart in person and two further anti-emperors who had appeared in Rome and on the Danube frontier. But what to do with the *basso continuo* of Persian harassment in the East? Almost sixty years previously the emperor Diocletian had established a system of power sharing to combat the practical difficulties of ruling so large an empire by instituting the system of Caesars, deputies who could act in his name. Although this system had been neglected once Constantine had made himself sole emperor, Constantius resurrected the idea and Gallus, on March 15, found himself, in Sirmium, promoted to Caesar—Constantius's military representative in the East.

Julian must have watched the ceremony with some sense of hope about the future. One of the witnesses wrote of the event in a speech addressed to the emperor referring to the three of them. "For of this fine pair, the one, like the morning star as dawn has risen with you who illuminates the great thrones, imitating your bright rays with his reflected lights; while the other, shining forth from the herd of young men, like some high-spirited bull that leads the herd, has leapt in the meadows of the Muses, like a young horse full of divine spirit."[32] The respective status of the three is clear. Constantius is the sun; Gallus, the morning star; and Julian is the young bull—not on the same level as the other two but worth mentioning and officially recognized.

To ensure Gallus's loyalty, the new Caesar found himself married to Constantius's elder sister Constantina. It was a political marriage more tasteless than most. Constantina was older than the twenty-five-year-old Gallus—probably by more than a decade—and had been married for a couple of years to his uncle, who had been a victim of the murders of 337. As with many women of the period, it is difficult to uncover what she was really like. Although she is represented as a saint in Christian hagiography, the more popular view of Ammianus has prevailed—that she was "a human Fury, constantly fueling her husband's rage and as insatiable as he for human blood."[33] If she was Ammianus's Fury, then it is at least understandable why she became so.

After his brother's promotion, Julian was able to continue enjoying the academic life especially with the freedom of travel that appears to have been organized for him by his brother when, in April, they met up again as Gallus headed south to take up his commission in Antioch. Julian must have been aware of the subtle shift in his fortune, but it is impossible to work out the extent to which he dwelt on it. For the next couple of years the nineteen-year-old continued his education through Asia Minor, studying in Pergamum and Ephesus.

As much as it was for his cousin and his brother, 351 was also a turning point for Julian personally and philosophically. It was the year he was to come under the pagan influences that were to set the flavor and standards of his reign; indeed, it was the year from which he himself dated his conversion and his critics dated his apostasy. Years later he wrote in a letter that he had walked along the path of Christianity "until his twentieth year," but for twelve years now had walked on the road of paganism.[34]

With hindsight it was only a matter of time before Julian left rhetoric and jumped feet first into philosophy. There is little doubt that Julian was ready to be influenced. Not only, as most intellectually inclined teenagers, had he pondered the questions of life and the universe, but he had had too much time at Macellum to do so. It is in this light that we should see the introduction of Julian's *Hymn to King Helios,* written seven years later:

> But this at least I am permitted to say without sacrilege, that from my childhood an extraordinary longing for the rays of the god penetrated deep into my soul; and from my earliest years my mind was so completely swayed by the light that illuminates the heavens that not only did I desire to gaze intently at the sun, but whenever I walked abroad in the night season, when the firmament was clear and cloudless, I abandoned all else without exception and gave myself up to the beauties of the heavens; I did not understand what anyone might say to me or heed what I was doing myself. I was considered to be over-curious about these matters and to pay too much attention to them and people went so far as to regard me as an astrologer when my beard had only just begun to grow.[35]

It is easy to take Julian at face value here—the language and metaphors the young man uses make it all too easy to see this as a pagan Damascene conversion. But of course it was not. It is wrong to suggest that Julian converted; indeed the word "converted" is rather a faux-ami. Ever since he had started formal study under Mardonius, Julian had been immersed both in the classical and the Christian traditions. He was in no way giving up one set of canonical practices for another. It is perhaps more useful to question why it is that Julian so totally rejected Christianity and embraced Hellenism. Part of it was certainly intellectual. As a man with an intelligent, enquiring mind, he was struck by the inconsistencies in Christianity and unable to look past them. Only someone so steeped in the Bible could appreciate referring to Christians as Galileans—a reference to St. John's comment that "out of Galilee ariseth no prophet."[36] Equally significant, part of it was also emotional. He was never going to be entirely happy worshipping the same God as the man who had murdered his family.

Julian's reason for coming to Pergamum, modern Bergama in Turkey, was to study with Aedesius, one of the greatest Neoplatonic philosophers of the age, then in his seventies. To all intents and purposes he was university principal, his status the result of having studied under Iamblichus, the "truly godlike man" who, Julian said, ranked "next to Pythagoras and Plato."[37] It was Iamblichus who was responsible for raising the intuitive and theurgic aspects of Neoplatonism and it is plausible that Julian's interest had originally been aroused by the fact that Iamblichus had been a correspondent of Julian's maternal grandfather.[38]

Keen to make up for time lost in the wasteland of Macellum, Julian had become an intellectual sponge. "He longed to drink down learning open-mouthed and at a gulp" is how he was described at the time.[39] More unpalatably, there is also the hint of the arrogance of youth, a rich boy refusing to take no for an answer. To make sure that Aedesius would teach him, Julian used to send him expensive presents, but Aedesius rejected them all. Accompanied as the young man was by a bodyguard at all times—almost certainly for Constantius's rather that Julian's protection—it is not hard to see why he really turned down the young man's suit, even though he used the excuse of age and infirmity. Instead he passed the buck to his own pupils, all four of whom were to play major roles in Julian's life.

The first two were Eusebius of Myndus and Chrysanthius of Sardis. The former appears to have been a philosopher in the modern sense of the word. It is hard not to see him as a rational, sensible character, and certainly he was respected. It was said that while lecturing he "shone like a bright star."[40] At the end of his lectures he used to remind students that all magic was bunkum. Julian cornered Eusebius to ask him what he meant. The philosopher answered at some length, which turned into a diatribe against Maximus, the third of Aedesius's pupils.

Maximus is one of the older and more learned students who, because of his lofty genius and superabundant eloquence, scorned all logical proof in these subjects and impetuously resorted to the acts of a madman. Not long ago, he invited us to the temple of Hecate. When he did so, he made us witness to his folly. When we had arrived there and had saluted the goddess he said: "Be seated, my beloved friends. See what happens and how superior I am to the rest of you." When he had said this and we had all sat down, he burned a grain of incense and recited to himself the whole of some hymn or other and was so highly successful in his demonstration that the image of the goddess began to smile and then even seemed to laugh aloud. We were all very disturbed by this sight, but he said: "Do not be afraid. Soon even the torches which the goddess holds in her hands shall be alight." Before he could finish speaking, the torches burst into flame. For a moment, we were amazed by that theatrical miracle worker. Do not wonder at any of these things—I certainly don't—but believe that the thing of highest importance is that purification of the soul, which is attained by reason.[41]

Eusebius's words had precisely the opposite effect of that intended. Julian told Eusebius to stick to his books and headed down the coast to Ephesus and Maximus. If there was any city where Julian was going to become seduced by theurgy, it would have been Ephesus. Home to the Temple of Artemis, one of the wonders of the world, the city was staunchly pagan. Theurgy or Neoplatonism was the intellectual's main alternative to Christianity at the time, but it is difficult for the modern mind to grasp exactly what it was. It had sacred scriptures, an emphasis on self-restraint and it was focused on the union of the soul with god, something achieved by magical rituals such as the animal sacrifices for which Julian was castigated when he became emperor.

The relationship with Maximus that Julian formed here shows him at his most gullible. Maximus was certainly bright—he wrote several books and a commentary on Aristotle—but there is a whiff of Rasputin about the philosopher, not helped by the fact that he affected a long grey beard, allegedly to draw attention to his hypnotic eyes. It is hard to see a pleasant side to Maximus, and few contemporaries, either pagan or

Christian, had much time for him—one dismisses him by saying that he worshipped "the penny far above the gods."[42] It was only Julian who regarded him as "superior to all men of my own time."[43]

The power he soon wielded was out of all proportion to his talents.[44] Maximus had none of the qualms that Aedesius seems to have had about consorting with the emperor's cousin, and the fraudster soon appears to have developed an almost Svengali-like relationship with the young man as he dragged him deeper and deeper into the pagan mysteries. Julian was swiftly initiated into cult after cult: first, the magic rituals espoused by Maximus which centered around the worship of Hecate; and then the worship of the sun god Mithras, especially popular with the army. It is curious how Julian's new beliefs remained undiscovered. While paganism itself was by no means illegal, sacrifice certainly was. It seems unwise for Julian to have followed these cults, surrounded as he was by spies and informers, ready at the drop of a hat to betray him to an emperor who was known for executing first and asking questions later.

For the next few years at his home in Bithynia it has been commonplace to view Julian and his set in the mold of the Apostles, the elite Cambridge debating society of the 1920s—gilded, overly literary, deliberately archaic fifth columnists. The reality was rather different.

It suited those writing afterward to portray Julian as a focus for pagan hopes long before he rebelled. Libanius is particularly guilty of this. "He kept the same appearance as before, since to reveal the change in his beliefs was out of the question. Aesop here would have composed a fable, not of an ass in lion's clothing, but a lion in an ass's hide," writes the old social climber.[45] The reference to Aesop (a not especially subtle in-joke as the ass was a symbol of Christianity and the lion a reference to Mithraism) gives the impression of inside knowledge, but, of course, news of Julian's paganism did not become public until November 361.

In fact, Julian survived precisely because he did nothing to rock the boat. Behind the smokescreen of the intellectual and scholar, he involved himself in running his estate, corresponding with friends, and even went as far as being instituted as a reader in the church of Nicomedia. If he was consorting with a small group of pagans headed by Maximus, it was as the head of an ostensibly Christian household, which would therefore not arouse comment. Certainly the pagans who came to see him did not regard it as a risky venture: unlike the teachings of their Christian brethren, paganism did not encourage martyrdom. It is also worth questioning to what extent Julian, without his knowledge, was a focus for the hopes of revolt. He was hardly the dashing military figure that the Roman Empire had come to expect from its revolutionaries.

If life had seemed too comfortable for the last few years, it was to take a turn for the worse in 354. The trigger was the execution of his brother for treason and Julian's summary recall to the court in Milan.

To history, Gallus is a mini-Nero, a bloodthirsty despot of the old school of Roman Caesars. With Constantina, the couple succumbed to excesses reserved nowadays for football players and pop stars. Gallus's case has not been helped by Julian himself, who saw his brother as damaged goods. With almost tangible regret, several years later he wrote about him after their years together in Macellum: "My brother was imprisoned at court and his fate was ill-starred above all men who have ever yet lived. Whatever cruelty or harshness was revealed in his character, was increased, having been raised in the mountains."[46]

All of this is unfair. Gallus was guilty of nothing more sinister than overstepping the boundaries of his job. He had been sent to Antioch to solve the military problem of shoring up the eastern frontier, which he did. One of the chroniclers swooningly refers several times to his considerable valor and bravery.[47] Certainly he was a successful enough commander for his actions to have been noted on the other side of the empire and to warrant an assassination attempt.[48] Gallus may have been inexperienced, but he was a natural soldier.

And that is the real problem. Gallus had been sent out as a figurehead, but the more military success he won, the more power he gained. Events came to a head in early 354, when the young Caesar was asked what he was going to do about corn prices. A large army and impending famine had pushed up prices, and landowners hoarded grain to push prices up even further. It was a perennial problem for the city and one that was later to haunt Julian. Gallus rightly referred all questions to the governor and left on campaign. Military and civil functions had been deliberately split in the previous century, a way to stop overly ambitious soldiers from being able to finance their own rebellions. This did not satisfy the people of Antioch and over the next few days the governor was lynched during rioting.

When Gallus returned in April, he decided to deal with the problem. He put out an order that food hoarders lower their prices, and when this was not obeyed, he sentenced the entire council of Antioch to death. In doing that Gallus essentially signed his own death warrant. He had acted illegally by interfering in domestic matters, and although his sentencing of the council was an obvious bluff born out of frustration, he had made enemies of the richest and most articulate members of society.

By now Constantius was concerned enough by Gallus's actions to want to recall his Caesar. Some nervousness on the part of Gallus as he left Antioch at the start of September is understandable and his wariness is well documented.[49] In a preemptive strike, he had sent Constantina to check the lay of the land and smooth things over with the emperor. That she died suddenly en route was both a personal blow and the removal of the last effective link between Gallus and the emperor.[50]

In October 354, in what is now the Croatian town of Pula, Gallus was executed—just like Crispus. This was to be a long-term cautionary tale for his brother and perhaps Julian's epitaph for him should stand: "He deserved to live, even if he was unfit to rule."[51]

What was regarded as Gallus's treachery triggered a bout of imperial paranoia. Gallus's associates were all investigated and, as his brother, soon it was Julian's turn. He was called to Milan. He did not take his summons seriously and his actions give the impression of a carefree student rather than an imperial prisoner. En route, Julian took time to visit Troy. In the hands of the citizens of Novum Ilium, the city of Hector and Priam had long become a tourist trap, the Trojan War Experience, designed to fleece young Roman aristocrats. They were shown the spot where the Greek fleet had landed, where Achilles had killed Hector, and where Achilles himself died, before they went on to look at the tombs and the temples to the fallen heroes. The excitement of a student comes through in his writing, and even though he was older when he put pen to paper, there is no hint of the danger that must have been hanging over him.

Hector has a hero's shrine there and his bronze statue stands in a tiny little temple. Opposite this they have set up a figure of the great Achilles in the unroofed court. If you have seen the spot you will certainly recognize my description of it. You can learn from the guides the story that accounts for the fact that great Achilles was set up opposite him and takes up the whole of the unroofed court. Now I found that the altars were still alight, I might almost say still blazing, and that the statue of Hector had been anointed until it shone. So I looked at Pegasius and said: "What does this mean? Do the people of Troy offer sacrifices?" This was to test him cautiously, to find out his own views. He replied: "Is it not natural that they should worship a man who was their own citizen, just as we worship the martyrs?" Now the analogy was far from sound; but his point of view and intentions were those of a man of culture, if you consider the times in which we then lived. Observe what followed. "Let us go," he said, "to the shrine of Athena of Troy." Thereupon with the greatest eagerness he led me there and opened the temple, and as though he were producing evidence he showed me all the statues perfectly preserved.[52]

When he reached Milan, Julian stood for only the second time before his cousin, the man who had controlled his fate for his entire life. What would Constantius have seen? A marvelously lifelike rock crystal intaglio in the Cabinet des Médailles in Paris from around this period shows a young man, hair carefully coiffed and brushed forward in the contemporary style, his expression one of benign innocence.[53] Many believed that he looked like his mother. There is a splendid description of Julian at the time. The church father Gregory of Nazianzus, who was to meet the future emperor later that year during his studies in Athens, describes the way his shoulders shook, his neck jerked, and his eyes jumped all over the place when he was excited; how he would get so wound up that his nostrils would flare, words would tumble out of his mouth and he would jump from one idea to the next.[54]

It is not a description that should be taken at face value and from an ideological opponent it is as cynical as it is jealous (it is notable that Julian did not think Gregory even worth mentioning). But through the caricature and the exaggerations it is possible to see something of the emperor's almost manic energy that was to stay with him until death. At the same time it is worth considering the extent to which Julian himself at this period played up to this image. Most famously the emperor Claudius kept up the appearance of idiocy in his youth, to divert attention, to make himself less of a threat, and to survive; and it is an attractive thought that Julian might have done something similar.

It was definitely in Julian's interest to appear as unthreatening as possible. The charges against him were anything but trivial. He was accused of having conspired against the emperor. Although Julian was cleared, he was kept in imperial stasis; not allowed to go free or to meet the emperor, for seven months.

What saved him was the intervention of the emperor's new wife, Eusebia (Constantius's first wife died before 350 without issue) who began the gradual rehabilitation and reintegration of the young man. It was Eusebia who lobbied for and eventually got Julian an audience with the emperor. Julian himself is effusive in his praise of her. "I could not have escaped from Constantius's clutches myself, if one of the gods had not wanted me to escape and made the beautiful and virtuous Eusebia favorably disposed toward me."[55] At times, Julian's comments on the empress are positively puppyish. Even given the artificial constructs of a panegyric, in his speech to Eusebia, written soon after he arrived in Gaul, she is clearly the feminine ideal. Among others, he compares her to the goddess Athena and to Odysseus's wife Penelope. That Eusebia was born in Greece was the icing on the cake for the rampant Hellenophile in Julian.

For him, she was always *the* woman, to all intents and purposes the only significant female relationship in his life. Moreover, it is easy to see why the young man held Eusebia in such high regard. Apart from saving his life—as he saw it—all sources agree that she was bright and he was obviously attracted to her, intellectually at least if not physically. Although there is no evidence for it, it is worth at least bearing in mind that for Julian it might have been more. She was, after all, much younger than her husband. It is feasible that she was as little as two or three years older than Julian. A romantic yearning in Julian's mind is not beyond the realms of possibility.

While it is easy to see what Eusebia was to Julian, the more interesting question is what Julian was to Eusebia. The absence of any real sex in Julian's life has tormented historians, and francophone writers especially tend to ponder the relationship between Julian and the empress. "The nature of the sentiment which united Eusebia and Julian can scarcely be doubted. But of all men who have owed their fortune to love, Julian is perhaps he who took least pains to please women. Eusebia must have had tastes somewhat unusual in her sex to have attached herself to so austere a young man," is the nineteenth-century French author Anatole France's rather harsh critique.[56]

Did she really feel empathy with the young orphan? For all the praise heaped upon her, there is the occasional discordant note that jars and it must be borne in mind that Julian might not be the best witness here. He was always too open to people who professed to like him. Did he completely misread the empress? It is very possible. There is one explicitly and cynically expressed view that has Eusebia putting Julian up for the job of Caesar because she did not want to go to Gaul herself. Her way of convincing the emperor was that it was a win-win situation: if Julian succeeded in Gaul, then he was useful; if he died, then they were rid of a potential usurper.[57]

In and of itself that is not convincing and could simply be court gossip, but there is a fair amount of circumstantial evidence to suggest that Eusebia's motives and actions were not only more manipulative than most have believed, but that she was acting as the mouthpiece of Constantius himself. Firstly, given how intelligent everyone agrees the empress was, it is worth stepping back and considering whether the new young wife of an emperor was really likely to have gone out on a limb so consistently in supporting Julian against the entire court. Secondly, it cannot be coincidence that the instances where the empress did intervene on Julian's behalf—sending him to Athens and later in making him Caesar—dovetailed perfectly with imperial policy. Thirdly, there is no sign that Constantius was displeased with his wife's interference. On the contrary, the emperor was later to rename the Pontic diocese in his wife's honor. He called it *Pietas,* a Latin word meaning "faithful"—not an action he would have taken for a subversive. And finally, for all of Constantius's faults, he was not stupid. Any appeal toward a man whose entire family you had murdered was likely to be knocked back. Using your bright, younger wife as your mouthpiece was less duplicitous and more pragmatic.

In this light, with Julian being saved for possible imperial use, it is understandable why he now found his reins loosened a little. He was not allowed back to Asia but encouraged instead to stay nearby in Como. It was a dull, provincial backwater and not at all to Julian's taste—there was no university and he was a long way away from his mentors. Eusebia came to his aid again and he was given permission to go to his family property in Bithynia. He was never to make it there. That summer, the political fallout from another—imagined as it turned out—conspiracy against Constantius brought a resurgence of imperial paranoia. Letting Julian return to an area where there was any kind of tradition of family support was suddenly out of the question.

Julian describes what happened next: "When I wanted to return home, Eusebia first persuaded the emperor to give his permission and then provided me with a safe escort. Then when some bad spirit, the one I think who dreamed up my former troubles or perhaps some unfriendly Fate, cut short this journey, she sent me to Greece, having asked this favor for me from the emperor when I had already left the country."[58]

He had won the lottery. As so many well-heeled Roman aristocrats before him, Julian was going to round off his education in Athens. "This had long been my dearest wish and I had wanted it more than I had wished to possess treasures of gold and silver," he wrote.[59] No matter that they had been dead for centuries, Athens was still the city of Plato and Aristotle, and for any philosophically and academically inclined student it had a status, a class and a reputation that Pergamum and Ephesus could never equal.

Horace may have mentioned its "academic groves of blissful green,"[60] but if Julian was being honest he might have admitted that Athens was a little past its prime and living off bygone glory. It is easy enough to imagine a student becoming increasingly disillusioned on his arrival. The road from Piraeus, the city's port, to the gates of Athens was long, hot, and flanked by the now distinctly tatty Long Walls. And as he passed the Dipylon Gates into the city the sights that greeted him were of decay not elegant classicism. But that was irrelevant to Julian.

This was Athens, the focal point of Hellenic culture. If Libanius is to be believed, Julian intended to live and die in Athens.[61] It is difficult to see what other options were open to him at the time and the fact that Athens was a bit of a backwater now must have calmed Julian a little. Surely the emperor could not accuse him of fomenting revolt from here?

The leading light at the university was Prohaeresius, professor of rhetoric. Although in his mid-eighties, his powers were undiminished and certainly impressed Julian. But as at Pergamum, Julian inclined more toward magical rites than rhetoric. He continued, under what kind of care and secrecy we can only guess at, his pagan studies. He sought out and found the fourth of Aedesius's students: Priscus of Thesprotia. Along with Maximus, he was to be the most important influence on Julian's intellectual and theological life. Tall, handsome, he kept his cards very close to his chest—characteristics that would have attracted and impressed Julian. The two men were to become very close friends and it was either through Priscus's introduction or through one of his colleagues that Julian met those who were able to initiate him into the Eleusinian Mysteries in late September.

Once he had arrived in Athens, it was always a matter of when rather than if Julian was to be initiated into this, the most famous of the ancient world's cults. Julian's initiation into the Greater Mysteries, which lasted nine days (another, shorter festival, the Lesser Mysteries took place in spring), began with the pilgrimage of the initiates from Athens to Eleusis. When he arrived in Eleusis, a mere fourteen miles away from Athens, he would have fasted throughout the day, before drinking a symbolic draught of meal, water and mint leaves. Julian would then have been allowed to enter the Hall of Initiation, the inner sanctum, after reciting a password. What happened inside is unknown—initiates were forbidden on pain of death to reveal its secrets—but as the cult was centered on Demeter, the goddess of grain, they are likely to have been based around the cyclical nature of life emphasizing rebirth. As with all other initiates, Julian's own writings reveal little. "Those who take part in the secret rites are wholly chaste and their leader, the hierophant, forswears sex. . . . On this subject I have said enough," is his sole comment.[62]

The most widely accepted view is that the rites included a reenactment of the story of Demeter and her daughter Persephone, who was abducted by the god of the underworld; Demeter's grief and the winter that descended on the earth; followed by Persephone's resurrection as she is reunited with her mother. Given the number of people who were clearly watching him it may sound strange that he did not get in trouble for it, but by now the Mysteries were as much tourist attraction as cult.

Julian was to spend only three months in his adopted city. He was summarily recalled to Milan in October with no explanation given. Julian must have thought his luck had finally run out. He left Athens obviously both heartbroken and fearing for his life. "What floods of tears I shed and what laments I uttered when I was summoned, stretching out my hands to your Acropolis, and imploring Athena to save her suppliant and not to abandon me. Many of you who were there can back me up. The goddess herself is my witness that I even begged for death at her hands there in Athens rather than my journey to the emperor."[63] Julian was of course laying it on with a trowel for the home crowd—the passage is from an open letter to the Athenians, written to justify his revolt against Constantius several years later—but it is probably not that far removed from what he was thinking.

Any disquiet he was feeling cannot have been in any way eased by his welcome in Milan. He was not allowed into the city, but remained under house arrest in one of the suburbs. Although he received several letters from the empress telling him to keep his spirits up, it was deemed unwise for him to communicate with anyone. Other letters did not get through—his servants were searched.

Still only twenty-three, it is to Julian's credit that this—he did not know it, but it was to be his final period of imprisonment—did not break him. Writing about his feelings at the time, he gives the impression of a much more stable and pragmatic character than many give him credit for: "I have imagined that I can devise wider schemes for myself than those who know all things. But human wisdom, which looks only at the present, with all of its efforts, may be thankful if it succeeds in avoiding mistakes even for a short time. That is why no man gives a thought for events that are to happen thirty years on or for those already past: the one is superfluous, the other impossible. . . . But the wisdom of the gods sees very far, or rather sees the whole, and so it puts you on the right path and brings to pass what is best. They are the causes of all that is now and all that shall be."[64]

Again Julian came to believe that Eusebia smoothed things over. He was not going to be executed. It was much, much worse than that. He was to be promoted to Caesar. "I felt like a man who can't drive a chariot and doesn't want to, but is forced to manage one that belongs to a noble and talented charioteer," he writes.[65]

The physical transformation from student to soldier is the one moment of high comedy among the terror and nervousness. Julian was landed on by teams of the Roman equivalent of style gurus and given a complete makeover to make him presentable: they cut off his beard, dressed him in a military cloak, and even made him walk differently.[66] However much he might have wanted to return to his books, that was no longer an option. Much like his brother before him, Julian was being offered a position that looked like a compliment, but could so easily be a death sentence. The gods had spoken. The transformation was complete. He was to become a soldier. He was to become Caesar. He was to go to Gaul.

2

A WRITTEN ORDER

On this day I gave to Mr. Fletcher Christian, whom I had before desire to charge of the third watch, a written order to act as lieutenant.

CAPTAIN WILLIAM BLIGH,
LOG OF HMS *BOUNTY*, MARCH 2, 1788

As he entered the town of Vienne in the middle of December AD 355 an old woman shouted out at Julian: "This is the man who will restore the temples of the gods."[1] Her foresight may have been remarkable, but it is unlikely to have done anything to calm the nerves of the young Caesar. For all the bright sunlight and the streets decorated with garlands and branches and greenery, the spare had become the distinctly unwilling heir.

He was in a foreign country with more ceremonial than real power; he knew that at the first hint of sedition the emperor would have no compunction about having him executed, just as he had his brother; worse, his promotion was one that could be withdrawn in typical Constantinian manner if the emperor had a son. As he was about to cross the border into Gaul, dispatches had reached him that one of the provincial capitals had been captured by the Franks. Little surprise that Julian was heard to mutter to himself that all he had achieved by the promotion was the prospect of dying with more work on his hands.

Gaul had dominated Constantius's thoughts for most of the latter part of that summer as it had periodically for the past five years. Although Magnentius, his brother's murderer, had been soundly beaten in an incredibly bloody battle in 351, the threat from the West had not been lifted by his suicide in August 353. The Western empire still reverberated with the aftershock of Magnentius's revolt.

To be sure of victory, Constantius had struck a deal with the Germanic tribes on the eastern side of the Rhine: he would turn a blind eye to their excursions across the river if they helped him get rid of this upstart. They did, but rather than politely withdraw to the right side of the river after Magnentius's defeat, the barbarians decided to stay and make a nuisance of themselves.

That summer, on August 11, 355, Claudius Silvanus, a much decorated general, in fact commander of the Gaulish army had himself proclaimed emperor at Cologne. The twenty-eight-day emperor was stabbed to death by his own men on his way to a Christian service at dawn on September 7 (rather more bloodily Julian writes that his soldiers "set on him as though he were a wolf and tore him limb from limb"[2]), but Constantius believed the situation remained volatile enough to warrant the posting of an imperial military representative, and took the step of promoting his young, inexperienced cousin.

On November 6, Julian found himself standing on a rostrum, surrounded by eagles and standards in front of all the troops that were stationed near Milan. With the over-formality for which Constantius was famous, the emperor took Julian by his right hand, told the assembled crowd of soldiers of his decision and put the purple robe round his young cousin's shoulders. As the troops cheered, the more observant noticed the grimace on the young Caesar's face and his look of dejection. It is said that as he took his place next to the emperor in the carriage Julian muttered to himself a line from *The Iliad*. He said that fate had just wrapped him in "death's purple."[3] It is probably a fair assessment of the way he felt.

Along with the purple, the emperor bestowed a wife on him—
Constantius's own unmarried Christian sister Helena. Julian had just
turned twenty-three and Helena was several years older, at least six
and possibly as much as seven or eight years. The fact that it was a
blood marriage is not surprising given the dynastic considerations, and
politically it mirrors the earlier marriage of Julian's brother Gallus to
Constantius's other sister Constantina.

Unlike many of his imperial predecessors, the one charge that even
his detractors could not make against him is of debauchery. Julian's
asceticism and self-control put even some of the fathers of the early
Church to shame. His marriage was one of convenience and political
expediency and his wife was certainly no Lesbia for him to worship in
her lifetime or a Beatrice to be mourned after her death. Julian himself
mentions Helena only three times in the writings we have, and in each
case it is either in passing or as if about a total stranger. In a speech in
honor of Eusebia, Julian thanks the empress—in the customary third
person—for a wedding present: "It would perhaps not be ungrateful
to mention, one of those gifts of hers, for it was one with which I was
myself especially delighted. She gave me the best books on philosophy
and history, and many of the orators and poets, since I had brought
hardly any with me from home, deluding myself with the hope and
longing to return home again, and gave them in numbers and such
amounts that even my desire for them was satisfied, even though I am
altogether insatiable for conversation about literature."[4] It is painful
to read. It is obvious that the new Caesar's real passion lay with the
books. The second time, during his tours of duty in Gaul, he notes in
passing: "My wife was still alive and I had gone to the upper room
near hers to rest alone,"[5] which sends a clear signal about the state of
the marriage.

And finally, in what comes across as a letter of rather Victorian prig-
gishness, he writes to his uncle from Constantinople, some time after
Helena's death: "I call all the gods and goddesses to witness, that I should
not have resented it even if someone had published abroad all that I ever
wrote to my wife, so temperate was it in every respect."[6]

We know next to nothing of Helena. She is barely a ghost in his
life and tiny details have assumed a major importance. Thanks to the

Renaissance writer and artist Vasari, for example, we have almost more details about the font at which she and her sister were baptized in the Church of Sant'Agnese fuori le Mura in Rome than about her looks or personality: "The font . . . was ornamented with sculptures made a long time before, notably the porphyry pillar carved with beautiful figures, some marble candelabra exquisitely carved with foliage and some *putti* low relief, which are wonderfully beautiful."[7]

The only stories we have of her are obviously palace tittle-tattle. In the first year of her marriage, Helena lost a son, supposedly through Eusebia's machinations. It was claimed that the empress bribed the mid-wife to kill the baby as soon as it was born by cutting the umbilical cord too short. Then, the following year, Helena joined Constantius and Eusebia on the emperor's state visit to Rome in 357. On that trip, out of jealousy of her own inability to conceive, Eusebia allegedly dosed Helena with a drug that would make her miscarry whenever she was pregnant.[8]

Despite both Eusebia's manipulation of the young Caesar and the intensely competitive and bloody nature of Constantinian family politics, the empress does seem to have been genuinely fond of Julian. And even if you wish to see Eusebia as jealous, unable to conceive a child, it is unlikely that she would have gone to the extreme of murder. Sadly the death of his offspring seems to have had little impact on the young Caesar, who never mentions them.

Helena was to die in childbirth five years after getting married. As with any sudden death at the time there were rumors that she had been poisoned, but as these were fueled by one of Julian's old enemies in Gaul, again they are unlikely to be true. It is hard not to feel sorry for Helena. She had been more or less ignored by her husband; her mother Fausta had been executed by her father, Constantine the Great; her sister only avoided execution by dying of fever; and after two miscarriages she was relegated to a footnote of history with not even the date of her death surviving. She was buried in Rome alongside her sister Constantina, in what remains one of the best-preserved mausolea of late antiquity, begun by Constantine and finished by Julian; now the Santa Costanza, on the via Nomentana. Helena's magnificent porphyry sarcophagus now rests in the Vatican Museum while Constantina's holds the relics of St. Simon and St. Jude and can be seen in the south transept of St. Peters.

On December 1, with a wife and a personal escort of 360 men in tow, the new ruler of Britain, Gaul, and Spain set off for Gaul. The number of companions he could take was severely restricted, but he did have one friend with him, the doctor Oribasius, who was to accompany Julian for the rest of his life.

History has neglected Oribasius. He was famous both as a doctor and a teacher in his lifetime, as well as a prolific medical writer. If he is known at all now, it is for his main surviving work, the *Medical Compilations*—an incredible encyclopedia of which just over a third survives, of the best medical thinking at the time. But it draws so heavily on Galen, the greatest doctor in the ancient world after Hippocrates, that Oribasius rather unfairly has often been called "Galen's ape."

The two had met at Pergamum, Oribasius's hometown, four years previously. The doctor was roughly a decade older than Julian and the position as personal physician to a Caesar was a significant move up in the world. Julian's promotion of him was to pay off: the doctor was to remain loyal throughout his life. In fact, the first version of the Medical Compilations was completed in Gaul and is dedicated to Julian. One can only speculate about their level of intimacy. Some have tried to see it as a slightly distant servant-master relationship, but considering the length of time they were together, through such momentous events, it is obvious that they were close.

At least there was someone in whom he could confide his thoughts en route to Gaul. If Julian had misgivings about the troops that were sent to accompany him—he snidely commented that the only thing they knew how to do was how to pray—the Caesar can't have failed to have been cheered by the weather. He is said to have enjoyed such brilliant sunshine on his journey that "they called it the season of spring."[9] Constantius accompanied him to a point marked by two columns on the Lomello and Pavia road. It was the last time that Julian was to see his cousin alive. Nor would either of them have been aware of the intense irony embodied in the columns that looked down on them as they said their good-byes. One was a military column, dedicated to the rebel emperor Magnentius, while the other was dedicated to the third-century emperor known as Caracalla, famous for murdering his coruler and brother to win the throne. Although the original site of the columns is now long gone, inscribed stones from them have recently been found in medieval buildings in Lomello.

Julian traveled on to Turin, where the first bad news reached him. Not only had one of the Frankish tribes called the Chamavi risen up and taken Cologne, the capital of the province, he also found out that he was one of the last to know. The imperial palace staff had already been fully updated on events, but had not mentioned them in case it upset preparations for the new Caesar's departure. What appeared to Julian a slightly patronizing approach is unlikely to have done anything to calm his fears that he was leader in name only.

As the late Indian summer continued, Julian and his companions headed toward the Cottian Alps. From Turin they followed the route of what is now the S25 for the thirty-one miles as far as Susa, and then crossed the Alps at the Col du Montgenèvre, the lowest Alpine pass and, given the time of year, the safest.

With the olive trees still heavy with their fruit on the French side of the Alps, the party headed up the Rhône valley toward Vienne, famous for the tradition that Pontius Pilate was buried there. Bloated with self-importance, the town sat along the river in the shade of Mount Pipet where the Rhône River joins the Gère River. The Roman provincial capital has always suffered from a reputation for dullness. Lawrence Durrell referred to it as the Bournemouth of the ancient world, while the poet Horace patronizingly hoped that even "they who drink the waters of the Rhône"[10] would read his poetry after his death. This is a little unfair. The town was still a major center courtesy of a military road north and its strategic position whereby it could keep an eye on the Alps and all roads from the East.

Many chroniclers would have us believe that Julian's first few years in Gaul were a time of humiliation. Libanius writes that Julian "had authority for nothing save to wear his uniform."[11] A picture emerges of a Caesar in name only as military command remained first of all in the capable hands of an extremely experienced general called Ursicinus—he had been a commander under Constantine, had played a major role in getting rid of Silvanus and was also the patron of Ammianus. After his departure for the eastern front, Ursicinus was replaced by Marcellus, a cavalry officer, whose prime recommendation for the job from Constantius's point of view appears to have been that as a Pannonian he was unlikely to start a revolution in Gaul.

To add insult, as Julian would like us to believe, to injury, the emperor had packed him off with instructions rather as if he were sending a younger relative to university. The one note of imperial largesse was that the emperor had made liberal provision for the expense of his cousin's table, something that stuck in the craw of the young ascetic.[12] It is just possible that Constantius had intended this as an affectionate gesture—he had written the advice, rarely for him, in his own hand—but it was certainly not perceived as such. Julian may have had carte blanche as far as his diet was concerned, but that is as far as it went. "I was sent not as a commander of the garrisons but rather as a subordinate of the generals stationed there. Letters had been sent to them and express orders given that they were to watch me as vigilantly as they did the enemy, for fear I should attempt to cause a revolt," he later wrote.[13]

The emperor's moves seem less a case of oppression and more ones of sensible balance and checks, even if some of Constantius's deputies were rather overzealous in following his injunctions. Julian's funds were certainly closely monitored—the emperor did not want Julian throwing money around and currying favor with troops who could end up more loyal to the Caesar than to the purple, but one may assume that Constantius thought as little as Julian did of the informer who reported the Caesar after he had slipped some money to a soldier for a shave.

While Constantius undoubtedly put brakes on his cousin, it was by no means as bad as Julian would have us believe. It would have been more surprising had Constantius allowed his cousin a freer rein. Look at it from the emperor's point of view. Why, after all, would he entrust the vast western half of his empire to an untrained, bookish youth, especially after what had happened when his brother had been promoted, on top of the tradition the region had for throwing up rebels? If anything, the initial few years in Gaul show Constantius in a good light—even if Julian was a puppet to begin with, the emperor had no qualms about loosening the reins of power once his cousin had proved himself.

The winter of 355 was a turning point for Julian personally. He could have decided to enjoy the trappings of power in the palace in Vienne and given himself over to a life of luxury. He could have withdrawn into himself and carried on his academic readings. Julian did neither of these things. He decided instead to become a soldier and a ruler.

If he wanted to survive, he needed to learn how to become one of the men. Julian put himself through basic training. Claudian, the last Roman poet in the classical tradition writing at the end of the century, gives a charmingly idealized account of training.

> *The sergeant gives the signal, cracks a whip,*
> *And then, as one, the men go through the moves,*
> *Bring down their bucklers to their sides, or raise*
> *Them up; the sound of clashing steel is heard,*
> *And, to a rhythm drummed by swords on shields,*
> *The song of steely weaponry rings out.*[14]

The reality was really rather different, as we can tell from the *Epitome of Military Science,* the single most influential military treatise in the Western world right up to the Renaissance. Written toward the end of the fourth century by Vegetius, a Spanish-born bureaucrat and horse breeder, it preserves a most unpleasant sounding account of the physical realities of square-bashing. Julian will have exercised with post and foils; practiced throwing javelins; trained in jumping and attacking at the same time; chopped trees, carried loads, swum, and run with a full pack.[15]

Rather than let himself be pampered when he returned to the palace, Julian made sure that it got about that he had turned his back on a bed with silk sheets and a duvet and slept, like regular soldiers, under a rough rug and blanket. He also spurned the luxuries of a spoiled young aristocrat—he ate and drank what the soldiers did. Out were delicacies like pheasant and sows' udders (some particularly unappetizing examples of recipes for the latter with asafetida and mulled wine have survived in the cookery book of the first-century author Apicius), and in were soldiers' rations of grain to be made into bread. Roman legionaries lived on a daily average of 3,000 calories, made up of almost a liter of grain, which could be made into bread, and probably a small amount of meat. Out too was wine, symbol of Roman easy living; in was beer, the drink of his troops. He even wrote a poem to it:

> *You're Dionysus? No, that can't be true!*
> *Bacchus, the son of Zeus I know, not you!*
> *He smells of nectar, you just smell of goats!*
> *Grape-less, the Celts pour barley down their throats,*
> *So you're less "Bacchus" than "Back-to-the-Earth,"*
> *Your oats are tame, not wild; in flour, not fire your*
>   *birth!*[16]

As well as learning to be a soldier, Julian also threw himself into reading everything that he could get his hands on that might be useful for his command. As might be expected, he continued with his study of poetry and philosophy, but he also got his Latin up to scratch, read everything he could on Gaul, and made sure that he knew Julius Caesar's *Conquest of Gaul* inside out. "Even when I take the field, one thing above all else goes with me as a necessary provision for the campaign, one narrative of a campaign composed long ago by an eyewitness."[17] The question of Julian's knowledge of Latin has been oft debated. Although it is obvious that he much preferred Greek, by the end of his life he must have been fluent in Latin too, partly because he needed to communicate with his Gaulish troops and partly to show up his uncle. Constantine's linguistic skills were so poor he needed an interpreter to help him translate into Latin.

Julian was lucky in having a Gaulish financial officer called Salutius Secundus to guide him. Now approaching middle age, Salutius was a stable and experienced administrator. He took the young Caesar under his wing and guided him through the intricacies of government. It was a happy pairing. A few years later Julian was to remember "the labors we shared and endured together; our unfeigned and candid conversation; our innocent and upright intercourse; our cooperation in all that was good; our equally matched and never-repented zeal and eagerness in opposing evildoers. How often we supported each other with one equal temper."[18] Indeed, it was a partnership that was broken only by Julian's death.

Salutius had probably begun his career under Constantine, had subsequently worked under Constans and now Constantius, and had both the governorship of southwest Gaul and of Africa under his belt before he met Julian. He seems to have been able to communicate with Julian in a way few others could, undoubtedly helped by the fact that he was also a pagan and a thinker—not only was he to write a manual of pagan theology called *On the Gods and the Universe* but he also corresponded regularly with intellectuals such as Libanius. The two men rapidly became close. Julian referred to him as "the excellent Salutius,"[19] later on dedicated his *Hymn to King Helios* to him and wrote a speech of consolation about him when he was recalled from Gaul by the emperor three years later. He became a father figure to the young Caesar, a replacement for his beloved Mardonius—a parallel the young Caesar himself noted when he wrote on Salutius's departure: "I felt the same anguish as when at home I left my teacher."[20]

It is likely that the first two of Julian's panegyrics, one to Constantius and the other to the empress Eusebia, date to this winter. Artificial in form and content, the panegyrics are remarkable for their adherence to formal rhetorical principles and their supreme flatness of style. Some have tried to distinguish in the former—a straight run-through of the emperor's life and career with a final prayer that he live a long and prosperous life—some kind of deception on the part of Julian, that he was willfully hiding his true pagan feelings. In fact, it is well nigh impossible to distinguish anything personal in the speech. The latter, although more of an exercise of style rather than content, is more interesting as at least some element of real feeling comes through.

At some point in the New Year, Augustodunum, modern Autun, had been attacked. A lively cosmopolitan place, the city, founded by Julius Caesar and famous for its school of rhetoric, was rich and powerful with a population of as much as 80,000. At its height, it was one of the jewels of the region boasting over four miles of walls, four impressive city gates, temples, theaters, and even two amphitheaters, one of which was the largest in Gaul. A force of Alemanni had attacked the city under cover of darkness. They had tried to scale the old and crumbling walls on ladders by an unguarded gate and the city was saved only by the swift action of some veterans. It was time for Julian to put some of his theory into practice.

Before looking at the campaigning season of 356, it is essential to grasp that whatever the focus that has inevitably been placed on Julian, he was part only of a much larger strategy. Constantius's first priority, as it had been over the previous two years, was the protection of the Gallic provinces. And, broadly speaking, this strategy of shoring up defenses was to characterize the rest of Constantius's reign too. It is a moot point how much of a disruption barbarian incursions into Roman territory actually were, but that is how they were perceived.

The loss of Cologne may have been merely embarrassing, but flying columns of raiders like this were penetrating deep into Gaul, and the Romans had effectively now lost control of a long strip of land on the west bank of the Rhine from Augst to the North Sea. This was one humiliation too far. Constantius and his council appear to have developed a strategy that relied on a simple pincer movement. The emperor was to advance east through Switzerland, while the army in Gaul, under the command of Marcellus, was to push north, herding the Germanic tribes back toward the Rhine. Both armies were then to meet up in Strasbourg.

In direct contrast to the impression Julian gives, not only was he not in charge of the campaign, he was barely invited along. Ordered by Marcellus to rendezvous in Reims, the young Caesar appears to have obeyed the letter of his orders rather than the spirit. Julian made an unscheduled side trip to Autun and entered the city on June 24, with a small detachment of cavalry and artillery units. Any young commander would have decided to teach the Alemanni a lesson and Julian appears to have gone out of his way to taste blood.

After a council of war in Autun—and briefings from spies—Julian took his guerrilla force and pushed on north, probably out of what is now called the Porte d'Arroux with its two main arches flanked by smaller entrances for pedestrians and its upper gallery topped by elegant pilasters, toward Auxerre. He rested there for a short while, but soon pressed on toward Troyes. If anything shows the naïveté of the young Caesar, this is it. Although the march through the forests is treated with brevity, the few titbits that emerge suggest that Julian narrowly avoided another Varian Disaster—the first-century massacre of three legions in the Teutoburger forest at Kalkriese that had traumatized the Roman psyche ever since.

We have hints of successive attacks while Julian had to resort to bribery to ensure that his men remained true to Rome—a fixed reward for every soldier to kill a barbarian. The effect on the slightly nervous soldiers was total savagery. Libanius mentions that the Roman soldiers "reveled in the killing"; that barbarians were "annihilated" and "their killers brought in their dead foes' heads as proof, for there was a price set on every head and much eagerness for headhunting."[21]

So foolhardy was the venture through the forest that when Julian and his troops arrived at the gates of Troyes, the inhabitants hesitated before letting them in, thinking they might be a horde of Germans. It was a fair presumption on the part of the people of the city. They were terrified of being attacked and many of Julian's troops were ethnically German. From there it was a simple march to the rest of the army at Reims. This sideshow may have been dangerous and unnecessary, but it did accomplish several important things. First, Julian had tried combat and won. Whatever the minor importance of Julian's fending off Germans, his success will have given the young Caesar faith in himself. As significantly, turning up, bloodied, with some captives in tow, will have raised the morale of the entire force. Roman soldiers were traditionally superstitious and had the habit of adopting people who would bring them luck. A Caesar of the imperial family who had won before they set off was someone to cherish.

The time, from July on, was spent clearing up the left bank of the Rhine. Reading between the lines, however successful this campaign might have been for Julian, it had become rather a damp squib for the Roman state. Constantius's forces had made a foray into the Black Forest, but the German army had simply gone to ground. After it became apparent that they were prepared to sue for peace, Constantius retreated. Rather a no-score draw.

It was left, therefore, to Marcellus and his army to mop up. The Alemanni occupied much of the province—territory bounded by the Vosges Mountains to the south, the Moselle to the west and the Rhine to the east and north—from Strasbourg, as far north as Mainz. An initial ambush, possibly near the town of Dieuze, in about the middle of July had the benefits of keeping the Roman army on its toes and reining in some of Julian's enthusiasm. Ammianus approvingly notes, "from then on Julian, thinking that he could not cross roads or rivers without the risk of an ambush, became wary and deliberate, qualities which are particularly advantageous in great generals."[22]

Brumath was the first town to fall back into the hands of Julian. The Caesar's attack was pure textbook. The *Epitome of Military Science* notes that there are seven ways to engage the enemy—number four is described as risky but can be swift and effective: "When you have ordered your line, at between 650 yards and 800 yards before you reach your enemy, suddenly spur on both your wings when he is not expecting it, in order to turn the enemy to flight by catching him unprepared on both wings and win a quick victory."[23] This is exactly what Julian did—he drew up his forces in a crescent and took the town.

From then until the end of the year, we have only the dimmest details of Julian's movements. He appears to have decided to retake Cologne, passing up the Rhine through Coblenz and Remagen. This extension to the campaigning season was by no means as dangerous a maneuver as has been suggested. One of the peculiarities of the Germanic excursions into Roman territory is that although they were destructive, there was no attempt at settlement—in fact the German tribes actively avoided occupying cities, believing that they were "tombs surrounded by nets."[24] Ever since Rome and Germany had clashed swords, as Tacitus noted: "It is a well-known fact that the peoples of Germany never live in cities and will not even have their houses set close together."[25] In many cases Julian must have done little more than enter the city.

There remains the question of under whose command Julian was now fighting. The ancient sources are little help on the matter, implying that Julian was by this point commander-in-chief. Despite his successes earlier in the year with the detour via Autun to Reims, it stretches belief to suggest that Julian had enough personal support yet to conduct a campaign into enemy territory without the backing of Marcellus and Constantius. Whatever the exact status of his command, there is no doubt about his successes.

By the end of September Julian had retaken Cologne. The city had enjoyed a long and glorious history. In the past four centuries it had been headquarters of the governor of Lower Germany, briefly capital of a splinter Roman Empire and remained a major manufacturing center of ceramics and glass. Julian, however, found the city in a shocking state—desolate and in ruins. This was a blow as fewer than fifty years previously Constantine had ordered the 22nd Legion to build a military camp that was connected to the colony by a bridge. The rather well-preserved foundations that can been seen at Castrum Divitium in Deutz are of sixteen barracks protected by fourteen towers, which indicates that the camp could have housed up to 1,000 soldiers.

The town's significance can be deduced from the time that Julian spent there. He remained for several weeks, negotiating a temporary peace treaty, patching up the city and its fortifications and installing a garrison. Winter was now starting to bite, so by mid-October Julian and his force marched to the town known in the later Roman period as Senones (after the Gallic tribe that Julius Caesar had beaten), now Sens, to set up his headquarters.

With the coming of winter, Julian could be forgiven for thinking that he had a quiet few months ahead of him. By most standards it had been a good year for him personally. He had proved his worth both to himself and to his troops, and—despite the impression that he gives in his *Letter to the Athenians* that he was already at loggerheads with Constantius—he enjoyed the full confidence of the emperor. A quiet time, however, was anything but what he got. Luck and youthful enthusiasm may have carried Julian through the previous year, but if anything 357 was to prove even more taxing.

What happened over the next month remains one of the many tantalizing mysteries of Julian's life and depends on how you regard Marcellus. The facts are brief. The cities along the Rhine had needed garrisons. Alemanni spies found out that this had left Julian relatively unguarded. A plan was hatched and a horde laid siege to Sens, trapping Julian inside. Retaliation was impossible; he did not have enough manpower. Instead, the Caesar's reaction was to barricade the gates, to repair the walls around the city (fragments of which can still be seen), and to wait for help. None came. Julian sat there for thirty days, before the Germans got bored of the stalemate and withdrew.

Marcellus, wintering nearby, could easily have come to relieve him, but instead left Julian to his own devices. Why? Some have tried to see in this the hidden hand of Constantius wanting to rid himself of a troublesome relative. As a theory it is implausible—it was not his style. While it was certainly not beyond Constantius's powers to engineer a barbarian revolt, a man who had slaughtered much of his family in cold blood and had not hesitated before having Julian's brother murdered, had far easier means at his disposal of getting rid of his cousin than laying siege to a city. Secondly, and even more convincingly, as soon as the emperor heard about the incident, Marcellus was cashiered and banished to his native Bulgaria.

It is also possible to construct a conspiracy theory, with the emperor's cabinet giving orders for the city to be left to fall. Attractive though the idea might be, there is no evidence for that either. The ancient sources are of little help. Ammianus gives us nothing and Libanius says only that Marcellus "showed cowardice in the face of the enemy and reserved his violence for his own people."[26] Even Julian is curiously reticent on the subject. He writes: "I had assigned the greater part of the force that I had to them [the cities along the Rhine] and so I myself was left isolated," and that "I was exposed to the utmost danger," but he goes into no more details and nowhere does he blame Marcellus directly. His final comment is so blandly factual as to raise eyebrows. "The commander-in-chief of the forces fell under the suspicions of Constantius and was deprived by him of his command and superseded."[27] The readers could make the connection if they wanted to.

The most likely explanation is that Marcellus was working on his own. He was a jealous commander seeing his own star eclipsed by this young blood. He could have justified his actions to himself in that Julian had proved himself no mean tactician so could get out of this one on his own. He might also have believed—wrongly, as it turned out—that were it to turn into a disaster for the garrison at Sens, there would be official condemnation from the capital and an unofficial pat on the back.

The difficulty is that whatever it was that caused him to act in this manner, Marcellus clearly thought that his grievance was justified and even if his opinions were in the end dismissed, he was heard out. On his way back to what is now the Bulgarian capital Sofia, Marcellus

petitioned the emperor personally and Julian had to send his chamberlain Eutherius to Milan to act in his defense. While we do not have the
exact charges, we do know that when Marcellus was admitted before
the council he "ranted and raged" and accused Julian of everything
under the sun.[28] Eutherius had all charges thrown out and Marcellus
was banished into obscurity. He pointed out that it was Julian's prompt
thinking in the face of Marcellus's dilly-dallying that had saved Sens
and offered his own life as guarantee that Julian was faithful to the
emperor.

Back on the western front, the fragile peace that Julian had arranged
unraveled in the New Year. Germans began raiding almost at once and
the Caesar's time was consumed with military operations—redistribut-
ing soldiers to trouble spots and discharging administrative matters—
and making sure that the army had enough to eat. Julian himself gives
us a snapshot of the state of the country before he set out on campaign
in late summer:

> A great number of Germans had settled themselves with impunity
> near the towns they had sacked in Gaul. There were about forty-
> five towns whose walls had been dismantled—not counting cita-
> dels and smaller forts. On our side of the Rhine, the barbarians
> controlled the whole country that extends from its sources to the
> ocean. Significantly, those who were settled nearest to us were as
> much as thirty-five miles from the banks of the Rhine and an area
> three times as broad as that had been left a desert by the raids so
> that the locals could not even pasture their cattle there. Then too
> there were certain cities deserted by their inhabitants, near which
> the barbarians were not yet encamped.[29]

There was a silver lining to the cloud that had begun to descend.
A side effect of the fallout from the Marcellus affair and an indication
that Constantius had increasing confidence in his cousin was that Julian
was made commander-in-chief of the army. With his promotion working relationships within the senior military command in Gaul improved
immeasurably, a trend that continued when Marcellus was replaced by
an experienced career soldier, the universally popular Severus.

There was little other good news. By July, when Julian set out from Sens, it was already late in the campaigning season, and events soon took a turn for the worse. The new infantry commander and head of the second army was Barbatio, a man promoted much above his talents and an old enemy of the family—it was he who had betrayed Gallus. He appears to have been happier with the cloak and dagger atmosphere of court than in the cut and thrust of the army. Ammianus knew him well and couldn't stand him—he calls him "an over-ambitious boor"[30]—and relished the fact that he was executed a couple of years later for treason.

The two armies were to follow the same strategy as the previous year. Julian and Severus eventually headed east toward Tres Tavernae, now Saverne in Alsace (sometimes still referred to in older accounts by its German name of Zabern), where he wanted to make his headquarters. Barbatio was to come up from Italy with a force of 25,000 men, cross the Rhine at Augst and push on north. It did not work out that way.

The Roman strategy fell apart as Barbatio made one mistake after another. Some have tried to imply that Barbatio was in some way out to subvert Julian's command. It was nothing as sophisticated as that. Barbatio was an incompetent. First he got stuck in Augst and could get no further—a result of greater than expected German resistance. Then a tribe of Alemanni slipped through between the two armies and raided Lyons. While the barbarians were unable to take the city, it was an inspired piece of terrorism on their part. An attack that far inside Roman territory, against Gaul's largest city, unnerved the Roman high command.

Julian reacted quickly. He sent his light cavalry to cut off the barbarians and to see if he could recover some of the loot. His three squadrons managed to block the roads from the Vosges and Jura mountains to the Rhine and all of the bounty that passed through that way was recovered. The third escape route for the barbarians, however, was over the Rhine at Augst. Julian sent two tribunes—a Gaul by the name of Bainobaudes and the thirty-six-year-old future emperor Valentinian—to liaise with Barbatio and to stop any barbarians escaping that way.

The petty-minded Barbatio refused to take orders from Julian and saw the presence of Bainobaudes and Valentinian as an attempt to interfere in another commander's turf. He decided to challenge the perceived threat to his authority rather than the Germans, and ordered the two tribunes to withdraw. The road remained unguarded and the barbarians and their booty got through unopposed.

If relations between the two commanders were bad now, they declined dramatically over the rest of the summer. Inaction on the part of Barbatio turned into deliberate obstruction. As it became clear to the barbarians that Julian meant business, they began to pull back slowly, but it was an organized withdrawal. Roads were blocked with tree trunks as many withdrew to the islands in the Rhine, from where they yelled abuse at the Romans on the banks.

Julian needed boats if he was to have any chance of ferreting out the barbarians. He didn't have any, but Barbatio, who had requisitioned a number to build a pontoon further south, did. The Caesar asked him for seven, but Barbatio burned them instead—a move that was perceived as childish pique. It did not help matters. Luckily for Julian, Barbatio's intransigence became an academic question—some captured spies revealed that the Rhine was fordable upstream. He sent a group of lightly armed commandos on to one of the islands. It worked. The Romans indiscriminately slaughtered everyone on the island, then found some barbarian boats and carried on raiding other islands. It sent the message that Julian wanted and the Germans withdrew.

Julian, who had reached the appointed spot, spent the next few weeks rebuilding Saverne—the Roman city occupied the site around what is now the parish church with some of the town walls visible along the canal. He made sure that it was more than adequately provisioned. This gave him a solid headquarters and blocked any ideas the Germans might have of raiding in the future. Again Barbatio was less than useful. He had requisitioned a grain convoy en route to Julian and, even though he almost certainly burned the wagons he did not need to stop the food falling into enemy hands, the rumors that it was a calculated move cannot have helped. Rather nastily Ammianus writes: "it is unresolved whether he committed so many monstrous acts as a result of his own vanity and self-destructiveness, or prompted by orders from the emperor."[31]

Barbatio now enters the story for the final time. He appears to have been ordered by Constantius to cross the river alone—possibly to make a Roman beachhead on the left bank. It was a disaster from the word go. As soon as the proposed pontoon that had caused the bad feelings a few weeks earlier had been built, the barbarians smashed it by cutting down trees upstream and letting them crash into the makeshift bridge. The Germans then attacked en masse. Barbatio's army was routed and driven back as far as Augst. His baggage was almost entirely looted and, realizing that this was one mistake too many, he withdrew to Milan to work on his defense against the inevitable prosecution.

By the end of August everything looked black for the Romans. Constantius, determined not to throw good money after bad, had no immediate intention of reinforcing that wing of the army that year. Julian and Severus were left high and dry, completely exposed in Saverne. Then word reached them that seven of the German tribes had united to march on Strasbourg.

3

HEART OF FIRE

The blood-red blossom of war with a heart of fire.
ALFRED, LORD TENNYSON, *MAUD*

Several weeks later, in the second half of August 357, with the corn ripe in the fields and waving in the wind, Julian sat on horseback at the top of a hill looking out over the massive German army that was rallying in front of him. It was forming itself into defensive wedges, much of it already in position. Just behind the barbarians was the River Ill and parallel to that, slightly further away, the River Rhine, with the town of Strasbourg, the traditional headquarters of the 8th Legion, in the far distance off toward his right.

The battle of Strasbourg is always presented as Julian's greatest victory. In reality the young commander followed the manual to the letter and, without minimizing his achievement, it was a defensive battle, not won by the Romans but lost by the Germans. As the Roman army entrenched itself behind hastily dug ditches, Julian knew that the odds were not in his favor. The Germans had finished mustering their troops on the eastern bank of the Rhine several days previously and were now crossing the river methodically. It was patently obvious that they out-numbered the Romans almost three to one. Everything would come down to Roman discipline.

The Roman army, at best 20,000 strong but more likely numbering around 13,000, had had a long day. It was after dawn when it had set off to march the twenty-one miles from Saverne to confront the barbarian army near Strasbourg. With the threat of ambush at every stage, it had been a slow and tense march. The infantry were stationed in the middle with the 600-strong cavalry contingent posted either side as protection. They were taking no chances. Among the cavalry were mounted archers and cataphracti—the tanks of the Roman army—riders in full armor with helmets and faceplates astride mail-armored horses.

Just after 11 a.m., hot and tired after a five-hour route march, Julian had called a halt, within sight of the mobilizing Germans, and had addressed his men. It is the first record we have of him making a speech. The exact words that the young Caesar used have not survived, but even though Ammianus's patron had been posted to the east that spring, taking our eyewitness with him, the historian was able to use Julian's own account of the battle, which has sadly not survived, as a reference.

It was a wonderful piece of rhetoric. Julian had a sense of drama, and in choreographing a speech to raise the spirits of men tired after a long march, he was following the manuals. Vegetius advises the commander before battle to "say anything by which the soldiers' minds may be pro-voked to hatred of their adversaries by arousing their anger and indigna-tion."[1] In a prearranged move, Julian's suggestion that the Roman army bed down for the night was publicly contradicted by Florentius, who with blatant jingoism asked the troops if they wanted to let the barbarians run away before they had a chance to fight. Given Julian's impetuous character, it is implausible that he would call a genuine halt. There is no doubt about the effect on the army. The soldiers responded by rattling their spears against their shields—a sign of approval—and with cheers the army marched toward the Rhine.

Coming toward the crest of a hill, Julian's outriders spotted four barbarian scouts keeping a lookout for the Romans. The three on horse-back made their escape, but one, on foot, was captured and interrogated.

He soon revealed that the German army was some 35,000 men strong. It stopped Julian and the Roman commanders in their tracks for the moment.

What was going through Julian's mind? Did he realize quite how much he had underestimated the Germans? Up to now he had treated the Germans as if they were recalcitrant children, but the head of the German combined forces, a towering overweight brute of a man called Chondomar, was anything but a pushover. Six years earlier he had seen off part of the imperial pretender Magnentius's army and had dealt with Barbatio as little more than an inconvenience.

His intelligence rivaled the Romans' too. Chondomar appears to have been aware of the ructions between the two commanders and was obviously informed of quite how far Barbatio had retreated. One of his spies had let him know that Roman forces in the area were depleted. It was this perceived weakness that had prompted Chondomar to rally six other German chiefs and meld them into a cohesive unit. His deputy was his nephew, Serapion. The boy may have been young—according to Ammianus he was too young to grow proper bristles[2]—but he too was no novice in the ways of the Romans. His father had gone so native that he had even been initiated into some of the Greek cults, and had changed his son's name from Agenarich to Serapion.

Chondomar was canny enough to try and play the Romans at their own game. A few days earlier he had sent diplomats to Julian, to try and give his battle plans authority with legalese. He complained that Roman soldiers were stealing German corn and cited several letters from Constantius giving them permission to settle the land. Faced with the authority of these documents, Julian pursued the only course of action open to him. He had the diplomats arrested as spies and thrown into prison.

Sitting on the gently sloping wheat-covered hills, just outside the modern town of Oberhausbergen, Julian realized that battle had to be joined that afternoon. Maybe he could already see Chondomar, who, with his distinctive flame-colored plume and javelin in hand, was giving orders.

The signal was given on the long straight bugle that the Roman army used, and in full battle formation the Romans advanced on the barbarian forces. Julian had stationed the cavalry to his right; he himself commanded the infantry in the center, to which he had given backbone with the armored cavalry; and Severus commanded the left wing, also made up of infantry with some more cavalry. A further strong unit of infantry had been stationed behind them, to be deployed as and when needed.

A spy had informed the German forces how Julian planned to fight and naturally enough Chondomar had set up his line to counter it. The barbarian chief took charge of his own troops, opposite the main Roman cavalry. To his right, the German center was made up of the bulk of the infantry, while off to his far right, opposite Severus, Serapion was hidden out of sight among the reeds in the waterlogged ground in the small valley that continued from the bottom of the hill—roughly where the old station of Dingsheim is today.

Even before it had engaged the enemy, the Roman line began to break slightly. Severus came across Serapion's hidden units and halted, blocking them from the rest of the field. This meant the line began to trail. Julian, with his escort of 200 cavalrymen, came within range of the enemy archers to rally the troops there and gave the order to attack, at the same time warning them to keep their ranks if they routed the Germans. Yet again Julian was following the textbook. "Often a previously routed army has recovered its strength and destroyed those in loose order and pursuing at random," is Vegetius's warning.[3]

The unity among the German troops was more apparent—hardly surprising given that the army was made up of seven tribes—and the Alemanni infantry started to show signs of revolt. With laudable egalitarian zeal but a distinct lack of military discipline, they demanded that their leaders get off their high horses and join the fray on foot—sensing that they would thus be less tempted to make a run for it if the battle did not go their way. There was no time for debate. Chondomar leaped from his horse and the rest followed suit.

After the initial and traditional exchange of missiles, the trumpets gave the sign to engage. The first wild moments of battle were chaotic—there was to be no swift victory for either side. When Severus engaged, the left wing almost immediately repulsed the Alemanni attack. The Roman right wing was not so lucky. At the combined onslaught of the barbarian cavalry, the Roman cataphracti were routed. In a blind panic, they were only given heart by the sight of Julian's pendant, the symbol of a purple dragon attached to the tip of a long lance and streaming in the wind "like the cast skin of a snake"[4] coming toward them. Somehow they rallied.

By now, the barbarians had turned their sights on the infantry—the heart of the Roman army—and their cavalry had charged, hoping for another easy rout. The two sides remained evenly matched until two units of veteran auxiliaries came up to support the Romans. Armed with shields and spears, these two regiments had more ethnically in common with those they were fighting than with Rome itself, but they fought on.

After releasing a volley of javelins, they too attacked. The Romans locked shields in the famous tortoise formation—hollow squares with twelve men on each side standing so close to each other that their shields overlapped making an impenetrable barrier—as the Germans hurled themselves at them furiously. Two more regiments were called up as reinforcements, but the battle still raged, arrows flying and swords slashing. The outcome still hung in the balance. The Germans had height, strength, and numbers on their side; the Romans had training and discipline.

The Germans had one last push in them. The leaders rallied their troops and attacked. It took the tired Roman front line by surprise. The Alemanni broke through and reached the center of the Roman forces. But there, the legionaries stood firm, fighting coldly and methodically, hacking away at any exposed enemy flesh. With that failed final push, Alemanni spirit and energy evaporated and the barbarians ran for it "like the crew and passengers of a wreck in a storm at sea, who are eager to get to land wherever the wind carries them."[5] To all intents and purposes, Gaul was free. It was a victory the like of which had not been seen along the Rhine for generations.

As for the barbarians, anyone who could made for the river. Julian gave the order not to follow the Germans into the water, and the rout became a massacre as the Romans lined the banks hurling arrows, darts, and slingshots at the panicked barbarians. The rest of the Roman army started on the cleaning up process—burying the dead, building a camp for the night along the Rhine and counting the cost. All in all, the Romans had lost only 243 men and four officers, one of whom had led the commando raid earlier in the summer to help clear the islands of the Rhine. The German dead on the field numbered 6,000 not counting those at the bottom of the Rhine, which could have been as high as 2,000 men.

Chondomar's part in the action is not mentioned until the very end. He needed to get back to his camp at Lauterbourg, about thirty-seven miles north of Strasbourg up the Rhine. He had even had some boats hidden before the battle for such an emergency. Winding a cloth round his face for concealment, the Alemanni chief was heading for the river when his horse slipped on the mud that had been churned through with blood, and threw him. He tried to escape to a nearby hill but was recognized by a Roman unit. All fight now out of him, Chondomar surrendered in person and alone.

Ammianus's description is so savage and humiliating that it is hard not to have some sympathy for Chondomar. "Like all barbarians, Chondomar was as submissive in disaster as he was the opposite in success. Finding himself in another man's power he was dragged along pale and dismayed, speechless from consciousness of his crimes, a different being from the man who after a course of wild and deplorable outrages trampled on the ashes of Gaul and uttered a string of savage threats."[6] Nonetheless, Julian spared him and a few days later sent him to the emperor's court in Milan. There, he was drafted into the imperial army and stationed at a military base in Rome for personnel seconded from the provincial armies called the Castra Peregrina (roughly where the Via Santo Stefano and Via Navicella meet). In the Eternal City he succumbed to disease, probably tuberculosis, and died soon afterward.

After the battle it would have made sense to head back for winter quarters in Saverne or Sens, but even though it was late in the year Julian intended to make sure that the Germans were suitably cowed and that there would be no repeat of last year's performance—a revolt as soon as Roman backs were turned. The left bank of the Rhine might now be subdued, but Julian intended to take the fight into the Germans' own territory.

In the first instance, Julian did withdraw to Saverne and spent several days dealing with disciplinary matters. First, he released the German diplomats he had arrested. Then the cavalry, which had caved before the barbarians' onslaught had to be punished. Rather than suffer execution, they were publicly humiliated instead, dressed up in women's clothing and led through the camp.[7] Finally he had to cope with the administrative aftermath of the battle—sending prisoners and booty to Metz for safekeeping, for example—before announcing to the surprised soldiers that he now intended to cross the Rhine.

The news was not especially well received. The soldiers had fought hard all year and had just won a major battle. Unsurprisingly they wished to bed down for the winter, but, as so often, they were won over by Julian's charisma, encouraged, as Ammianus claims, by the fact that he shared their work, conditions, and drudgery.[8]

In early September, the army marched north and crossed the Rhine on pontoon bridges near Mainz. The Romans were on the wrong side of the Rhine. As Julian had predicted, it was a move that completely flummoxed the Germans. First they sent envoys to sue for peace; then they sent envoys to threaten the Romans unless they evacuated the region.

Julian did not even bother to reply. Just as he had done earlier in the summer when he was clearing the islands in the Rhine of barbarians, he put together a hefty commando unit of 800 men and sent them in boats upstream to destroy anything they could find. They did their job well. When the main force of the Roman army appeared the next morning, the soldiers found nothing but burning farms and homes. The Germans had fled east and south across the Main to warn their families. Whenever Julian's forces came to a farm it was checked for prisoners and then razed to the ground.

It was now the end of September and getting extremely late in the year for campaigning. The first snow had fallen and after a march of around ten miles the army hit forest. The advance was halted for a time while what Ammianus calls "a German deserter,"[9] though more probably a spy fed the Romans the line that there was a huge force hiding in the forest in underground tunnels and trenches.

We should not underestimate quite how uneasy the Romans would have been. Germany, especially on the wrong side of the Rhine, made them very nervous. It had always been the backdrop to Rome's worst defeats. The first extant geographical work in Latin, *Description of the World* (also known as *The Cosmographer*), written in the first century by the Spanish-born Pomponius Mela, elegantly sums up the Roman point of view—there are too many rivers, the mountains are severe and the rest is impenetrable because of the forests.[10]

Forests certainly made it even worse. The Hercynian Forest, although strictly speaking further east, was used as a blanket term for all forests along the Rhine, and as such had an image of impregnability and sheer size that daunted the Roman mind. Given how well Julian knew Caesar's *Conquest of Gaul,* one phrase of his may have stuck in his mind: "No western German claims to have reached the eastern extremity, even after traveling for two months or to have heard where it ends."[11] It certainly scared Julian. In a fragment that has survived either from a letter or Julian's own account of these campaigns, he writes that compared to other regions within the empire that claimed to be impassable, "for difficulty of approach they are trivial indeed compared to the Hercynian Forest."[12]

One can only guess with what Julian had to bribe his soldiers to continue, but probably against their better judgment, they began to advance through the forest. Although there were no Germans lying in wait for them, the army found its path blocked by trees. Not yet prepared to give up, it made sense to find a proper base and Julian headed for Ladenburg. Now a rather pretty town, then it was the edge of the world. By AD 200 it had become a fairly impressive frontier town (the remains of which can be seen underneath the St. Galluskirche), but the town was destroyed by the Alemanni sixty years later and limped on in an increasingly decrepit state, the object of occasional bouts of vandalism. At the time Julian arrived, Ammianus says that Ladenburg had recently suffered a violent attack.[13]

Julian spent until the end of November rebuilding the town. A garrison was stationed, the empty granaries were refilled, and the surrounding tribes soon got the message that this was no guerrilla raid. Rather than wait for the Romans to finish their work and then destroy the entire area, the Alemanni sent diplomats to sue for peace. After making them wait for an answer and no doubt letting them ponder the consequences of a Roman town in their midst strongly defended with artillery, he agreed to a ten-month peace. Quite how much Julian had rattled the barbarians can be seen in the terms of the treaty and in that they were kept: three of the kings who had sent help to Chondomar were made to swear allegiance to Rome—according to their own oaths, not Roman ones they could wriggle out of—and they promised not to attack the fort and to supply corn whenever it was asked for.

It was finally time to return to winter quarters. Fate, however, had other plans. Severus formed the advance cavalry guard and en route to Paris via Cologne and Jülich (sometimes referred to by its French name of Juliers) bumped into a large band of Franks—Ammianus says 600, Libanius says 1,000—near the River Meuse. Realizing that Severus was only the advance guard, the Franks took fright and shut themselves into two forts along the banks of the river.

Rather than risk a direct attack, Julian decided on a siege. It was a much longer affair than he had planned. The barbarians held out for fifty-four days, right through December and January. Increasingly frustrated, and possibly aware that a large army of Franks was coming to the rescue, Julian realized that a frozen Meuse was giving the Franks opportunity to slip out under cover of darkness.

He ordered his soldiers to row up and down the river all night, making sure that no ice formed. That did the trick. Frankish resistance soon collapsed through hunger and lack of sleep and the barbarians surrendered, while their potential rescuers realized that an all-out attack might not be such a good idea and quietly dispersed. The coda to the story is that Julian sent the entire band to Constantius, who, pleased to receive such a strong and brave band immediately enrolled them in one of his auxiliary units.

At the end of January 358 it was at last time to seek out winter quarters. Julian had been on campaign without a break for the past seven months. In that time he had fought numerous battles and inspired his soldiers with an almost manic drive to succeed. Those who were with him said that he always had either books or arms in his hands. This was a compliment from an army that was not especially bookish—but he could do anything he wanted provided that he kept winning, handing out honors, and allowing them to plunder at will. Nobody took any notice of those at court who sneered that his live fast and die young attitude was merely a ploy to avoid meeting the same end as his brothers. Gratefully,

Julian and his army headed for Paris, the city he referred to as his "beloved Lutetia,"[14] a city that has adopted him as one of its own.

Only vague ghosts and shadows remain of the Paris that Julian knew. From the time of Julius Caesar to the middle of the third century the city had grown from a barbarian fort of the tribe known as the Parisii into an elegant city and important river port. At its height, much of the city sprawled across the present Left Bank, centered on Sainte Geneviève. There was a forum in the area of the rue Soufflot; an arena, built to hold 20,000 spectators, off the rue Monge; and a theater at what is now the corner of the boulevard St. Michel and the rue Racine.

But the city had barely survived the upheavals of the third century. For a start, the palace had moved back to the Île de la Cité and you have to look closely to find any traces of the fourth century. Paris had been sacked and burned by the time that Julian arrived and resettlers had preferred the safety of more southern cities like Vienne. The rue Saint Jacques lines up with the only bridge that remained—the Petit Pont, which crossed the Seine through Île de la Cité to both right and left banks. The most famous remnants from that period, however, are the Roman baths—now the Museum of the Middle Ages and Cluny Museum, where the Roman parts are still easily distinguishable both from outside and inside the building.

Julian himself gives a vivid snapshot of the city: "It is a small island lying in the river; a wall entirely surrounds it and wooden bridges lead to it on both sides. The river seldom rises and falls, but usually is the same depth in the winter as in the summer season, and it provides water which is very clear to the eye and very pleasant for one who wishes to drink. . . . A good kind of vine grows thereabouts and some people have even managed to make fig trees grow by covering them in winter with a sort of garment of straw and with things of that sort, such as are used to protect trees from the harm that is done to them by the cold wind."[15]

From this winter we can detect a slight shift in the relationship between Julian and Constantius. Neither can have been especially conscious of it at the time and there is nothing specific beyond growing mistrust on both sides and Julian's general dissatisfaction. Julian will have had time to dwell on the fact that Constantius had sent out communiqués wreathed in laurel to the provinces lauding his victory over the Alemanni and claiming that he had received Chondomar's surrender in person. In itself, there was nothing sinister about this; the emperor was generally credited in person for wins his armies had anywhere in the empire, but even though this was normal policy, the lack of mention in dispatches clearly rankled with Julian.

After the breach between the two had become more permanent, he wrote:

> At Strasbourg, even though the gods gave into my hands as prisoner of war the king of the enemy, I did not begrudge Constantius the glory of that success. And yet, even though I was not allowed to triumph for it, I had it in my power to kill my enemy, and moreover I could have led him through the whole of Gaul and exhibited him to the cities, and thus have luxuriated as it were in the misfortunes of Chondomar. I thought it my duty to do none of these things, but sent him at once to Constantius. . . . So it came about that, though I had done all of the fighting and he had only traveled in those parts and held friendly conversations with the tribes who live on the borders of the Danube, it was he who held the triumph, and not I.[16]

If Julian was suffering from a bruised ego, Constantius too had reason to be wary of his cousin. In the immediate aftermath of the battle of Strasbourg, Julian's soldiers had hailed him as Augustus. It was certainly only over-exuberance on the part of an army that had just won its first major battle in the region for years—and Julian angrily, publicly, and pointedly rebuked them—but Constantius cannot have failed to have been reminded of all the usurpers who had started that way. It would have taken a much more secure emperor than Constantius not to have been unnerved by his Caesar's growing popularity. Certainly, Julian's mail was still monitored. In a note to Julian that winter, Libanius went so far as to append a convoluted and sycophantic note to his minder, which leaves the reader in little doubt about how free Julian was thought to be.[17]

At court things were little better. Figuring that the way into Constantius's favor was to belittle Julian's achievements, gossips nicknamed Julian "Victorinus," a pun meaning both "little victor" and a reference to a rebel from Gaul a hundred years previously. The jokes and the backbiting will have done nothing to calm either man's fears. Neither was aware of it, but the victory at Strasbourg had changed their relationship irrevocably.

As spring turned to summer, Julian concerned himself with two problems, both of which involved finance. Julian's role, as commander-in-chief of the army, was to look after the safety of Gaul. Although he was military leader, Julian was not the administrative head. The two positions—which reported directly and independently to the emperor and not to each other—had traditionally been split for reasons of security. It made sense to keep the man who held the purse strings and the man who commanded the soldiers separate, but the impetuous Caesar now came up sharp against the senior civil administrator, the praetorian prefect Florentius. Although relations had hitherto been cordial, they rapidly soured—the more that Julian's actions were perceived by Florentius to have been counter to the wishes of Constantius. Even though we have a less than pleasant image of Florentius, he appears to have been a solid, reliable bureaucrat who, to start with, had the absolute confidence of the emperor.

The economy is one of the most complex and least understood areas of ancient history, only now getting the attention it deserves. While Julian's military successes in Gaul have overshadowed his other achievements, this is the one area in which he consistently won nothing but praise. The taxation of Gaul, when Julian arrived, was both badly thought out and inefficiently collected. Not only was the poll tax assessed on information that was hopelessly out of date—taxes were in no way means-tested depending on war or a bad harvest—but the answer to the current budget deficit was to slap a supplementary tax on the few who had already paid.

Florentius, whose idea the supplementary tax had been, took what he saw as Julian's meddling badly. Already something of an intellectual bully, Julian not only gave Florentius chapter and verse of why such a tax did not work historically, he then took the praetorian prefect through the books and proposed a tax cut. Events rapidly came to a head. Julian would throw Florentius's proposals on the floor without reading them and the praetorian prefect had to appeal to Constantius, who slapped his Caesar across the wrist and told him not to undermine Florentius's authority. The letters went back and forth, but it cannot have helped that Constantius eventually sided with his cousin.

Julian's solution was not to increase taxes, but to make sure that the taxes levied were actually collected, specifically those on the rich. What had permanently muddied the books was the practice of indulgences, by which back taxes were periodically wiped out. In theory it was a windfall for all, but in practice it only benefited the better off. The poor had to pay their taxes on the nail, while the rich could cosy up to the collector—traditionally a civic honor—and postpone payment until the next round of write-offs. Julian's measure worked. Relieved from the worry about supplementary taxes, people actually paid what they owed and his measures had such a marked effect on the exchequer that during Julian's four years in Gaul, taxes were reduced by more than two-thirds.

We get some idea of the bad atmosphere that had grown up in Paris in a letter that Julian wrote to a friend. Although Julian does not mention him by name—for both stylistic reasons (it was a sophistic affectation) and security—he is evidently referring to Florentius.

> With regard to my behavior toward him, the gods know that I often
> kept silent at the expense of my own honor when he wronged the
> provincials. Some charges I would not listen to, others I would not
> admit, others again I did not believe, and in some cases I blamed
> his associates. But when he decided to make me complicit in such
> a scandal by sending those shameful and absolutely abominable
> reports for me to sign, what was the right thing for me to do? Was
> I to remain silent or to oppose him? The former course was fool-
> ish, servile, and hateful to the gods; the latter was just, manly, and
> liberal, but not an option open to me as I was engaged in other
> affairs. . . .
>   In a case like this, what was the right conduct for a zealous
> student of Plato and Aristotle? Should I have looked on while the
> wretched people were being betrayed to thieves, or have helped
> them as far as I could, for they were already singing their swan
> song because of the criminal scams of men of that sort? It seems a

disgrace that while I punish my military tribunes when they desert their posts (they ought to be put to death at once and not even granted a proper burial), I should myself desert my post which is for the defense of such wretched people; whereas it is my duty to fight against bandits of his sort, especially when god is fighting on my side, for it was he who posted me here. And if any harm to myself should come of it, it is no small consolation to have proceeded with good conscience.[18]

As if the issue of tax collection had not caused friction enough, Julian and Florentius came to loggerheads again at the start of that year's campaign. Indeed, it is the very fact that the campaign season did not begin until the harvest in July that highlights Constantius's strategic imperatives throughout 358. The problem was grain. Even though the Alemanni had been effectively subdued, northern Gaul—as the brief winter sortie on the River Meuse had shown—was still wide open. A quick look at a map shows that the obvious logistical answer was to use British grain. Julian had realized this and had amassed a fairly major grain fleet with ships "larger than galleys"[19]—"I had collected a fleet of six hundred ships, four hundred of which I had built in less than ten months,"[20] he wrote.

The problem was that with control of the English Channel compromised, it was impossible to guarantee grain imports from Britain. Instead, supplies had to travel a long and tortuous route from southern France, which did not reach their depot in Reims until midsummer—too late to supply an extended military campaign.

Constantius's plan, therefore, was twofold. From a military point of view, he wanted to reinforce and reestablish the chain of forts from the Channel down to Cologne as a counter against any threats from the Frankish tribes—specifically the Chamavi, who had been responsible for attacking Cologne three years previously and were disrupting the grain convoys. The emperor, however, also had a broader social agenda. He wanted to repair the damage that had been caused by the barbarian invasions and the troubles of the third century. Huge tranches of northern and eastern Gaul had been depleted or destroyed, land had been left to go to waste and the countryside had been all but deserted. If the emperor could guarantee safety in these areas, it would significantly help their resettlement. This was not an entirely altruistic move. If the region was repopulated, then not only could taxes begin to flow again, but one of the traditional recruiting grounds of the Roman army could start defending the empire.

Florentius's answer was a bureaucrat's one and an instant fix. If the barbarians were hijacking grain ships from Britain, then pay them a "tax" to stop. Florentius cannot have imagined that it would have caused any difficulties. Constantius had had no problems with coming to arrangements with the barbarians in the past, and he cannot have thought that this occasion would be any different. Julian, however, pulled him up short. Some indication about just how fraught those discussions must have been can be seen in Julian's account of the matter: "The situation seemed so impossible to Florentius that he had promised to pay the barbarians a fee of two thousand pounds of silver in return for safe passage. When Constantius learned of this—Florentius had informed him about the proposed payment—he wrote to me that I should carry out the agreement, unless I thought it absolutely disgraceful. How could it fail to be disgraceful when it even seemed so to Constantius, who was only too much in the habit of trying to pay off the barbarians? No payment was made."[21]

Julian's solution? To take the offensive. While his resolve is admirable, his actions must have seemed foolhardy if not verging on the insane. Without waiting for supplies, Julian managed to source three weeks of hard rations and set off at the beginning of May against the Franks who had settled between the River Meuse and the River Scheldt. By the time he had made it to Tongres, the Franks were ready to negotiate. After lulling them into a false sense of security with consideration of a treaty, he and Severus cowed them completely after a couple of lightning attacks.

Then, the real object of the campaign: the Chamavi. Julian headed east to their territory between the River Meuse and the River Rhine. Julian's own account of that part of the campaign reads like dispatches and disguises what must have been a terrifying campaign of destruction. "Since the gods protected me and were present to help, I received the capitulation of part of the Salian tribe, drove out the Chamavian tribe and took many cattle, women, and children. I so terrified them all and made them tremble at my approach that I immediately received hostages from them and secured a safe passage for my food supplies," he wrote.[22]

After the defeat, the standard pattern of rebuilding forts continued and Julian reconstructed three of them along the Meuse. As he neared the Rhine though, the Caesar was pulled up short by a near revolt among his soldiers, triggered by a lack of food. Julian had given some of the rations that the soldiers had carried to provision the forts and had gambled on being able to requisition grain from the Chamavi, but it was June and the corn was not yet ripe.

As Napoleon was later to find out, an army always marches on its stomach and what started out as whining threatened to become mutiny. The other issue was pay. A Roman soldier received a regular income that he was used to being paid at fairly wide intervals as well as donatives in lieu of looting. Understandably, as Constantius was less than keen on giving Julian all of the tools he needed for a revolution, he made sure that his cousin had no authority over the purse strings, even though he had managed to arrange some one-offs in the past. He was shocked how rapidly the soldiers turned on him. From their hero, he became "the bloody wog," "a liar," "a fool," and "a wannabe philosopher."[23] It was only quick thinking, fast talking, and basic bribery that saved Julian.

For the second time, Julian crossed the Rhine. If Julian had thought he had command problems up to now, matters suddenly got worse. Severus began to act oddly. His advance was sluggish, and rumor had it that he had threatened to have his scouts charged and executed if they advanced too rapidly. Severus was certainly an old man and he had loyally aided Julian for the past two years. It appears to have been a medical problem, and a nervous breakdown brought on by exhaustion is a plausible diagnosis. He was certainly ailing and died of natural causes soon afterward. While it is often pointed out that Julian acted like a common soldier, it is perhaps more accurate to suggest that he acted like a perfect common soldier. It cannot have been easy for those like Severus to live and work with a man who seemed to have no vices and appeared inured against fatigue.

In quick succession, two more of the chiefs who had supported

Chondomar were subdued, more Roman prisoners were released, and Julian was back in winter quarters in Paris by the early autumn. It may have been notably earlier than the year before but this was almost certainly due to the earlier uprising. Julian also had much to feel satisfied about. By the winter of 358 Chondomar was dead in Rome, three barbarian chiefs had signed nonaggression treaties the previous year, two that year and with Serapion presumed dead, Julian had dealt with all of those who had risen up at Strasbourg.

If the previous three years may be characterized as arrival, war and consolidation, 359 was the year of the split between Julian and Constantius. On the surface, however, it was business as usual.

Julian sent spies across the Rhine to check out the lie of the land, and then intended to follow with his troops. For all the military successes against the Franks the previous year, Julian needed not only to confirm that the ships could get through, but also that the granaries that had been destroyed in various raids were rebuilt. For security, a line of seven towns was reoccupied, old frontier posts on the lower Rhine stretching from Fort Hercules, just south of the Rhine by Arnhem, across to Bingen in Germany.

An indication of quite how much the barbarians had been unnerved by the events of the previous year is given by the rapidity and the efficiency with which the local chiefs sent building materials to help the work. Julian then crossed the Rhine for the third and final time, accepting peace treaties from several chiefs on the usual terms—nonaggression, the release of all prisoners, and supplies when needed.

Julian's own assessment of his time in Gaul is fair:

> It would take too long to enumerate everything and to write down every detail of the task that I accomplished within four years. To sum up: I crossed the Rhine three times when I was Caesar; I demanded and received one thousand Roman prisoners that had been held captive on the far side of the Rhine; I took ten thousand prisoners in two battles and one siege—men in the prime of life, not of unserviceable age; I sent Constantius four levies of excellent infantry, three more of average infantry and two very distinguished cavalry squadrons. I have now, with the help of the gods, recov-

ered all the towns and by that time I had already recovered almost forty.[24]

If militarily it was business as usual, elsewhere enough little cracks were starting to appear to make a final break inevitable. There was little sign of it on the surface—laws for example, were still being issued in both of their names—but much like an iceberg, the real danger was out of sight.

If we are looking for a catalyst, then it is the death of the emperor's wife Eusebia. It is unclear how she died. One of the more entertaining theories has it that she died as a result of anorexia nervosa, brought on by an unsatisfactory sexual relationship with Constantius, a theory that neatly accounts for her childlessness. It is perhaps more plausible to suggest that she died of cervical cancer.[25]

While she was alive, she could act as a counterpoint to the backbiting at court and do much to reassure Constantius. With her gone, there was no one. Julian was mocked for his pretentiousness, for his purported cowardice, and his appearance. The jokes and the sneering began to hit home and there was no one who might be able to smooth over the cracks.

It makes sense to date the second oration to Constantius to that spring. The strains in the relationship between Julian and the emperor are now obvious. Julian uses Homeric parallels to praise his cousin and finds a Homeric counterpart for every event in Constantius's life. The effect is mechanical and over-egged, and eyebrows will have shot up about parallels drawn between Achilles and Agamemnon in the speech's opening paragraphs. Was Julian really suggesting that he was Achilles in this relationship and had quarreled with the king? It is all too easy to read the speech as an extended needling of the emperor. In an early passage, for example, he compares Constantius to a number of Homeric heroes, rejecting each one for a specific failing, which could quite easily be read to mean the emperor. "There is the archer Pandaros in Homer— but he is treacherous and accepts bribes. And anyway he had a weak arm and was an inferior soldier. Then there are Teucer and Meriones. The latter uses his bow against a pigeon while Teucer, although he distinguished himself in battle, always needed a sort of bulwark or wall.

Accordingly he keeps a shield in front of him—and that not his own, but his brother's. He aims at the enemy at his ease and cuts an absurd figure as a soldier as he needed a protector taller than himself. It was not in his weapons that he placed his hopes of safety."[26]

But Constantius was far away and Julian's more immediate worry was Florentius. He may have won some administrative battles the previous year, but his praetorian prefect now began to outflank him at every turn and Julian was becoming increasingly isolated. Then came the final break.

Julian's honesty was already the stuff of legend, but it was not necessarily popular. During one notable trial for embezzlement, Julian's failure to convict led the defendant's lawyer to ask: "Will anyone be found guilty, your highness, if denial is enough to secure acquittal?" Julian merely replied: "Will anyone ever be acquitted if accusation is enough to secure conviction?"[27]

When Florentius was caught with his hand in the till, the affair was blown out of all proportion. One of the praetorian prefect's cronies was being prosecuted for fraud and as Florentius was presiding over the case, he attacked the prosecutor. Such blatant corruption did not go unnoticed and the upshot was that Florentius himself came under investigation. As a senior member of staff, he invoked an "all boys together" code and tried to get Julian to oversee the case in private. Julian refused to cover up for him. He used the excuse that he did not have the power to do so, but it was apparent that it was just that—an excuse.

Florentius was incandescent with rage. Julian had broken an unwritten rule. Florentius went on the attack and sent urgent dispatches to Constantius that Julian's closest adviser, the quaestor Salutius, was a bad influence on the impressionable Caesar, encouraging the young man to act too big for his boots. Salutius was summarily recalled. It is hard to interpret this as anything other than vindictiveness.

Despite popular support from both locals and soldiers, by the winter of 359 Julian was increasingly alone. He could expect little help from Severus's replacement, an arrogant and greedy Christian called Lupicinus. Several letters to friends asking them to come and visit him have survived from this period. To Priscus, his former tutor in Greece, he initially wrote with some bravado, but soon followed this up with a rather more plaintive letter. "As regards a visit to me from your good self, if you plan to, make your arrangements now, with the help of the gods, and hurry," he wrote.[28]

It is easy to imagine history stopping here. The intrigues that threatened Julian by now—both at court and around him in Paris—were such that it is a surprise that he survived. His popularity with the soldiers would have been enough to have him murdered like Gallus, or any of the others Constantius had dispatched over the years. But in his time in Gaul, Julian had gained a confidence, an arrogance, which carried him through. He had learned how to fight and proved that he could command. He had learned how to administer a country—not without treading on people's toes, but more effectively than anyone else. Without realizing it, Constantius had trained his successor.

4

OUT OF THE DARKNESS

In my mind's eye a Temple, like a cloud
Slowly surmounting some invidious hill,
Rose out of the darkness.

WILLIAM WORDSWORTH,
IN MY MIND'S EYE A TEMPLE

It was a letter from Constantius in January 360 that turned the Caesar into a rebel, and then the rebel into an emperor. The letter contained orders to send troops to the eastern front. But within a few weeks this simple order had been rejected, the Gaulish soldiers had risen en masse, surrounded Julian's palace in Paris at midnight with cries of "Julian for Augustus," and had openly declared him emperor. When he reluctantly appeared, they raised him aloft on an infantry shield—the ritual honor for kings among the barbarian troops that were the backbone of Julian's support. Whatever reforms he later instituted, Julian never forgot that it was the army that had made him emperor. The solemnity of the occasion was broken only briefly when the soldiers could not find a suitable diadem with which to crown him. He was asked whether his wife had a necklace or some piece of jewelry that would do. Julian protested that this would be rather an inauspicious start to his reign. Then the standard-bearer for one of the legions removed the torque from around his neck and placed it on Julian's head. Like so many emperors before him, he was crowned by his troops.

Julian describes what happened in some detail:

> The legions arrived. I went to meet them as was customary and ordered them to continue their march. They halted for one day and until then I had no idea at all of what they had decided. I call to witness Zeus, Helios, Ares, Athena, and all the other gods that no such suspicion even entered my mind until that very evening.
>
> It was already late, when about sunset the news was brought to me, and suddenly the palace was surrounded and they all began to shout while I was still considering what I ought to do and feeling by no means confident. My wife was still alive and to rest alone, I had gone to the upper room near hers. From there through an opening in the wall, I prayed to Zeus. And when the shouting grew still louder and the palace was all in tumult, I begged the god to give me a sign. He showed me a sign and bade me yield and not to oppose the will of the army. Even after these tokens had been given to me I did not yield without reluctance, but resisted as long as I could and would not accept either the title or the diadem of emperor.
>
> But since I could not control so many single-handedly, and the gods, who willed this to happen, spurred on the soldiers and gradually softened my resolve, somewhere around 9 p.m., some soldier or another gave me the torque and I put it on my head and returned to the palace, as the gods know, groaning in my heart. It was my duty to feel confident and to trust in Zeus after he had shown me the sign, but I was terribly ashamed and sank into the earth at the thought of not seeming to obey Constantius faithfully to the last.
>
> Since the palace was in complete uproar, the friends of Constantius thought they would seize the occasion to contrive a plot against me without delay and bribed the soldiers, expecting one of two things—either that they would cause a split between the troops and me or that the latter would attack me openly.

But when a certain officer, one of the commanders of my wife's escort, saw that this was being plotted, he reported it to me. When he saw that I paid no attention to him, he became frantic and like one possessed, began to cry aloud before the people in the marketplace: "Fellow soldiers, strangers, and citizens, do not abandon the emperor!" The soldiers, berserk in their anger, all rushed to the palace, weapons at the ready. When they found me alive, in their delight, like men who meet friends whom they had not hoped to see again, they pressed round me on this side and on that, and embraced me and carried me on their shoulders. And it was a sight worth seeing. They were like men seized with a divine frenzy. After they had surrounded me on all sides they demanded that I let them punish Constantius's supporters. The gods know what fierce opposition I had to fight to save those persons.[1]

It is a wonderful story with all the motifs of legend: the spontaneous uprising, the sign from the gods, the unwilling prince raised to emperor then magnanimously protecting his enemies. As with all the best propaganda, it has the advantage that some of it was even true. It is certainly how Julian wanted the rebellion to be remembered in the justificatory manifestos he wrote the following year. But Julian's account not only compresses events, it deliberately misleads by omission.

The events of that January evening point to an opportunistic revolt, leapt upon by Julian and his advisers on the spur of the moment to take advantage of popular sentiment, and not an organized revolution. Julian's uprising was less one born out of suppression and more one of bravado.

First and foremost, the demand for troops was not a matter of personal animosity at all. While Julian does not strictly lie, he is not exactly telling the truth when he complains that Constantius had written him insulting letters and threatened Gaul's security with the withdrawal of Julian's best troops.[2]

There is no mention in Julian's account that the military demands of the empire had changed. After the successes of the past few years, for the whole of the previous year Gaul had been enjoying a stability it had not seen in a while. Other parts of the empire were less peaceful. For a start, trouble was being fomented in Britain, and that winter the Scots and Picts were causing chaos along the empire's northernmost frontiers. Julian immediately dispatched his deputy Lupicinus to London together with two regiments of reserve troops.

Although Lupicinus must have succeeded in quelling the revolution, it was a quick fix rather than a solution. Disturbances broke out four years later and in 367 the province revolted, more seriously this time. Contemptuously treating Hadrian's Wall like a Maginot Line, the Picts simply sailed round it. They had killed two important local officials before the emperor Valentinian sent a senior army officer with four regiments to pacify the province.

So when the orders arrived from Constantius at the start of the year, Julian already had a depleted army. The emperor was frantically mobilizing the empire after defeats on the eastern frontier and intended to take charge of the campaign personally. However much Julian wanted the demand for his troops to be seen as a way of curbing his own popularity by the emperor, it was a perfectly logical military move for Constantius. He had just lost six legions after the disastrous seventy-three-day siege of Amida, now Diyarbakir on the banks of the Tigris in southeast Anatolia, which had ended in Roman humiliation. He was desperately in need of reinforcements.

Unaware of the situation in Britain—the news cannot have reached the emperor in time—Constantius ordered Julian's four best regiments to march for the East, under Lupicinus and Sinitula, another senior officer. This would have reduced Julian's force by between 30 and 50 percent. The order had instant repercussions. Most of the soldiers in Julian's army were native to Gaul and understandably reluctant to leave their homes. But what turned personal disquiet into a political powder keg is that Julian had personally promised his troops that they would never serve beyond the Alps.[3]

In the days after the letter's arrival Julian had no option other than to carry out Constantius' orders. But he was working alone. All his advisers had conveniently left him and Sinitula had vanished eastward as soon as the orders had arrived taking with him the best of the light-armed troops.[4] Julian turned to the praetorian prefect for assistance, writing to Florentius who was in Vienne, and suggested that he return to

Paris. Given the state of their relationship, Florentius was not especially inclined to help. Realizing that Julian suspected, perhaps not without good reason, that it was his dispatches to the emperor on the stability of the region that were behind the decision to remove his troops, he decided to stay put. He claimed he had to source supplies, which is certainly a plausible excuse—riots had almost occurred six years previously when supplies had been stopped from Chalon and the then praetorian prefect had to apologize personally to the troops. Another letter from Paris followed, in which Julian threatened to resign unless the praetorian prefect reported for duty, but much in the same way that Julian had avoided Florentius' memos on tax, this request also went unanswered. From now on, Florentius strenuously avoided all contact with the Caesar. After Julian's elevation to emperor, he ran to Constantius' apron strings. He was rewarded with the position of prefect of Illyricum, but after Constantius' death went into hiding with his wife, was condemned in absentia, and only resurfaced after Julian's death.

With Lupicinus in Scotland, Sinitula rushing to the emperor's side with thoughts of promotion and Florentius absent without leave, Julian did call his troops out of their winter quarters. They were less than impressed. Already feeling unrewarded and put upon by Constantius, they were now expected to leave their homes and travel to the other end of the empire. As Libanius rather histrionically puts it: "Those women, especially who had borne children to the soldiers, pointed to their children, not least to the babes at the breast dandled before them and begged their fathers not to desert them."[5] Anonymous samizdats began to appear in the camps of two of the legions complaining about Constantius's betrayal of the army. "We are to be driven off to the ends of the earth like condemned criminals while our nearest and dearest, whom we have only just freed from captivity after desperate fighting, will become slaves of the Alemanni again," one pamphlet stormed.[6]

Julian recognized that this was a potentially explosive situation and took steps to calm the soldiers down. He listened to the grievances of his troops and not only announced that their families could travel with them, but even put the public transport service at their disposal. In an attempt to diffuse the situation further, he went to meet the legions as they arrived on the outskirts of Paris and spoke to them about the honors that were awaiting them on the eastern front. They received this blatant jingoism in silence.

But what was it that happened in the ensuing hours that turned the soldiers who had greeted him in sullen silence into a mob prepared to commit treason and raise their commander to emperor? The events of the early evening are missing from Julian's own account, and there is a discrepancy of three hours in the emperor's story. He writes that the soldiers surrounded the palace at around 9 p.m. Most other chroniclers either agree on midnight or, aware of the confusion, fudge the issue.

What happened in those missing hours is that Julian invited his senior officers to dinner, as Ammianus blandly puts it, "to make any request it was in his power to grant."[7] There is nothing strange about the commander of an army dining with his officers the night before a campaign and that in itself does not suggest a preplanned revolt. Nonetheless, it requires not too much imagination to see that in conversation over dinner they must have discussed the implications and extent of the troops' unease and the anonymous pamphlets, and how that in turn became a forum to sound out individual officers about their units. It would be a very short step for the atmosphere over dinner to become seditious.

While some speculation is required to come to this conclusion, what makes it more compelling is that the guest list that night for supper also included Julian's pagan intimates in Gaul, his doctor Oribasius, an otherwise unknown Libyan called Euhemerus, and possibly five others.[8] The guests at dinner are all likely to have been individuals in whose company Julian felt comfortable, certainly so if he could invite fellow pagans. If his guests did not already know about or actively encourage his dreams of the purple, they were not the group to discourage them.

We do know that Julian had not shied away from sharing his ambitions with at least one person at dinner. He had written to Oribasius the previous year:

> I too this very day saw a vision of the same sort. I thought that in
> a certain very spacious room a tall tree had been planted and that
> it was leaning down to the ground while at its root had sprouted
> another, small and young and very flourishing. Now I was anxious

on behalf of the small tree, in case someone pulling up the large one should pull it up as well. And in fact when I came close I saw that the tall tree was lying at full length on the ground, while the small one was still erect, but hung suspended away from the earth. When I saw this, I said in great anxiety: "Alas for this tall tree. There is danger that not even its offspring will be preserved." Then Hermes said: "Look carefully and take courage. Since the root still remains in the earth, the smaller tree will be uninjured and will be established even more securely than before." So much for my dreams. God knows what they portend.[9]

The sentiments of the letter and the unsubtle imagery, which Julian must have worked out—the large tree is the emperor and the sapling is his cousin—show where he saw his future.

It is patently obvious that Julian's thoughts if not deeds had long been in revolt—possibly as far back as the aftermath of the battle of Strasbourg. It should not be a surprise that a man convinced in his own mind that he is destined for the throne finds the signs he is looking for from the gods. And with a group of friends as well as the soldiers he had led on three successful campaigns lauding him, one wonders only at how long it took the group to convince him.

When, some time after supper (presumably just long enough for the officers to get back to their units and round up their men) the soldiers surrounded the palace at midnight shouting "Julian for emperor," the die had already been cast. Although he waited until the morning before accepting the accolade publicly, Julian had crossed his Rubicon almost twelve hours earlier. He must have cut a slightly odd figure that winter's morning in Paris—a slight man wearing a purple cloak and surrounded by a bodyguard of armed soldiers as a safeguard against objections to the new political realities. Playing out the role expected of him as a putative emperor, he made a short speech of acceptance and promised the statutory donatives of five gold pieces and a pound of silver to every soldier.

Julian now had to come to terms with his actions. Although in a strong position in Gaul, to the rest of the empire he was a rebel. A more foolhardy soldier would have marched against Constantius immediately, but Julian realized that he was in no position to take on as seasoned a veteran as his cousin, however distracted he might have been by an eastern campaign. Instead what Julian decided to do was to play a waiting game. He took a gamble that if he made no overt and immediate attempt at becoming sole Augustus, then Constantius might do nothing, continue to focus on the East and so give Julian scope to plan his moves in the West.

At the end of February Julian wrote the first of several letters he was to send to Constantius. It was simple, straightforward, and offered some compromises. He reported what had happened outside the palace in Paris; made suggestions how he could help Constantius with reinforcements, mostly from Spain and to whom he had made no promises about not having to cross the Alps; and said that he would accept any praetorian prefect that the emperor suggested. Admittedly the last point was not an especially large concession given the well-known lack of love lost between Julian and Florentius. Be that as it may, the overarching aim was to show Constantius that Julian recognized him as ruler of the empire. He even signed the letter "Caesar" not "Augustus" as a mark of deference.

The letter was entrusted to Eutherius, Julian's faithful chamberlain, and Pentadius, chief of the secretariat. They caught up with Constantius in Caesarea in Cappadocia, modern Kayseri in Turkey, preparing for that season's campaigning in the East. The emperor, although forewarned about events, did not take the news of Julian's unauthorized promotion well. So angry was he that Ammianus reports that Julian's emissaries left the meeting fearing for their lives.[10]

Despite Constantius's fury, Julian's gamble paid off in the shape of a diplomatic back and forth that lasted in one form or another for almost seventeen months. As predicted, faced with a recalcitrant relative and the Persians, the emperor appears to have assessed the danger from the West as containable. Julian was making no hasty moves, while the Persian monarch Shapur II was on his doorstep and baying for blood. After weighing up the various options with his councillors, rather than abandon the eastern campaign, he continued mobilization and contented himself with a sharp letter sent to Julian in the care of his imperial secretary and chief legal counsel Leonas. In it Constantius warned Julian not to have ideas above his station and reshuffled the senior officers in Gaul—a reprimand for those who should have stopped such a situation occurring in the first place. He ordered Nebridius, Julian's quaestor, to replace Florentius as praetorian prefect; and Pentadius and Lupicinus, still in Britain, to be replaced as chief of the secretariat and as cavalry general respectively.

Although Leonas had served the emperor well the previous year when, on a diplomatic mission, he had single-handedly bullied a council of 150 bishops at Seleucia and reversed what had started off as a three-to-one majority against the emperor's views, he was an appalling negotiator to send to Julian. When he arrived in May, he delivered the letter and then berated Julian for the thanks he had shown to the cousin who had raised an orphan and made him Caesar. "Is my father's murderer seriously reproaching me for being an orphan?" was Julian's sharp answer.[11]

The imperial secretary was given a clear indication the next day that he was not dealing with a wayward child who could be slapped down. In a public relations masterstroke, Julian decided to read out the letter on the parade ground. It had the hoped-for effect. When Julian got to the passage where Constantius condemned the events in Paris, the soldiers rallied round shouting "Julian for Emperor" again. His diplomatic tail between his legs, Leonas was sent back to Constantius. He now had firsthand experience of the rebel's popularity with the rank and file and was carrying a simple message from Julian saying that he accepted the appointment of Nebridius, but had already filled the other positions.

Julian's first act of open insubordination was a snub that should have resulted in instant military reprisal. But because it was in everyone's interests to keep the diplomatic channels open, the exchange of letters continued and, before the year was out, at least one more envoy from Constantius made an approach to Julian, with much the same result. In the meantime, each Augustus looked to more immediate issues. Constantius marched as far south as Edessa—Sanliurfa on the Turkish/Syrian border—then on to inspect the ruins of Amida and finally back to winter camp in Antioch.

Julian on the other hand acted to consolidate Gaul. His support rested on having subdued the province and were that to be in any way compromised, then so too would his authority. Before he could do anything else, he had to neutralize Lupicinus who was still in Britain. Uncertain whether the old soldier would declare for him or for his cousin, Julian could not risk an attack from behind. Instead he stationed an officer at the port in Boulogne to prevent anyone leaving the mainland who might tell Lupicinus what had been going on and then to arrest him when he returned. Amazingly this worked, and Lupicinus and his three senior officers were picked up as soon as they made landfall, while one of Julian's own officers took over the British army. (It has been suggested, and it is certainly an attractive theory, that Lupicinus was the owner of the fabulous Mildenhall Treasure, now in the British Museum, and that it was subsequently hidden by his family or staff after his arrest.[12]) The rest of the summer and early autumn was spent subduing the Frankish tribe of the Attuarii, and then on a tour of inspection of the Rhine fortresses up as far as Basle and Besançon before deciding to winter in Vienne.

Despite recent military successes, it was in a lonely and slightly dispirited mood that Julian started 361. He had celebrated Epiphany on January 6, in the Christian church in Vienne.[13] Although he knew it would have been unwise of him to declare his true beliefs just yet if he was aiming for the greatest base of support possible, the stress and irritation of living a lie must have been taking its toll. He was feeling very much alone. His wife had died six months beforehand, and however little she had featured in his life, he did feel her loss. It was around this time that he arranged for her remains to be sent back to Rome for a Christian burial. Worse than this, he was missing his friends. He wrote of this time to Maximus several months later and the unhappiness is palpable: "Then I approached Besançon. . . . Near the city I came to meet a certain man who was dressed like a Cynic philosopher with his long cloak and staff. When I first caught sight of him in the distance, I imagined that he was none other than yourself. And when I came nearer to him I thought that he had surely come from you. The man was in fact a friend of mine though he fell short of what I hoped and expected. This then was one vain dream I had."[14]

The start of the year went from bad to worse. The time for diplomacy with Constantius was running out and it was becoming apparent to all that the only outcome could be civil war. A distraction kept Julian preoccupied in early spring. Groups of Alemanni under their chief Vadomar raided across the Rhine into the regions around Raetia, now eastern Switzerland. Julian ordered two legions out of winter quarters and sent them to teach the recalcitrant tribe a lesson. It all went horribly wrong. Despite being outnumbered, their unfortunate commander forced an attack and was killed near Säckingen.

Far more significant than the defeat itself, Julian discovered that the attacks had been encouraged by Constantius. It may seem surprising that the emperor was prepared to use barbarians against Romans, but in the battle against a revolutionary, anything went. Hard evidence was found in letters from Vadomar when a messenger on his way to Constantius was arrested by Julian's sentries. In these letters Vadomar had written: "Your Caesar is not obeying his orders." It is hard to tell which hurt Julian more: Vadomar's betrayal or the fact that in all his correspondence with Constantius, the barbarian chief referred to him as "Caesar," not "Augustus." Vadomar thought of him as a Caesar in revolt, not an emperor in waiting.

Now was not the time for another campaign. Rather than subdue the Alemanni by force, he tricked Vadomar onto Roman territory and had him arrested while he was having dinner—a no doubt justifiable breach of hospitality. Julian did not blame Vadomar for what had happened. As the head of a small state, he was merely trying to avoid getting crushed as two heavyweights sized each other up, so Julian packed Vadomar off to Spain.

He appears to have been rapidly forgiven. Within four years he was a governor of Phoenicia under the emperor Jovian—a significant position as one of seven leading commanders on the eastern front. To make sure that Vadomar's troops got no further ideas, Julian sent a guerrilla force of lightly armed auxiliaries to cross the Rhine in the dead of night and surrounded them. There were some casualties in the ensuing fight, but most were pardoned in return for promises of good behavior.

The time for diplomatic bravado was over. Constantius was getting ready to march on his cousin. News had already reached Julian that the emperor had bribed the kings and Persian provincial governors beyond the Tigris to keep the peace, had embarked on a massive recruitment and requisitions drive, had established supply dumps of grain along the borders of Gaul and along the passes of the Cottian Alps, and had sent an agent to Africa to guard the coast and make sure that no supplies slipped through to Julian. The impact was severe with the side effect of making people reluctant to support Julian; indeed, the actions he later took to alleviate the embargo on Rome show quite how effective it had been. An arms race had begun and Julian responded in kind. "[The Celts] loved me so much, because of the similarity of our dispositions, that not only did they venture to take up arms on my behalf, but they gave me large sums of money besides," he wrote.[15] At the same time he attended to logistical matters, making sure, for example, that there were enough boats to carry his force down the Danube.

The question was no longer whether it would come to war, but where war would take place. The two cousins were, after all, at opposing ends of the empire. The options facing Julian were to remain in Gaul where he was strongest, or risk taking Italy and Illyricum. What spoke in favor of a move eastward is that the way lay unguarded. There is little doubt that the goal was Constantinople. Most of the soldiers who might have opposed his army's march had already been sent to the eastern front. The disadvantage was that Constantius had considerable superiority of numbers. At best Julian had 23,000 troops that could be spared for campaign. He needed to keep a force to defend Gaul and it would have been folly to withdraw completely from Britain. In a quandary, he prayed to the gods for a sign. Unsurprisingly he got one from them. Considerably more surprising, it was incredibly specific, referring to the emperor's death when an uncommon conjunction of stars occurred that autumn:

> *When Zeus had crossed Aquarius' broad domain,*
> *And Cronos reached the five and twentieth day*
> *Of Virgo, then Constantius, Asia's king,*
> *Shall end his life in pain and misery.*[16]

That decided it; he would march—as long as the soldiers would come with him. To celebrate her festival, on June 3, Julian sacrificed to Bellona, the goddess of war. It was his first semipublic acknowledgment of paganism. The rites were carried out in private, but since everyone knew about them, it also seems to have been a way of sounding out the army. It can't have harmed his case that Bellona was, naturally enough, a favorite with soldiers.

In early summer, he assembled his troops in Vienne. As he gave them their orders, his soldiers clashed their shields in the mark of Gaulish approval and swore to follow him to the death. The officers all followed suit, swearing allegiance to the young emperor—all except Nebridius, who tactlessly decided that now was a good time to mention that he would not swear an oath against an emperor who had supported him, helped him, and been his benefactor. Having been whipped into a frenzy by Julian's rhetoric, the soldiers who heard this tried to lynch the hapless praetorian prefect, and it was only because Julian covered the man with his cloak—the sign of imperial protection—and escorted him back to the palace that he was not murdered on the spot. When they got to safety, Nebridius asked for Julian's hand in friendship. "I'd have nothing to offer my friends if I gave you my hand," Julian laconically remarked.[17] Nebridius took the hint and retired to his home in Tuscany. He would later reappear as praetorian prefect of the East in 365.

Julian must have breathed a sigh of relief—he had asked his soldiers not only to support a rebel, but also to undertake the journey that had led to their rebellion in the first place. The army then marched to Augst, the site of a major bridge over the Rhine since the time of Augustus. Augusta Raurica was at the crossroads of two major routes—north to south from Italy to the Rhineland over the Great St. Bernard Pass and from east to west between Gaul and Raetia. The A5 motorway seven miles downstream at Basel fulfills the same role today. It was also a perfect springboard for his next move. It was large enough to support his army and even though it had been both battered by an earthquake and seen considerable military activity over the past hundred years, Augst had the right military infrastructure, as it was the headquarters for one of the West's crack legions.

Julian realized that he had to move more swiftly. He took the time to reorganize his economic and military high command. He appointed one of his men as praetorian prefect in Gaul, then he split his army into three to hide his lack of numbers from spies—after all, although many of Constantius's troops had been sent to the eastern front, the Illyrian army had not been totally depleted and Julian could not guarantee that they would support him. The cavalry commanders Jovinus and Nevitta were both put in command of around 10,000 men each, with Julian himself taking command of the remaining 3,000 or so. Jovinus was to march through western Switzerland, across northern Italy via Milan and Cremona, then head for the Danube. Nevitta was to cross Raetia and Noricum, turn south near Salzburg and descend into Pannonia following the Danube. The rendezvous point was probably Sirmium, now Sremska Mitrovica in Serbia, twenty-five miles northwest of Belgrade on the Save river.

It is to be presumed that Jovinus and Nevitta's journeys were fairly painless; certainly, we have no records of any events out of the ordinary. For Julian's march, however, we are fortunate to have several sources, including a speech of thanks to the new emperor given in the Senate house in Constantinople in the morning of New Year's Day by the consul for 362, Claudius Mamertinus. Speed was of the essence. Ammianus writes that Julian "rushed like a fireball or a blazing dart straight to his goal"; Libanius notes, "he rushed on like a torrent" and Mamertinus that he "flew over the heads of rulers and spurning them beneath his feet, appeared suddenly and unexpected in the very midst of Illyria."[18]

Although most accounts we have of the emperor's march are partisan, by reading between the lines, it is possible to see that the march was not exactly a walk in the country. Food appears to have been in short supply, Julian's guerrilla force was told to be on a constant state of alert and he went out of his way to avoid all kinds of attention. When he had to fight, he won with trickery rather than by force of arms. On one occasion he seized a city by dressing his soldiers in captured armor, so that when they approached the gates, the duped inhabitants let them in.

After the march through the Black Forest Julian reached the Danube in the beginning of July. The rest of the journey proceeded a little more smoothly. As planned, there were around a hundred boats waiting probably at or near Ulm to carry his force downstream.[19] "What ceremonious progress that was! The whole right bank of that famous river was fringed with an unbroken line of inhabitants of both sexes, people of all walks of life, armed and unarmed, while on the left bank we could see the barbarian hordes fallen on their knees in miserable prayer."[20] That was how Mamertinus wanted Julian's voyage to be seen—almost a stately pageant. Given the urgency Julian felt and the fact that the journey took less than a fortnight,[21] more plausibly he and his force sailed as rapidly and as secretly as possible making landfall at Bononea, possibly the town of Beocin, nineteen miles north of Sirmium, in the middle of July.

Needless to say, it was optimistic to hope to move 23,000 men half-way across Europe without news of it leaking out. Reports of the armies' advance had already reached Lucillianus, commander of Pannonia and father-in-law of the future emperor Jovian. He had mobilized two legions and a cohort of archers in Sirmium, ready to stop Julian.

Going round the city was not an option. Sirmium, the capital of Lower Pannonia and birthplace of Constantius, was key to the region and could not be bypassed. Diocletian had recognized the town as one of the capitals of the empire in his reforms of 294. Part of the reason was military. It was an important fleet station and overlooked the junction of roads linking Italy, Dalmatia, and the Danube. At the same time, the proximity of the often explosive Danubian frontier meant that the town frequently headquartered large numbers of Roman troops and it had developed attendant infrastructure. It housed, for example, important arms factories and Illyricum's major arsenal. As a governmental head-quarters and the capital of the praetorian prefect of Illyricum, the town also housed a mint, founded by Constantine, which struck gold bars with the figure of Fortuna, patron goddess of the town. It was too good an opportunity for a propaganda coup and after he had taken the city Julian lost no time in issuing coins in his own name.

As he was yet to be joined by Jovinus and Nevitta, it would have been ridiculous to expect his band to attack the town, so he relied on a swift commando operation. There Julian appeared "like an underwater diver who is hidden under the surface of the sea and unobserved by watchers on the shore for as long as he likes."[22] He sent Dagalaif, prefect of the household troops, to ride from Bononea to Sirmium and acquaint Lucillianus of the new political realities. The first that the old soldier knew that something was wrong was when he woke up surrounded by soldiers he did not recognize. He was brought before Julian to pay homage to him. To give Lucillianus his due, when he realized that he was not in any imminent danger of being slaughtered, he rapidly recovered his cool. "It's rather foolhardy and reckless of your majesty to venture into another man's territory with so few soldiers," he suggested. "Keep your good advice for Constantius. I have allowed you to pay homage not because I want your help, but to stop you being afraid," Julian replied.[23] Lucillianus, although relieved of his command, was allowed to live in peace in the city.

The next morning, Julian reached Sirmium and received the welcome he expected; he was met with flowers and cheers by a crowd of soldiers and civilians, who greeted him as "Augustus" and "Lord" and escorted him to the palace.[24] He had claimed the biggest prize of the campaign so far, his blitzkrieg had shocked them into submission. He was in control of the empire as far as the Balkans and held the key to Constantinople—and he had achieved it all with hardly any bloodshed.

In a mood to celebrate, Julian held chariot races the next day, possibly in the hippodrome attached to the palace. Recent excavations have revealed traces of one, along with sections of the barracks. All that was left to do was to reassign the troops Julian had found in Sirmium. He could hardly leave them where they were and because he could not guarantee their loyalty, he sent them to Gaul where they could do little damage.

It was already time to move on. Nevitta had reached Julian and by the middle of September, the much expanded army set out for Naissus, now Nis in Serbia, to wait for Jovinus and to make winter quarters. Constantinople, his goal, was only twenty-two days' ride away, and the town commanded the Morava-Vardar and the Nisava river corridors, the two principal routes from central Europe to the Aegean. This can still be seen today. The main rail line from Belgrade divides at Nis for Thessalonica in Greece and Sofia in Bulgaria. As significantly, the town also housed state arms factories—control of which was essential for a revolutionary.

Aside from the strategic reasons, there was a crucial symbolic reason for choosing the city too. Julian was now a rebel and what he needed more than anything else at this moment was validation. Naissus's long connection with the house of Constantine went some way to giving him it: the city was known as the birthplace of Constantine, but it was also where Constantius had peacefully accepted the abdication of another pretender to the throne. It was a town that everyone in the empire had heard of and that in people's minds was associated with nonviolence.

Up to November, Julian's military actions were all defensive. He could not push through to the capital as the province of Thrace stood between Illyricum and Constantinople. It was a formidable obstacle. Along the main route stood huge fortresses at Plovdiv and Edirne. Any attempt to cross the mountains would inevitably end in disaster. What Julian did was continue to play a waiting game. Between him and Thrace stood a huge range of mountains, to the north the Haemus range and to the south the Rhodope range. There was only one way through—the Succi Pass, now the Ihtiman Pass in Bulgaria, where you can still see the remains of Roman barracks. Securing that gave him two advantages. The first was military: once garrisoned, he was unassailable and would have until the spring to work out what to do next. It was also a psychological help as the pass had marked the geographical boundary between Constans's and Constantius's territory. This allowed Julian still to claim, however speciously, that he wanted to rule with Constantius. Consequentially Nevitta was ordered to garrison the pass.

Bad news was to greet him when he reached Naissus. The two legions and the cohort of archers from Sirmium had reacted badly to what was effectively a banishment. Stirred up by a firebrand called Nigrinus, a cavalry tribune, the troops got as far as the northern tip of the Adriatic before barricading themselves in late summer into the port of Aquileia, a town northwest of Trieste and where Julian's uncle Constantine II had been killed by his other uncle Constans. It is a difficult event to view with any kind of objectivity. Ammianus is so keen to have us see Julian as the emperor-in-waiting that it is easy to forget that it is Julian who is the rebel and Nigrinus who is fighting for the emperor. In taking the town, Nigrinus and his colleagues had blocked the main communication route between Illyria and Italy as it sat at the junction of the Via Postumia with roads north and east to the provinces of Illyria, Pannonia, and Noricum. Worse, the troops were stirring up the locals who came over to their side, presumably because they believed that Constantius's victory could not be far off and they feared reprisals, rather than through conviction.

It was a major blow. Not only was Aquileia one of the largest towns in Italy, but also Julian took this revolt personally. He had previously praised the city, describing it as "very prosperous and teeming with wealth."[25] It is easy to see that Julian was not exaggerating the town's affluence from the rich remains that are still in evidence. All Julian could do was to send word to Jovinus, then near modern Ljubljana in Slovenia, to return and besiege the city.

If his military measures were defensive, administratively the time at Naissus was one of consolidation. Replicating his financial policy in Gaul, Julian reduced several taxes and attempted to deal with a corn shortage in Rome, caused by Constantius's blockade in Africa. At the same time, he made several promotions. Among them, Aurelius Victor, author of a recently published history of the emperors, was made governor of Lower Pannonia, while Mamertinus who had effectively been made minister of finance several months earlier, was now designated both prefect of Italy, Illyricum, and Africa and consul elect for the following year.

But Julian was guilty of two major errors of judgment. The first lay in a series of letters he wrote to Rome and Athens as well as to the cities of Sparta and Corinth to justify his revolt. They were received badly. Rome had always tended toward support for Constantius—the emperor had gone out of his way to curry favor with the city, visiting it in 357 and having an obelisk erected in the Circus Maximus, which now stands in front of St. John Lateran. At the same time Julian was blamed for the continuing grain blockade. Rome could forgive anything, even a usurper, but it could never forgive bad manners. In the letters, gone was any attempt at appeasement. From the opening paragraphs, in the only surviving letter, the one to the Athenians, Julian accuses Constantius of murder and attacks his cronies throughout. Eusebius, Constantius's chamberlain, who had been the principal agent in the death of Gallus and had always been suspicious of Julian, is referred to only as "that execrable eunuch" while Florentius, who had fled as prefect of Illyricum as Julian's army advanced, is "greedy."[26]

The blatant propaganda and attack on Constantius and his court were bad enough, but one promotion in particular beggared belief. Mamertinus's colleague in office was to be the faithful Nevitta. The Senate was beside itself. The man was an uneducated boor and, worst of all, a Gaul. It was a potentially dangerous miscalculation. When Julian's letter was read out, it was heckled as the nobility shouted: "Show some respect for the man who has made you what you are today."[27] If there was no more fall out from these actions, it is only because the empire was overtaken by events.

The situation in the East had changed. The Persian king had withdrawn leaving Constantius time to focus on his cousin. Spies told Julian that the province's commander had mobilized Thrace. What he could not yet know was that Constantius was withdrawing troops from the East to support them too. As winter descended things looked ill for Julian. Behind him the revolt of the two legions holed up in the impregnable town in Aquileia was having a demoralizing effect on the whole of Italy. If they so decided, Nigrinus and his rabble could close the Julian Alps and cut the rebel commander off from his provinces in the West. The blockade of Rome was starting to become a worry. If a serious corn shortage developed, then all support for Julian would vanish in the Italian peninsula. And worst of all, the armies of the East were starting to mobilize on the other side of the Succi Pass.

And then, on November 3, the deus ex machina. On the way back from the Persian front and Antioch to the capital, on the road toward the Cilician Gates at the foot of Mount Taurus, Constantius died. The forty-four-year-old emperor had passed through Tarsus, where he contracted a fever. Needing to reach Constantinople as rapidly as possible he pressed on. The next day the fever gripped more tightly, his breathing became shallow, and he died soon after being baptized like his father before him.

His death was totally unexpected. To the public Constantius was still, if not young, then not an old man and had shown himself full of vigor over the last year. His actions and counteractions against Julian are not those of an ill man. Yet, the various disasters both political and personal, had taken their toll. Over the last two years, his troublesome cousin had risen against him, on the back of military disasters in the East, and at the same time his wife, Eusebia, had died in 359. Little surprise that the emperor had complained of nightmares.

Julian heard toward the end of the month when two German senior military officers as envoys arrived from the Succi Pass. They told him the news he needed to hear—not only that his cousin was dead but also that the armies of the East had sworn an oath of allegiance to him.

At once Julian gave up any public pretence of Christianity. He stopped shaving, grew a beard, and affected the dress of a pagan philosopher. At the same time public sacrifices started. He wrote to the philosopher Maximus in Antioch: "I worship the gods openly and the whole mass of the troops who are returning with me worship the gods. I sacrifice oxen in public. I have offered many great public sacrifices to the gods as thanks offerings. The gods command me to restore their worship in its utmost purity and I obey them, yes and with a good will."[28]

It was time for him to return to the city of his birth. He forced a march along the military highway through Sofia, the Succi Pass, and Plovdiv toward the Hellespont. It was time to return to Constantinople.

5
THE SHADOW OF
SACRED PLUMES

After that Constantine the eagle turn'd
Against the motions of the Heaven, that roll'd
Consenting with its course, when he of yore,
Lavinia's spouse, was leader of the flight;
A hundred years twice told and more, his seat
At Europe's extreme point, the bird of Jove
Held, near the mountains, whence he issued first;
There under shadow of his sacred plumes
Swaying the world, till through successive hands
To mine he came devolved.

DANTE, "INFERNO," *DIVINE COMEDY*

When Julian entered the city of his birth on December 11, 361, it was as sole ruler of the Roman Empire. The people of Constantinople had turned out en masse to cheer him on. "It seemed like a dream that this man of slight build who had just reached maturity should, after a series of notable exploits and bloody victories over kings and peoples, have flown from city to city with unheard of speed, acquiring accessions of might and strength wherever he appeared, and that, after seizing everything with an ease that rivaled the flight of rumor, he should finally have received the imperial power by the decree of heaven without the infliction of any loss upon the state." So wrote Ammianus.[1] The city's son, indeed the first emperor born there, had returned.

Julian entered the city through the Golden Gate (the ruined church and mosque known as the Isa Kapi Mescidi marks the spot), one of the main gates along the two and a half mile length of walls that Constantine had built to protect the city. Marching east along the main thoroughfare, Julian would have been able to see the Church of Saint Sophia up on a hill in the distance at the other end of town. Not the imposing structure we now know, but rather the first of the three churches with that name on the same spot, dedicated the previous year, on February 15, by his cousin. An observant viewer may also have been able to see the emperor frown at the Church of St. Eirene a little behind it. Constantine had knocked down shrines to Aphrodite and to Apollo to build it, the capital's first church. But before he got there, Julian turned south just after he had passed the forum (all of which now stands is the rather tatty remnants of the Column of Constantine, often referred to as Cemberlitas or the Hooped Column) toward the palace on the eastern side of the Hippodrome.

One of Julian's first actions was to hold Constantius's funeral—a ceremony he conducted with dignity and honor. For all of the sniping at his cousin before his death, after it, Julian spoke of him with reverence. This had little to do with not wishing to speak ill of the dead, rather it was a way for Julian to maintain his support with the legions that had been under Constantius's direct command in Rome and the East.

Although Julian had traveled post haste to the capital along the military highway, the former emperor's cortege traveled north more slowly through the Taurus Mountains, now the Toros Daglari. The body was accompanied by a staff officer called Jovian, a member of an elite corps in the army. In only eighteen months that same staff officer would be emperor.

When Constantius's body reached Constantinople, Julian himself went down to the Great Harbor on the Bosporus to greet the procession and stood, bare headed and anonymous, as the coffin was unloaded from the galley. He then walked at the head of the funeral procession up the hill toward the Church of the Holy Apostles, its facade covered in brass and the dome clad in gold to reflect the light. Inside it was as impressive as outside—porticoes ran along the four sides and the high ceilings were decorated with multicolored marble slabs right up to the dome. Constantius was then buried in a porphyry block to the right of his father Constantine (who had chosen the site of the church himself even if it had been built by Constantius). It was the last time that Julian would set foot in a Christian church. Neither the church nor the sarcophagi remain, although a miniature in the Vatican Library gives some idea of the building's magnificence.[2] Its bricks served as the quarry for the Fatih Camii, the enormous mosque of Mehmet the Conqueror built in the 1460s which now stands on the spot.

With his rival firmly buried and himself emperor both in name as well as deed, Julian could start to right what he saw as some of the wrongs of his predecessor—and settle some old scores into the bargain. If convention and a desire for unity meant that Constantius could not be attacked, he had no such compunctions about his predecessor's lackeys. Soon after he had been appointed emperor, Julian wrote to a friend in Egypt: "I had little hope of hearing that you had escaped the three-headed hydra. Zeus be my witness, I don't mean my brother Constantius—he was what he was—but the wild beasts that surrounded him and cast their evil eyes on all men. They made him harsher than he was by nature, though on his own account he was by no means of a mild disposition even though he seemed so to many. But one should not speak ill of the dead, as they say. I do not want these others to be punished unjustly, but since many people are bringing charges against them I have appointed a court to judge them."[3]

At the end of the month, he appointed Salutius Secundus, his friend from Gaul, both administrator of the East and president of a commission to purge the state of Constantius's more over-enthusiastic ministers—all of them civilians. The court, mentioned in the letter above, sat at Chalcedon, modern Kadiköy, opposite Constantinople across the Bosporus. It was a suburb rather looked down upon by the urbane citizens of Constantinople, much in the same way that Manhattanites look down on the other boroughs of New York.

Local wits referred to the area as "the city of the blind"—its inhabitants clearly hadn't looked around when they built their town. But the court's distance from the capital was an attempt to ensure that the trials were perceived as impartial and independent from the seat of government. This was underlined by the fact that Julian played no public role in them.

Some have seen the Chalcedon Trials as either a Stalinist purge or a military kangaroo court. In reality they were neither. Still, it is stretching the truth to suggest, as Libanius does, that the trials show Julian as the noble defender of the people.[4] Although they did not exhibit Julian's customary magnanimity, they constituted a sound political move by an emperor trying to establish his authority and reassert his influence over the army. If anything at all can be said in their favor, the unpalatable business was done as clinically as possible, like ripping off a bandage.

The commission was made up of six worthies—all of whom could be relied upon to come to the right conclusions. Along with Salutius, the court comprised Julian's loyal commanders Nevitta and Jovinus and Nevitta's co-consul elect Mamertinus. The final two members, in a patently political move, had been public supporters of Constantius: Agilo and Arbetio. Nonetheless, Julian must have been fairly sure that they would reach the verdicts that he wanted. Agilo was not only a former tribune of some of Julian's most loyal troops (regiments called the Gentiles and Scutarii), he was to work with Mamertinus during the ongoing siege of Aquileia. It was only Arbetio, one of Constantius's commanders in Thrace, who can be said in any way to have been truly hostile to Julian's aims. Be that as it may, the commanders of the eastern army had long resented the influence of Constantius's clique in Constantinople, and however much they may have disliked Julian, they had few qualms about sticking the knife into the stalwarts of the previous regime.

Whatever the legal delicacies of the trials—only lip service appears to have been paid to niceties like evidence—it is unlikely that many tears were shed for its main victims. Constantius's appointments had been notoriously corrupt. Many will have been relieved to see his two most infamous spies, Paul and Apodemius, in the docks.

The notary Paul, Constantius's Beria, had been nicknamed "The Chain" for his habit of stitching up prisoners with chains of lies, and the Spaniard certainly comes across as a proto-Torquemada. Libanius contented himself with the conclusion that "he deserved to die thousands of times both in Europe and Asia."[5] The fact that he had come down so heavily on supporters of Magnentius, who now made up much of Julian's army, sealed his fate. Apodemius was little better. Nicknamed "The Sycophant," he had been the one to execute Julian's brother Gallus. He had mutilated the body and then taken his shoes as evidence to the emperor in Milan. They were both condemned and burned alive.

Eusebius, Constantius's chamberlain, who had spent so many years dripping poison about Julian into the emperor's ear, was as much loved by the armies of the East as by the new emperor and he too was condemned to death, probably by burning as well.

As for the others, Florentius, the thorn in Julian's side in Gaul, was still hiding out so he was condemned in absentia and Taurus, the prefect of Italy who had deserted his post as Julian's army approached, was exiled to Vercelli, a rather miserable town in Piedmont. (St. Jerome describes the town as "once important, but now sparsely peopled and fallen into decay."[6]) Although Julian never defended his brother openly, he took exception to those who had attacked him. So Palladius, former marshal of the imperial court, who had accused Gallus, was exiled to Britain, while Pentadius—perhaps, though not definitely the same man who had acted as a go-between for the two cousins just after the Paris acclamation—accused of acting as the note-taker during Gallus's interrogation, was acquitted. Four others were exiled on charges no longer extant.

If it had been left at that, then the trials would have passed more or less without comment. But the execution of Ursulus, one of Constantius's finance ministers in charge of taxes and accounting of public finances, aroused universal disapproval and has overshadowed the way the Chalcedon Trials have been perceived ever since. Ursulus was a former mentor of Julian—he had been Constantius's finance minister in Gaul when Julian was first sent there. But he was deeply unpopular among the military, due to an unfortunate tendency to call a spade a spade. He was overheard mocking the greed of the army while looking at the ruins of Amida. "See with what courage our cities are defended by men

1. *The Louvre holds the only life-size statue of the Emperor Julian.*
(AKG London/Erich Lessing)

2. Colossal head of Constantine the Great in the Museo dei Conservatori in Rome. (Bridgeman Art Library)

3A. Aqueduct in Antioch.
(AKG London/Erich Lessing)

3B. Sassanid bas-relief showing Mithras and Shapur facing
Ahura-Mazda. The fallen emperor is usually identified as Julian. The fact
that it is a god standing over the emperor's head suggests that Julian's
death is the result of divine intervention. From Taq-i Bustan, Iran.
(Bridgeman Art Library)

4. *Simone Martini painted ten frescos illustrating the life of St. Martin of Tours, which are in the chapel of San Martino in the lower Church of San Francisco in Assisi. This detail depicting Julian is from* St. Martin's Renunciation of Arms.
(AKG London)

5. In 1702 Antonio Verrio decorated the King's Staircase at Hampton
Court Palace with themes from Julian's The Caesars.
(Historic Royal Palaces)

6. The largest intact brick arch in existence—the east-facing doorway of Shapur's palace at Ctesiphon. (Giraudon/Bridgeman Art Library)

7. Julian the Apostate Presiding at a Conference of Sectarians *by Edward Armitage, painted in 1874.*
(Walker Art Gallery)

8A. *Bronze coin of Julian with a pearl-diademed helmet, holding a spear in his right hand and a shield in his left hand. From the mint in Rome.* (Murdoch)

8B. *Bronze coin of Julian's half-brother Gallus, bare-headed, wearing a cuirass and cloak. From the Constantinople mint.* (Murdoch)

8C. *Bronze coin of a youthful Constantius II wearing a laurel wreath. From the Aquileia mint.* (Murdoch)

8D. *Bronze coin of Jovian from the mint in Heraclea.* (Murdoch)

whom the resources of the empire are exhausted to pay,"[7] he said, his words dripping with sarcasm, before depriving the legions of gifts from the emperor in a cost-cutting measure. No one likes a smart aleck especially not a penny-pinching one, and he was the one pawn sacrificed by Julian to the demands of the army. Julian at least had the decency to feel guilty about this and, although Ursulus's property had automatically reverted to the state (as did the possessions of all criminals), the emperor renounced a large portion of it in favor of Ursulus's daughter soon afterward.

Within six weeks—by the end of January 362—the commission was dissolved and Julian could turn his attention to other matters. He replaced Jovinus and put Agilo in charge of the siege that was still dragging on. As the most senior infantry officer in the East, he thought Agilo well enough known to tell the resistance within Aquileia that Julian was now emperor. Eventually they believed him and the inhabitants threw open the gates to greet the soldiers. The subsequent inquiry found Nigrinus, the instigator of the revolt, guilty and he was burned at the stake, while two members of the town council were also executed for their part in the proceedings.

Julian's glare focused on Constantius's court. He cut through it rapidly and efficiently, prompted to do so by a haircut. Soon after his arrival in the city, Julian had sent for a barber. When a gaudily dressed peacock presented himself, the emperor commented: "I sent for a barber not a treasury official."[8] Julian interviewed the man more closely about the terms and conditions of his employment. Not realizing that he was committing professional suicide, the barber told him that he earned twenty men's allowances of bread and the same of fodder for his cattle daily, as well as a salary and other profitable sidelines. Julian fired him on the spot.

The problem of excesses at court was a by-product of a deliberate policy of Diocletian's. Together with his corulers, Diocletian wanted to stamp his authority on an empire that had bordered on anarchy for too long. A result of this was that the emperor became an untouchable figure, closer to the gods than at almost any stage previously, and the court developed a style of Eastern obsequiousness that the West had never seen before. This distancing of the emperor from the people was a tradition that had continued throughout the subsequent reigns of Constantine and Constantius. Look at the colossal heads of the two of them on display in the courtyard of the Museo dei Conservatori in Rome. The eyes are focused upward toward heaven and not on earthly matters. Constantius went so far as to behave like a statue in real life, whenever he appeared in public. "He was like a dummy, gazing straight before him as if his head were in a vice, turning neither right nor left. When a wheel jolted he did not nod, and at no point was he seen to spit or to wipe or rub his face or nose or to move his hands about," is Ammianus's eyewitness description.[9]

The lucky few to gain an audience with the emperor had to do so on bended knees, and the minutiae of ceremony, pecking order and bureaucracy soon emerged. Libanius writes: "There were a thousand cooks, as many barbers and even more butlers. There were swarms of waiters, eunuchs more in number than flies around the flocks in spring, and a multitude of drones of every sort and kind."[10] This venality had even affected the army. The easy life had softened them. Not without the jealousy of a man who did not get a commission in the capital, Ammianus grumbles that the soldiers now slept on mattresses not stone; that instead of marching songs, they sang cabaret numbers; and that the soldiers' cups were now heavier than their swords, so ornate were they, and that to drink from earthenware was beneath them.[11]

None of these are unique charges. In the second century, for example, the satirical poet Juvenal acidly portrayed the emperor Domitian's courtiers "faces drawn and pale from the emperor's friendship," that is, from the effort they put into sucking up to the emperor. Although it is an obvious exaggeration, it was how the public perceived the throne and the court. Julian intended to do something about it. For a man who would rather be seen as the stoic Marcus Aurelius than Constantine, they all had to go. In one fell swoop he streamlined the palaces. He got rid of the eunuchs saying they were unnecessary as he had resolved not to marry again; he fired the cooks because he liked simple food; and he let the barbers go because he said a single one could cope with a large number of clients.[12] He even got rid of most of the hated imperial informers, a hallmark of Constantius's rule and a group that had plagued Julian over the years. A couple of them offered to reveal where the hapless Florentius was hiding in return for reinstatement. They had badly misjudged the emperor. Julian told them that such techniques were beneath him and confirmed their dismissal.

Some complained that he was cheapening the role of the emperor and one Christian apologist in a fit of pique wrote: "The expulsion of the cooks and barbers is in a manner becoming a philosopher indeed, but not an emperor."[13] But they were lone, sour voices. In general, this moderation was popular.

Even before he had swept the administrative chaff out of the palace, Julian was already putting the pieces in place to rebuild the empire. Although he would be in the East for the rest of his life, Julian made sure that time was taken to concentrate on the details of defense in the West. For example, walls were rebuilt and strengthened in Thrace and pay and logistical issues were addressed on the Danube. Then he turned to appointments. As well as the promotions of Mamertinus, Nevitta, and Salutius Secundus, other notable appointments included his maternal uncle, Julianus, who was made prefect of the East (previously he had been governor of Phrygia), and Anatolius, who was confirmed as minister of finance—a position he had held since 360.

But this was just the start. The death of Constantius had prompted a burst of letter writing to anyone he thought talented enough to have a position in the new regime as well as to old friends. As might be expected, the first tranche of letters were to pagan intimates, and the enthusiasm of the young emperor is palpable. To his friend Maximus he writes: "Too many things crowd into my mind at once and choke my speech, as one thought refuses to let another run ahead of it."[14] To a former tutor called Eustathius in Athens he scribbles: "Come then, lose no time, fly here as we say. A kindly god will speed you on your way with the help of the Maiden of the Crossroads. The state post will be at your disposal if you wish to use a carriage and two extra horses."[15] Both Maximus and Eustathius came as soon as possible, the arrival of the former causing frowns among Constantinople's establishment when Julian ran out of the Senate to greet him.

Not all rushed to take the emperor's shilling, either unwilling to side with a new regime or wanting first to see which way the land lay. Although Priscus was among the first to whom Julian had written, at the end of 362 the emperor could complain to Libanius that his former tutor had still not come in person.[16] And Chrysanthius in Lydia, another former tutor, remained unmoved by his former pupil's pleas despite letters to him, to his wife, and messages via friends.

Intriguingly, three of the people to whom Julian wrote were known and influential Christians. He appears to have been motivated to seek them out partly out of respect for their talents, but rather more for the influence that these men had in their respective back yards: Antioch, Cappadocia, and Athens. He recalled Aetius of Antioch, an old friend of his brother's, with whom he had spent time in Bithynia;[17] and he asked St. Basil, one of the most brilliant thinkers of the early Church, to come to Constantinople—effectively to head up a think tank. Basil was a force in Cappadocia—a resolutely Christian area that was described as "Christian to a man."[18] During the reign of Constantius the citizens of Caesarea, the region's capital, had taken it upon themselves to pull down the temples of Zeus and Apollo, and Julian badly needed some sort of voice there.[19] Finally, he wrote to Prohaeresius at the university in Athens, then in his late eighties, and invited him in the most ingratiating terms to write his official biography.[20]

Despite the personal connections—Basil and Julian had been students together, and both of them had been taught by Prohaeresius in 355—only Aetius accepted the invitation to Constantinople. Prohaeresius stayed where he was, teaching to the very end, to die at the age of ninety-two in 367. Basil, on the other hand, remained in Cappadocia, and any hope that the emperor had of gaining influence in the region was dashed when the people of Caesarea carried on their impromptu civic renovations by destroying the temple to Fortuna. Julian refused to give them the satisfaction of making them martyrs. Instead, the emperor deprived the town of its city status and it reverted to its old name of Mazaea.[21]

Although much of the initial enthusiasm in the end came to nothing, Julian's appointments and attempted promotions did send the clear message that people were to be appointed on merit rather than on influence, money, or even political affiliation. In the past Julian had written that an emperor should not choose his deputies carelessly or at random, rather he should be as rigorous a judge of quality as a lapidary or a goldsmith, and it is a belief to which he tried to adhere.[22]

Those like Anatolius had served happily under the previous emperor and even if it might have been dangerous to replace some of the military commanders in the East like Agilo, there is no sign of any curbs to their power at all. There were, until the issue of religion raised its ugly head, few complaints about any of Julian's domestic appointments either, and however rapidly his idealism may have worn off, the letters he wrote to Christian thinkers show that he was not motivated by religious intolerance either.

For his own part, Julian appears to have had a clear and consistent view of what kind of ruler he wanted to be. It is a version of Plato's benevolent despot from *The Republic* filtered through Marcus Aurelius's stoic reason. What is significant is that it is something that Julian thought a great deal about—not just because of who he was—but what he was. In his letter to the philosopher Themistius, written just after Julian had been made Caesar, he had gone into the subject in some depth.

> He who governs . . . ought by every means in his power to observe the laws, not those that pass as a reaction to some sudden emergency or established as now appears, by men who were not wholly guided by reason; but he must observe them only in case the lawgiver, having purified his mind and soul, in enacting those laws keeps in view not merely the crimes of the moment or immediate contingencies; but rather recognizes the nature of government and the essential nature of justice, and has carefully observed also the essential nature of guilt and then applies to his task all the knowledge thus derived and frames laws which have a general application to all citizens without regard to friend or foe, neighbor or kinsman.[23]

It is a dramatic step for an emperor to believe not only that he is not above the law, but also that the law is an end in its own right. Even though power was a novelty to Julian when the above was written, this is a point to which he returns again and again in his writings. "Law is reason exempt from desire," he writes. It behoves an emperor to "behave toward the people and the magistrates like a citizen who obeys the laws, not like a king who is above the laws." In short, an emperor should "do good to all men and imitate the divine nature on earth. To show mercy even in anger, to take away harshness from acts of vengeance and to display kindness and toleration to your fallen enemies."[24]

Was this idealistic? Yes. Did Julian always adhere to his principles? No. But the very fact that he attempted to do so is one of the most admirable aspects of Julian's character. A telling insight into the way his mind worked is seen in the anecdote of a case Julian was to try in Antioch. The case's dismissal hinged on the defendant's use of forged documents. Even though Julian knew that the defendant was guilty, the prosecutor was unable to prove it. In his summing up, Julian said that he was aware of the fraud, but because the prosecutor was too incompetent to see it, he had to find in favor of the criminal.[25] It is a curious sight to witness an emperor wrestling with some of the finer concepts of law and justice. It is hard to imagine an Augustus or a Constantine suffering from any similar form of self-doubt.

A further consequence of the reforms of Diocletian, and Constantine's movement of the capital from Rome, was that they had both required a rapid bureaucratic expansion. While difficult to quantify, it has been estimated that a civil service that stood at a few hundred at the end of the second century had swollen now to around 35,000. Constantinople had grown at the expense of the cities, resulting in many of the problems seen during the Industrial Revolution in Britain. Several of Libanius's letters are references for young men eager to exchange the sticks for the lights, money, and titles of the city. There was little to stop the rise of the talented even if they had neither money nor titles. The empire was showing distinct signs of a meritocracy. But there was a price to pay—the cities were drained of talent while the capital stagnated under the weight of bureaucrats.

Julian's solution to the administrative faults around him was to strengthen the town councils so that they could act as a counterbalance to the capital. It is a policy that has been much criticized, but he died before anyone could see whether it had worked or not. What shines through is that his policies were an attempt to take pressure off central government and inject money and talent into provincial cities. It has become received wisdom to suggest that Julian was attempting to set up an alternative power base to the Church—loyal to the emperor rather than God—and that he wanted to restore the prestige of the councils to the level they had enjoyed in previous centuries and before the carnage of the third century. There was a greater pragmatism to Julian's reforms than that. It was a policy of decentralization. He believed that if cities were able to look after themselves with the best people taking part, then the stresses on central government and its coffers would be reduced.

He set the tone for his reign on New Year's Day, at the inauguration of Mamertinus and Nevitta. Rather than summon the Senate to the palace, as had become customary, Julian himself went on foot to the Senate house to hear Mamertinus's speech. This was far from being a one-time event. Julian went regularly, often took part in debates and even as staunch a critic of the emperor's as the fifth-century ecclesiastical historian Socrates Scholasticus grudgingly noted that he sat up all night writing speeches and he was the first head of state since Julius Caesar to deliver them in person.[26] To back up these public moves, on February 5, the emperor passed the law which can be understood as his credo in these matters: "The rights of the senators and the authority of that class—in which we also count ourselves—must be defended from all injustice."[27]

In retrospect it is easy to see what the emperor was trying to do: to raise the standing of the Senate while underscoring the point that he, as emperor, saw himself as a servant of the Senate. Few were convinced by this humility. He was criticized for what was seen as an affectation, portraying himself as an ordinary citizen. Julian could not understand this condemnation. He would have argued that he was an ordinary citizen. But then again he was able to; he was the emperor.

Julian in fact had a more immediate problem in restoring the status of the councils than trying to turn back the tide of history. The problem was that serving on the city council was both time consuming and expensive. Councillors had to do everything from collecting taxes and running the local police, to organizing state requisitions—and all of this for no money. Worse, the councillors were personally liable for all of these services. The emperor tried to ease their difficulties. On March 13, he relieved senators of some of the more arduous work—debt and poll tax collecting among others—that he, and almost certainly they, regarded as beneath their dignity.[28]

This he hoped would stop people finding excuses not to serve on the councils. Members of some specialized professions—such as doctors and teachers—had long been exempt from public service and did not have to serve as councillors. But since a ruling of Constantine's forty-nine years previously, the clergy had also been exempt. It is in that light that we should see his law, also of March 13, directed at those who used Christianity and claimed to be clergy as a way to escape public service.[29] They were to start paying taxes again. This was not a law specifically against Christianity, it was a law primarily against avoidance, as can be seen in the letter he wrote to a town in Northern Africa: "I have restored all your senators and councillors to you whether they have abandoned themselves to the superstition of the Galileans or have devised some other method of escaping from the Senate and have given exemptions only to those who have filled public offices in the capital."[30]

At the same time, the emperor considered that if the councils themselves were on firmer financial ground, then the issue of financial liability would be less of a deterrent. So he gave them property.[31] Although criticized by the Church, which lost land in the move, it was a relatively simple way of giving the cities assets which they could then lease, thereby giving them what must have been a significant source of revenue.

And finally, at the end of April he made the presentation of golden wreaths—a tribute paid by the cities—a voluntary affair, and capped it at a fixed sum.[32] Cities had traditionally given the emperor a golden wreath every year, a free-will offering of thanks for his protection. In reality, however, it had become a crippling tax as cities competed with each other to see who could give the emperor the heaviest wreath. It was another cost that the councils could probably do without and although Julian did not go so far as to ban them—indeed those who continued to present them to him were well received—his legislation did limit the excess.

It is hard to find fault either with the intention or wording of his laws. The problem was implementation. Not everyone grasped what he was trying to do. Antioch, a city of which Julian is able to boast "I increased the register of your Senate by two hundred members and spared no man,"[33] appears to have missed the point entirely. The following winter, you can see the emperor shake his head as he complains: "Would you like me to remind you of a single instance?" he writes. "You nominated a senator, and then before his name had been placed on the register and the scrutiny of his character was still pending, you thrust this person into the public service. Then you dragged in another from the market place, a man who was so poor that he belonged to a class which in every other city is counted as the very dregs, but who among you, since in your infinite wisdom you exchange rubbish for gold, enjoys a moderate fortune. And this man you elected as your colleague."[34]

All of Julian's laws that are cited survive because they were collected together in the fifth century by a sixteen-man strong commission that collated every law from the time of Constantine into a single work called the Theodosian Code. Looking at Julian's legislation more broadly, the emperor's laws that have survived do go beyond stimulating the life of the councils. His aims appear to have been to rid the empire of layers of bureaucracy—he simplified, for example, the laws on appeal—while his economic policy was to avoid corruption and waste. He was proud of the latter and able to boast that "I have not levied gold money or demanded silver money or increased the tribute, but on top of the arrears, one fifth of the regular taxes has been in all cases remitted."[35]

The best-known example of controlling costs was his overhauling of the imperial courier system, which began toward the end of February.[36] The system provided transport for those traveling on official business throughout the empire while the cities picked up the tab. The animals were overused and the system had become abused almost to breaking point. Libanius paints a distressing picture of beasts that never saw the inside of a stall, were regularly lashed and often dropped dead as soon as they were unhitched.[37]

Although other emperors had tried to come to grips with this problem before—Hadrian had ordered that expenses be defrayed from the imperial purse, but the costs had long reverted back to the cities—Julian both introduced a strict quota on the number of passes that could be issued and restricted who could issue them. Some territories, such as the heavily mountainous area of Sardinia,[38] which made the use of horses both unprofitable and difficult, were not deemed important enough to enjoy the full service any more. Julian's efforts appear to have had some effect and even his critics had good words to say about him on this matter.

To alleviate corruption he hit the accountants and government tax collectors at the end of January. They were given formal warning that, after every five years in office, they had to go on gardening leave for one, a system to ensure they were open to prosecution from any citizen who might have a complaint. Those found guilty of fraudulent accounting practices were to be tortured.[39] Two weeks later, Julian passed a law discouraging payment up front for favors. He realized that the favor system was so ingrained in the empire that it could not be banned, but it could be limited.[40] This move was perhaps the result of his experience with a party of particularly litigiously minded Egyptian lobbyists who had laid siege to the palace in Constantinople demanding restitution for money they had paid around seventy years previously to men in the capital for patronage. The solution was a wonderful piece of political legerdemain. Julian ordered that they should go to Chalcedon and that he would shortly join them and settle all of their claims. As soon as they had gone, Julian gave orders that no ferry should allow an Egyptian on board and eventually the mission went home with its tail between its legs.

To prevent future abuses of the system, on March 13, Julian announced that there could be no taxes imposed or old taxes remitted without his approval.[41] It is a sign of how important an issue he considered this that he took personal control, and some sign of what would now be dubbed the open government that he was trying to engender. Certainly, Julian was no mere figurehead in these matters. His apprenticeship in Gaul had stood him in good stead and his dealings with financial petitions show that his decisions are not those of a young man feeling his way—they are those of a seasoned politician.

Quite how directly he was involved can be seen in his reply to the Thracians who had petitioned the emperor to reduce their taxes.

> Since I have not made it my aim to collect the greatest possible sums from my subjects, rather to be the source of the greatest possible blessings to them, I shall cancel your debts. It will cancel the whole sum absolutely, but there shall be a division of the amount and some shall be remitted to you, some shall be used for the needs of the army, since you definitely benefit from their presence—peace and security. I remit the whole sum that is in arrears for the period down to the third assessment [up to AD 359]. Thereafter you will

contribute as usual. The amount written off is sufficient indulgence for you, while I must not neglect the public interest. I have sent orders to the prefects so that your indulgence may be carried into effect. May the gods keep you prosperous for all time.[42]

It was the perfect decision for all concerned. The Thracians were happy to pay less than had been demanded and did not seem to notice that rather than having the whole amount remitted, they were still left with a hefty bill. Central government was happy because it no longer had to shoulder the cost of the army—that expense had been palmed off on the locals. Best of all, by conceding something and appearing to be magnanimous, Julian himself came out of it smelling of roses.

This apparent focus on internal affairs had not distracted the emperor from preparations for war with Persia. Envoys had arrived in Constantinople from Shapur to negotiate, indeed had given every indication of making concessions. The emperor, however, was in no mood to compromise.[43] An epigram has survived from one of Julian's statues in the city which shows his determination for war. "Julian, whom you see in setting up walls to protect his people, has erected a trophy, a symbol of his vigilance. He is eager to slaughter his enemies at a distance rather than wage war in front of the city."[44]

In spring Julian had written to a friend in Cappadocia: "The first signs of spring are here already, the trees are in bud and the swallows, which are expected almost immediately, as soon as they come drive our band of campaigners out of doors and remind us that we ought to be over the border. We shall travel through your part of the country so that you would have a better chance of seeing me, if the gods will it, in your own home."[45] By midsummer preparations were ready and it was time to move to Antioch.

Antioch was the Roman Empire's traditional base for military campaigns in the East. Apart from being one of the largest cities in the empire, it was strategically important for the eastern front. The city was the key to northern Syria and of the four legions that were stationed in Syria, three of them had headquarters within striking distance of the city. As such it had become a center of military manufacturing. The city housed three state factories: a mint, an arms factory and a factory for making dress uniforms for officers. An imperial move there will have been interpreted as serious mobilization.

Julian's final gift to Constantinople was a series of public buildings. He started work on a new harbor on the Marmara side of the city; finished off a public library started by Constantius; carried out various other monumental works including the transport of an obelisk from Egypt (very possibly the obelisk of Egypt's warrior king Thutmosis III that was eventually put up by the emperor Theodosius and still stands in the remains of the hippodrome); and finished work on the city's walls. But in the second half of May or early June, Julian set out for Antioch. The pressures of government business as well as his attention to detail were starting to take their toll. In a long letter to his uncle, Julianus, prefect of the East, mostly concerned with details about his arrival in Antioch, he complains: "I do not even offer up many prayers, though naturally I need now more than ever to pray very often and very long. But I am hemmed in and choked by public business as you will perhaps see for yourself when I arrive in Syria."[46]

The emperor headed along the main roads that had been in use, in one form or another, for the last millennium. It took him only five weeks or so to march the six hundred eighty-three miles to Antioch even though at times it appeared as much of a progress as a march. The surviving sources deal with the journey briefly, but it is possible to gather more details from archaeological and other literary sources. We can trace Julian's progress on one of the earliest Roman maps to have survived—the Peutinger Map, sometimes also called the *Tabula Peutingeriana,* named after Konrad Peutinger who owned the manuscript in the early-sixteenth century.[47] Although the original is long gone, a copy was made by a monk in the thirteenth century, and we have a fair representation of the Roman Empire at the time of Julian that stretches from southern England as far as Sri Lanka.

Almost twenty-three feet long, though only thirteen inches wide so that it could be carried easily rolled up, the map does not conform to the rules of any projection, nor is it possible to apply a constant scale to determine distances. Geographic rigor was sacrificed in favor of administrative efficiency, and it is perhaps most useful of all to think of it as we do the map of the London Underground. Nonetheless, as well as beautiful in itself, it provides a wealth of information. Roads, rivers, and mountain ranges are marked in red, green, and brown respectively; important cities are shown with town walls, while towns, harbors, spas, and granaries all have their own ideograms.

Three cities are given special prominence. Rome, surrounded by a golden ring, is clearly still the center of the civilized world. Personified as a female figure sitting on a throne, she holds a scepter in one hand, a spear in the other, and has a shield next to her. Constantinople—labeled "Constantinopolis" not "Byzantium" from which the mid-fourth-century date has been deduced—is altogether more martial and triumphal. She is represented by a helmeted female figure seated on a throne, holding a spear and a shield in her left hand. With her right hand she points to a high column topped by a statue of (possibly) Constantine.

The representation of Antioch, the third largest city in the Roman Empire, is perhaps the most interesting. Also depicted as a woman, it appears to be a picture of Tyche, the city's patron goddess. Sitting on a throne, a spear in her right hand, a much smaller naked male figure, the personification of the River Orontes, rests near her left foot, while the arches of an aqueduct from the nearby suburb of Daphne, bring water into the city. It is an image of the city that will have been instantly recognizable—it would have been familiar as many logos are today.

Julian crossed the Bosporus and headed for Nicomedia. Although the emperor had strong personal connections with the city—he had, after all, spent some of his childhood there—this was a state visit, to see a city that had suffered a catastrophic earthquake four years previously. The emperor was hugely upset when he saw the city. Libanius wrote to him: "It is possible for you, if you so wish, to restore the city, but for your despair for those who died may consolation come from somewhere in heaven. I congratulate Nicomedia even in her ruins. She should be standing yet, but still in her fall she has been honored by your tears. . . . It will be your concern that the city of old shall become a city again."[48]

There are few ancient remains of any description in the modern city of Izmit, which we now know lies along the North Anatolian fault line. It is a disaster that has been repeated throughout history, most recently on August 17, 1999, when the city was hit by an earthquake, measuring

7.4 on the Richter scale, which left 6,000 dead. In a style of reportage that is depressingly contemporary Ammianus writes:

> At dawn on August 24 . . . a terrific earthquake entirely destroyed the city and its suburbs. Since most of the houses were built on slopes, they fell on top of one another and the whole air echoed with the vast roar of their destruction. The hilltops re-echoed the various cries of people searching for their wives, children, and those close to them. At last, just after 8 a.m., the day, which was now bright and clear, revealed the full extent of the carnage. Some had perished under the sheer weight of the debris which had fallen on them; some were buried up to their necks in the heaps of rubble, and might have survived had anyone helped them, but died for lack of assistance; others hung impaled upon the sharp points of projecting timber.
>
> Most were killed instantaneously, and where there had been human beings a moment before, now all there was to be seen were piles of jumbled corpses. Some were imprisoned unhurt by the fallen roofs of their houses, only to die in agony and starvation. Among them was Aristaenetus, governor of the recently created diocese which Constantius, in honor of his wife, Eusebia, had named *Pietas*. He breathed his last after protracted suffering. Others, who were crushed by the sudden, overwhelming shock, lie buried under the ruins to this day. Some with fractured skulls or severed arms or legs hovered between life and death and were abandoned, in spite of their loud cries for help from others in the same situation.[49]

After making a generous donation to the city's restoration fund, from the ruins of Nicomedia, Julian made only one unscheduled stop—to visit the ancient shrine of Cybele at Pessinus. Now called Ballihisar, you can at least get some idea of its former majesty from the remains of the temple, ritual bath, and Ionic portico. Julian had written his *Hymn to the Mother of the Gods* in her honor that spring, probably at the time of her annual festival in March, so his detour to visit the temple is not surprising. As was to happen so many times in his reign, Julian was upset by the neglect he found at the shrine. In a letter that compares her troubles to those of Odysseus's wife Penelope, he appointed a priestess, a woman called Callixeine who had kept the faith despite the oppression by Constantine and his son.[50]

Cybele had a long history of worship in that part of Turkey and was the first of the oriental religions to be adopted by the Romans. Julian's adherence to the cult was, for once, more Roman than Greek. The Greeks had long shied away from its excesses, but Julian was a dedicated acolyte of the Mother of the Gods.

It was a cult linked to the seasons. The climax of her festival on March 24, was called "the day of blood," as it symbolized the death and resurrection of Cybele's beloved Attis, both her lover and her son. Attis is normally portrayed as a beautiful youth who deserts the goddess. In a spirit of remorse he eventually returns, and as the Roman poet Catullus wrote:

> *Over the high seas Attis, carried in a speedy craft,*
> *When he touched the grove in Phrygia eagerly with*
> *   hurrying feet*
> *And approaching the goddess' gloomy forest-girt*
> *   domain,*
> *There by raving madness goaded, his wits astray,*
> *He tore off with a sharp flint the burden of his groin.*[51]

Attis then dies of his wounds beneath a pine tree, violets springing up where his blood drops to earth. His barrenness symbolizes winter and his restoration to Cybele was the coming of spring.

The cult of Cybele and indeed her popularity had been linked with the glory of Rome for the last 450 years. In the dark days of the Carthaginian Wars, the Sibylline oracle had predicted that if Rome housed "the most holy statue of the goddess,"[52] then Hannibal could be beaten. Julian relates the story in his *Hymn,* of how the Senate and the people of Rome rushed to greet the ship which stuck fast in the Tiber until the priestess took off her girdle, fastened it to the ship's prow and pulled it upstream.[53]

The goddess brought the city luck as promised. The Third Punic War ended with the destruction of Carthage and a huge temple was built that sat on the Palatine Hill in Rome; until it was knocked down to make way for Saint Peter's Cathedral which now stands on the temple's site.

The difficulty that the more squeamish had with the cult was its blood-curdling nature. The worship of Cybele was conducted by cross-dressing, castrated priests called Galli. The first example of one in Britain was recently found near Catterick, buried wearing a jet necklace and bracelet, a shale armlet, and a bronze expanding anklet.[54] The cult was orgiastic in the extreme, accompanied by the sound of such frenzy-producing instruments as drums and cymbals. Perhaps most distasteful of all, the service culminated in scourging and self-mutilation. With considerable leg-crossing detail, the second-century Syrian-born writer Lucian of Samosata describes the ritual: "The young man whom Fortune has given to do this casts off his clothing and rushes into the center with a great shout, and takes up a sword, which has stood there many years for this purpose, I believe. Then he immediately castrates himself and runs through the city bearing in his hands those parts he has cut off. And from whatever house into which he shall cast these, he gets female clothing and womanly adornments."[55]

Imperial interest in the cult appears not to have been endorsed by the citizens of Pessinus, and Julian had later to write a stiff letter to the high priest of Galatia from Antioch: "I am ready to help Pessinus if her people succeed in winning the favor of the Mother of the Gods. But if they neglect her, they are not only not free from blame, but not to speak harshly, let them be aware of reaping my enmity too."[56]

After a brief visit to Ankyra, now Turkey's capital Ankara (sadly one of the best-known tangible remnants of the emperor's reign, the Column of Julian, which stands forty-nine feet tall on Ankara's Hükümet Meydani, was probably not erected before the sixth century), Julian headed for the Taurus Mountains. There is still really only one place to cross these majestic mountains: the Cilician Gates, now Külek Bogazi, a pass that follows the gorge of the River Gökoluk and has served for centuries as a natural highway linking Anatolia with the Mediterranean coast. The route, also crossed by both Cyrus the Great and Alexander the Great, is now followed by the main railway line between Istanbul and Beirut.

Once over the mountains on the Cilician plains, it was an easy ride from Tarsus to Adana, round the Gulf of Iskenderun and across the plain of Issus. From Iskenderun, the town Alexander the Great built to celebrate his victory over the Persians in 333 BC, it was a simple day's journey on horseback over the Amanus Mountains, through the pass called the Syrian Gates to Antioch, "the magnificent jewel of the East."[57] Julian had finally reached his destination, the key to northern Syria and the city from which he was going to conquer Persia.

6

SUNG IN VAIN

Urg'd with his fury, like a wounded deer,
O'er these he fled; and now approaching near,
Had reach'd the nymph with his harmonious lay,
Whom all his charms could not incline to stay.
Yet what he sung in his immortal strain,
Though unsuccessful, was not sung in vain;
All but the nymph that should redress his wrong,
Attend his passion, and approve his song.
Like Phœbus thus, acquiring unsought praise,
He catch'd at love, and fill'd his arm with bays.

EDMUND WALLER,
THE STORY OF PHOEBUS AND DAPHNE

Julian would have heard the shrill notes of flutes and the wailing of both men and women long before he entered Antioch, modern Antakya, through the Bridge Gate on July 18, 362.[1] As the emperor drew closer, he would have seen and smelt the clouds of incense rising over what he might eventually have recognized as the effigy of a man, washed in water, anointed in oil, and dressed in red. The emperor's arrival coincided with the feast of Adonis, the lover of Aphrodite who was killed by a boar. The god's funeral was celebrated annually around the midsummer, and especially enthusiastically throughout Syria.[2]

Julian marched north through the city along the colonnaded Street of Herod and Tiberius, which still follows the path of the city's main road to its very heart, the fountain called the Temple of the Nymphs. Stopping to admire a sight much praised by ancient writers, with its gleaming marble, colored pillars, numerous paintings, and fountains, the emperor and his retinue turned left toward the Orontes river, which splits just north of the city, making a small island on which the palace and the hippodrome stood.

As he marched up toward the island he passed the Tetrapylon of the Elephants—four arched vaults linked to one another in rectangular formation. It was here that Julian later and fatefully was to publish *The Beard Hater*. Passing on, it was a short walk to the palace quarter—roughly where the present Hatay Museum stands—the place from where his brother had ruled the city.

Libanius is filled with customary civic pride as he describes the palace. "Of all the palaces in the world which are called palaces from their size or are far famed for their beauty, this palace quarter is in no way inferior to the first and is far superior to the second," he writes. Indeed, "it is divided up into so many rooms, colonnades and halls that even people long acquainted with the place can lose their way when going from one door to another," he boasts.[3]

It should have been a magnificent entrance to a magnificent city. But the Cassandras who took the emperor's arrival in the middle of funeral celebrations as a bad omen were proved right. A wave of enthusiasm greeted the new emperor and Julian, the consummate politician, was charming in return. Libanius met him on his arrival in the city and wrote to a friend about their first meeting: "Almost as soon as the emperor left you he met me. He almost passed me by in silence since my face is so ravaged by time and illness, but his uncle and namesake [Julian's maternal uncle, Julianus, prefect of the East] told him who I was and he was remarkably excited as he sat on his horse. He grasped my hand and would not let go, and he showered me with jokes most delightful and sweeter than roses, and I did not refrain from jesting myself. He was admirable both for the remarks he passed and those he suffered."[4]

But when Julian left nine months later, the honeymoon had ended in acrimonious divorce. In the beginning, Julian had been excited to be there. His Hellenism would never be comfortable in the West and, remembering his first impressions, he later wrote: "I intended to make it a city of marble,"[5] echoing Augustus's sentiments on Rome three centuries previously when he had become emperor.

The emperor soon reacted against both the city's Christianity and what he saw as its innate frivolity. To him it was a latter day Sodom. This was no new charge; the emperor Hadrian had been so infuriated by the city that he had tried to remove some of the territories under its jurisdiction in an attempt to curb its influence.

The Antiochenes in turn had little time for Julian's pompous self-denial. A fragment that appears to come from an edict to the people of Antioch makes the emperor sound rather like a classical Miss Manners: "When I enter the theater unannounced acclaim me, but when I enter the temples be silent and transfer your acclamations to the gods."[6]

Although population figures in the ancient world are notoriously difficult to gauge, current estimates suggest that Antioch had what was getting on for half a million inhabitants. To give some idea for comparison, Alexandria in the later Roman Empire had a population of around 600,000 and Constantinople had just over one million people.

Antioch shared many of the same characteristics of other third cities of an empire. It had all of the power and none of the class. It might have been important, but had made its money through trade, and compared to the possibly more refined taste of the capitals it was regarded as a bit nouveau riche. As a defense mechanism the city had become infamous for its sense of humor—it was the Antiochenes who dubbed the followers of Christ "Christians" or "Christ-groupies."

Julian appears genuinely to have underestimated quite how Christian the city was. There had been a large Christian emigration into Antioch after the stoning in Jerusalem of Stephen, the first Christian martyr, and it was here that the faith not only shifted from a rural to an urban movement, but stopped being a Jewish/Hebrew one too. The Gospel of

Matthew, for example, was written here and it is worth remembering that it was written in Greek. The Christian community of Antioch had rapidly become extremely diverse, consisting of a large proportion of Jews, but with Hellenes and a predominant number of Gentiles. And it also became the missionary center, spearheaded by St. Paul, from which Christianity spread. Since the fall of Jerusalem, Antioch had effectively reigned as the center of Christianity. After all it was here that Ignatius, bishop of Antioch who died in AD 110, used the term "Catholic Church" for the first time. This was a depth of belief that Julian could not wash away with a few laws.

None of this was helped by the fact that the people of Antioch had taken both Constantine and especially Constantius to their hearts. The latter had been stationed in the city from 355 until Constantine's death and as a sign of his affection for the city had constructed several build-ings there. By 346 the new harbor had been finished at Seleucia Pieria, just twenty miles west of the city. More relevant to Julian, however, his cousin had finished the Octagonal Great Church (often called the Golden Church) that Constantine had started. With its tall walls and gilded wooden dome it would have been visible from miles away after its dedication on January 6, 341. Worse that that, as far as Julian was concerned, it had been built right next to the palace on the island.

All of this frustrated Julian beyond belief. After the relationship between emperor and city had broken down almost irrevocably, Julian put pen to paper, but what starts off rueful, ends up as well-vented spleen. "It was my fault that I did not understand this city's charac-ter from the beginning even though I am absolutely sure that I have read no fewer books than any other man my age," he begins.[7] Then (in what reads like a remarkably Darwinian argument) Julian explains that because the city's founder was an idiot, no one should be surprised that the locals are too.[8]

As difficult as the city was for Julian to understand, it is even more difficult for the modern mind. First and foremost, we have little real concept of what Antioch was. Rome appears familiar—however false that sense of familiarity might be—through films such as *Ben Hur* and *Gladiator;* Athens with its Acropolis is one of the most photographed of all ancient cities; and even Istanbul's classical past is recognizable, if only from *The World Is Not Enough* and *From Russia with Love,* when James Bond punts his way through the great cistern of Justinian. But not only has little of classical Antioch survived, it has changed hands and been destroyed both by human and natural disasters so often, that there is not even a sense of what went before.

The city remained a powerhouse in the Middle East until it was sacked in the thirteenth century and all its inhabitants were either slaughtered or sold into slavery. Antioch was never to recover and slowly sank into the mud that washes down from Mount Silpios. By the mid-nineteenth century, the city had become a village. Even the indignity of anonymity was not enough. In the twentieth century, Antioch became a counter in an international game of frontiers and the city changed hands three times. During the time that United States archaeologists had their hands buried in the mud excavating in and around the city in the 1930s, the city around them which had started out as part of the French mandate of Syria when they arrived, then flirted briefly with independence before it was annexed by Turkey in July 1939.

The high point for the archaeologists from Princeton was the discovery of beautiful mosaics. A bittersweet reminder of the city's past elegance and grandeur, by far the best examples came from the suburb of Daphne, now Harbiye, a famously beautiful spot almost thirteen miles south of Antioch. The clean spring air and views had turned it into the city's summer retreat, indeed Antioch was renamed Epidaphne or "near Daphne," by wags. Anyone who was anyone had a home there.

Daphne was one of the major reasons that Julian came to Antioch, but its significance for the emperor had nothing to do with either the climate or the city's demimonde. It was that Daphne was home to the shrine to Apollo. And the temple caused the breach in the emperor's relationship with the Antiochene Senate for good.

The temple, like Antioch and Daphne, had been built in the third century BC by Seleucus, the most able of Alexander the Great's generals. He had been seduced by the story of Daphne, a river nymph, who had run away rather than give in to the attentions of the god Apollo.

The myth is one of the most moving of all classical legends. After an argument with Cupid, the god of love had shot Apollo with one of his love arrows and then maliciously shot Daphne, the daughter of the river god Peneus, with one that repelled love. Apollo pursued her as assiduously as she avoided him until, as he was about to catch her, Daphne prayed to her father for help. At the last moment, she turned into a laurel tree.

It was the romantic and dramatic intensity of this final moment that attracted so many Renaissance artists. Bernini's life-size statue in white marble in the Galleria Borghese in Rome, for example, catches Daphne at the point of change. As bark starts to sheathe her body, we see leaves begin to sprout from her fingers and her hair. At the same time Apollo's hand on her breast can still feel the human heart beating inside. Despite her metamorphosis, the god's passion remained undiminished. Apollo made a crown of the leaves of his beloved and swore to make the laurel his tree. Tradition had it that Apollo haunted the spot in her memory ever after.

With a myth so firmly attached to one place, little surprise that soon after he had founded Antioch (named after his father), Seleucus found the very laurel of the legend. In honor of the spot he had the shrine built with a massive statue of Apollo commissioned from Bryaxis.

The statue was magnificent. Over forty-two feet tall—the same size as the statue of Zeus at Olympia—Apollo's body was made of vine wood and fitted together with such astonishing skill that it seemed as though it was made of a single, indivisible piece. The statue was draped in a golden tunic that allowed the nude and ungilded parts of the body to shine with inexpressible beauty. The god was posed as the leader of the Muses holding a lyre. His hair intertwined with a crown of laurel was gold plated, like his mantle. And in place of eyes were two enormous violet gems.

Over the years the shrine—a younger sister to the famous Pythian at Delphi—had matured as emperor after emperor lavished money on it. After dipping a leaf of the laurel into the waters and reading what was written on it, Hadrian had learned that he would become emperor. Soon after taking the throne, he ordered the fountain to be blocked up so that no one else might be tempted to look into the future. It should therefore have surprised the Senate little that Julian wished to consult the shrine.

While still at Constantinople, Julian had written to his maternal uncle, Julianus, prefect of the East: "First, reerect the pillars of the temple of Daphne—take those that are in any palace anywhere and have them transported there. In their place use other pillars taken from the newer houses. If there are not enough even from that source, let us use cheaper ones made of plaster and cased in marble as a stopgap. Piety is to be preferred to splendor and when it is practiced, gives much pleasure for the righteous in this life."[9]

When he finally made a visit to the temple, however, preparations had not gone entirely to plan. Despite the almost comic description of events in *The Beard Hater,* the emperor was quite clearly furious. "I saw in my mind's eye, the sort of procession it would be, like a man seeing visions in a dream—beasts for sacrifice, libations, choruses in honor of the god, incense, and the youths of your city attired in white and splendid raiment surrounding the shrine, their souls adorned with all holiness," he wrote. But when he got there, he found that nothing had been prepared for him. Following what must have been an embarrassed silence after Julian asked what sacrifice the city intended to make to Apollo; the priest appeared with a goose he had brought with him from home.[10]

The emperor lost his temper. The speech he made to the Senate afterward, the culmination of a series of frustrations with Antiochene lubricity, shows quite how infuriated he was. More of a rant than a speech, he complained how on one hand the city's *jeunesse dorée* were quite happy to fritter away their money on parties, but when it came to religion, they kept their purse strings tightly closed.[11]

One can easily imagine what the effect of that tantrum was. But relations rapidly deteriorated even further. When Julian went as a suppliant to the Pythian at the oracle to ask why it had gone silent, he was told: "The dead prevent me from uttering. I will say nothing until the grove is purified. Break open the graves, dig up the bones, move the dead."[12] This was a blatant reference to Julian's brother Gallus, who, while governor of the city, had not only neglected the shrine, but had in fact built a church to one of the local saints, St. Babylas, former archbishop of Antioch, right next to it.

A popular local saint, Babylas exhibited many of the diplomatic traits of the early Christian martyrs. The great historian of the early Church

Eusebius tells the story that he once refused an emperor—several are suggested and Philip the Arabian is as good as any—entry to his church at Easter until he had confessed his sins. While Philip apparently took no offence at this instance of lese-majesty, Babylas was imprisoned by a later emperor for refusing to take part in pagan sacrifice, tortured and then beheaded with three of his pupils in AD 251.

The act of building the church was almost unforgivably offensive to pagans and highlights one of the fundamental differences between pagan and Christian belief. Christians had a clearly articulated vision of the resurrection of the flesh—the dead had intrinsic value, they sanctified and protected. For pagans, the dead polluted and were to be interred in *nekropoloi*—cities of the dead. It was a debate over which there could be no compromise.

Julian still maintained a placatory stance and only suggested that the body of St. Babylas be moved—out of a sense of self-preservation perhaps, the Pythian did not mention the saint by name—but the population reacted very badly. As the cart carrying the archbishop's stone sarcophagus made its way back to the martyrium just outside the city walls from where Gallus had moved it, the road was lined with a massive number of people, especially women, singing the fourth-century equivalent of protest songs, taken from the Bible: "Confounded be all they that serve graven images, that boast themselves of idols: worship him all ye gods."[13]

Better leaders have been frustrated by passive resistance. Julian's already frayed temper snapped and it is difficult not to have some sympathy with the emperor. One of the Christian nobles, a certain Publia who was the choir mistress and mother of the city's chief presbyter, used to taunt the emperor every time he walked past by singing another psalm: "Their idols are of silver and gold, the work of men's hands. . . . / They that make them are like unto them; so is every one that trusteth in them."[14]

Asked to refrain from such behavior when the emperor was passing the irritating matriarch continued with: "Let God arise, let his enemies be scattered: let them also that hate him flee before him. / As smoke is driven away, so drive them away: as wax melteth before the fire, so let the wicked perish at the presence of God."[15] He cracked and told his guard to box her ears, and she was carried off still singing.

Julian never considered a full-blown persecution of the Christians such as had been seen in the past, but he had to do something to stop the demonstrations. He ordered the ever-faithful Salutius to round up the usual suspects and make an example of them, which the prefect did unwillingly—he knew the difficulty that martyrs would create for law and order. Nonetheless, several people were arrested and tortured with scourges and metal claws.[16]

But these were all minor skirmishes compared to what was to come. A couple of days later, on the evening of October 22, there was a fire at the temple in Daphne. A passer-by raised the alarm. Julian's uncle, Julianus, was roused from his bed and rushed to the scene, but it was too late. By now the main beams of the temple were collapsing and the statue itself had already gone up in smoke. A crowd of spectators was watching but was unable to help, such was the heat.

A guilty party was needed rapidly. Aware of how this would go down with the emperor, the officers in charge of the temple were flogged for negligence, but they swore blind that the fire had been started by a thunderbolt. It was a view corroborated by some peasants who were produced to back up their story.

The unfortunate priest of Apollo was next in the firing line and brought before the tribunal of justice set up for the inquiry that comprised Libanius and two other commissioners, Heliodorus and Asterius. When the hapless priest proved unable to name anyone, he was flogged to see if that would jolt his memory. Needless to say that did not work. At the close of the inquiry, the chief suspect was Vitalius, a Christian who later became proconsul of Asia under Jovian. He was eventually acquitted as an innocent bystander, but the solution left no one happy and the fallout dragged on for many months.[17]

With no obvious guilty party, in the end all Julian could do was use the incident as an excuse to close the Golden Church—something he had presumably been looking to do since his arrival in the city. He asked Julianus, Felix the imperial treasurer, and Elpidus, the emperor's private treasurer, to nail the church shut and confiscate its valuables, which were considerable. The church had benefited greatly from imperial largesse over the last two reigns. When he saw the sacred vessels Felix, a

Christian who had renounced his faith, commented: "Behold with what vessels Mary's son is served." Julianus is alleged to have committed an "act of gross indecency"[18] on the altar—the cleanest version of which has him taking the sacred vessels, throwing them to the ground, beating them flat, and sitting on them.[19]

Both Julianus and Felix were not to survive the winter and, rather like the death of Lord Carnarvon soon after opening the tomb of Tutankhamun, their fates were ascribed to the vengeance of God. Felix kept vomiting blood from his mouth, all day and all night and died the next day, while Julianus suffered from some wasting disease. The whole gamut of ancient medicine was tried. Physicians sacrificed fattened and exotic birds and placed them near the putrefied limbs while they invoked the maggots to come out. It failed.

Although the historians rapidly split into two camps—pagans who still believed the temple was burned by Christian insurgents, and Christians who thought that it was an act of God—the most plausible solution, if the least glamorous, is that it was an accident. It is unlikely that a temple that had until recently been almost abandoned would have been looked after that well. Ammianus mentions that a philosopher friend of the emperor's, a certain Asclepiades, had visited the temple and, after placing a silver offering at the feet of the statue, had lit a number of tapers and gone away. Past midnight, when everyone had gone home, it was a stray spark that caught some dry wood and turned the temple into an inferno.[20]

7

NOTHING IN EXCESS, AUGUSTUS

"Observing, then, that there is great contempt for
    the gods among us"—he says in his solemn way.
Contempt. But what did he expect?
Let him organize religion as much as he liked,
write to the High Priest of Galacia as much as he
    liked,
or to others of his kind, inciting them, goading
    them on.
His friends weren't Christians; that much was
    certain.
But even so they couldn't play
as he could (brought up a Christian)
with a new religious system,
ludicrous in theory and application.
They were, after all, Greeks. Nothing in excess,
    Augustus.

CONSTANTINE CAVAFY, JULIAN SEEING CONTEMPT

 The fire at Daphne may have been the spark that ignited the discord between Julian and the people of Antioch, but the destruction of the temple of Apollo was a smoke screen for two much larger issues—people's bellies and their souls.

Soon after the emperor's arrival in the city he was greeted by a distinctly unhappy mob at the theater chanting: "We've got the grain. Why the pain?"[1] A corn crisis had been long in the making. The stresses on the local economy had been severe for the last two and a half years. Constantius had made the city his headquarters before his campaigns in Persia and the strains on food reserves from the military and imperial administration had been compounded by the famine that had gripped the city for the past year. A lack of rain over the previous winter had wiped out the season's wheat. It is a sign of Julian's awareness of the problem that he remitted Antioch's tribute as early as the start of 362 and boosted the number of local senators by 200 to increase city finances. Since then, however, what stocks there were had been further depleted by a poor harvest that summer that should have been collected while Julian was approaching the city, and reserves were being stretched by the army's demands. A growing sense of panic over the state of that winter's crop was to be proved justified—it too failed.

Julian moved to act at once. The day after the demonstration in the theater he met with all those involved and tried to get them to lower prices; and by August 18, he had limited the number of civil servants drawing rations.[2] It was typical that the emperor took charge of the problem personally. He had a track record of fixing large problems since his successful reorganization of taxes in Gaul and knew the extent to which it had an immediate knock-on effect in popularity. But his measures did not work, and in the second half of October the emperor was forced to intervene again. As in Gaul, he took the step of reducing taxes, turned over 3,000 lots of land to cultivation to help the small farmers and increase food production, and then acted more directly on the market.[3]

Julian's interventions failed both economically and socially. While the blame was largely laid at the feet of the emperor, instead it was the Senate's fault. Julian had enough economic commom sense to recognize that the problem was twofold. The first part of the problem—the lack of grain caused by the drought—was easy enough for him to address even if the solution was expensive. As his brother had done, Julian mobilized grain deliveries from Syria. It was a smart move as soldiers stationed in the region were used, which had the effect of alleviating the immediate demand in the city as well as providing the much-needed grain. This had a fairly rapid impact and gave Julian breathing space as the city waited for more significant amounts to come from Egypt, while the large grain donations from his own property will have shown imperial largesse.

The second problem was more awkward: that of prices. These had spiraled as demand had increased to the extent that the cost of corn, if Julian is to be believed, had doubled since the summer. And this is where disaster struck. The emperor introduced price controls within the city, naively underestimating the cynicism of the Antiochene merchants and landowners.

Rather than easing the problem, speculators ran wild, with the smarter ones playing the spread. As rationing was not introduced, richer locals could buy up vast quantities of grain and either play a waiting game and hold it in storage or, as the majority did, buy the subsidized grain cheaply in the city and then sell it at the market rate outside the city in the countryside, where there was huge demand and no controls. Poorer merchants, caught between Julian's artificially low price and landowners' high one simply went bust. In a state of extreme embarrassment, Libanius admitted that the town should have shown its disapproval of the merchants rather than of the man who brought the prices down.[4]

In the end, Julian broadened price controls to include bread—a commodity with a limited shelf life and therefore unhoardable. But this too was a failure. With bread the only affordable food, the streets of Antioch became flooded with the region's urban and rural poor desperate to feed themselves and their families.

Everyone ended up disillusioned, not helped by an imperial tact worthy of Marie Antoinette. When someone complained to Julian that there was neither shellfish nor much poultry in the market, he replied that a well-conducted city needs bread, wine, and olive oil, but meat only when it is growing luxurious.[5] With a city swelling with refugees, little food and profiteers running rampant, little wonder that Julian's popularity remained low. The poor felt they were getting a raw deal and had stomachs that were no fuller; merchants have always balked at state interference and complained that Julian's meddling had paralysed business;[6] and the landowners hated him anyway.

The food crisis may have strained the relationship between the emperor and the people of Antioch, but what severed it completely was Julian's obsessive paganism. Almost as soon as he had taken the purple, the emperor had begun his counter-reformation, what is collectively seen as his anti-Christian measures. For all future commentators, and certainly those in the centuries immediately after Julian's death, it was these policies that elicited almost all criticism. Even today it is the most controversial aspect of the emperor's reign, reflected in the fact that he is still most commonly called "the Apostate."

Technically, since Constantine's initial laws restricting the practice of ancient beliefs in 320–321, paganism had been outlawed.[7] But the reality was rather different and how far these laws were enforced was entirely dependent on local conditions. During a grain shortage in Rome in 359, for example, as high profile a man as the city's urban prefect was happily able to sacrifice at the temple of Castor and Pollux to make sure that the seas remained calm so that ships could get through. Twenty-two years after Julian's death, a middle-class woman from Arles called Egeria was to dismiss the town of Carrhae, now Harran, writing in her travel diary: "I found hardly one Christian in that city, with the exception of a few clergy and holy monks—if any such dwell in the city; all are heathen";[8] and St. Augustine was to rail several times against "crowds of simpletons" and "Roman idolaters."[9] Even as late as the early-fifth century, after a law forbidding the public celebration of pagan rites and festivals, the bishop of Hippo writes of "certain impious rites" which took place in front of one of the churches in North Africa. When the clergy tried to stop it, they were pelted with stones and when the bishop reported the town to the authorities the people ran riot again and attacked the church.[10] How truly Christian was the empire?

Despite what we can now see as the inexorable rise of Christianity, when Julian came to the throne it was mostly an urban phenomenon that had been carried along Mediterranean shipping lanes from the Middle East. In many cities Christianity was little more than a veneer. There is a difference between signing up to something and believing it. The traditions that had grown up around paganism were by now so embedded in Roman society that it would take more than legislation to shift them. Most Romans will have seen nothing wrong in celebrating the pagan holiday of Saturnalia (which continued up to the end of the fifth century) while proclaiming themselves Christian, and we should not be surprised that the Romans were able simultaneously to maintain two mutually opposing beliefs. Few today have problems coping with the contradiction inherent in celebrating the Resurrection of Christ and the entirely pagan tradition of handing out, on the same day, patent fertility symbols in the form of Easter eggs.

Julian saw Christianity as a sickness infecting the Roman Empire. As a philosopher he resented the morality of this cult, which had always targeted and been most popular among slaves and women. But as an emperor he was fundamentally opposed to any belief that conflicted with the interests of the Roman state; it was not their right to worship that caused the problems, rather it was the intractability of Christians toward Rome's own gods. To him it was an illness, and this image of Christianity as a contagious disease both for an individual and more broadly for the empire crops up repeatedly in Julian's writings. "We ought to pity rather than hate men who in the matters of the greatest importance are in such evil case. . . . We suffer in sympathy with those who are afflicted by disease but rejoice with those who are being released and set free by the aid of the gods," he writes.[11] Julian even saw himself as having been poisoned by Christianity. In a particularly vivid allegorical passage in one of the emperor's essays on religion, Zeus talks to the sun god Helios about Julian. "Swear on my scepter and yours that you will look after him carefully and cure him of this illness. You see how he is, as it were, infected with smoke, filth, and darkness. There is a danger that the spark of fire, which you planted in him, will be snuffed out, unless you put on your war strength. Look after him and raise him. The Fates and I charge you with this task."[12]

Julian's most explicit attempt to wrestle with this interloper theologically is his treatise *Against the Galileans,* in which he sets out why "the fabrication of the Galileans is a fiction of men, composed by wickedness."[13] Long considered, he worked on it during the winter nights and finally published it in early 363.

There are some powerful passages that display theological pragmatism and Julian's wider belief in a need for unity. Discussing the Ten Commandments, for example, Julian asks: "Except for the commandment 'thou shalt not worship other gods', and 'remember the Sabbath day' what nation is there, I ask in the name of the gods, which does not think that it ought to keep the other commandments?"[14] But the work appears rather disjointed. What remains is disappointing, and it is not just because only around a third has survived. The passages we have are those garnered from an extensive refutation of the work by Cyril of Alexandria in the early 440s. By definition it is the weakest passages that have survived. Not only are the passages Cyril excerpted naturally enough the ones he disagreed with, but also they are the ones that he felt he could refute.

The passages that have survived are a considered attack on Christianity, pointing out discrepancies in the Bible, the introduction of practices not mentioned in either the Hebrew or Christian scriptures such as the cult of martyrdom and, more broadly, the Church's vicious attacks on heretics when they professed to follow the paths of forgiveness and love. Although Julian's schooling in Christianity is evident, as is his familiarity with the texts, *Against the Galileans* reads more like the essay of an overly enthusiastic student than a work of philosophy. It was certainly not unique. Several others had produced attacks before, most notably the Platonist Celsus, writing during the reign of Marcus Aurelius, whose great work *The True Word,* stands out as an intellectual call for Christians to abandon their separatism and rejoin their pagan brethren.

Like all Julian's religious measures, *Against the Galileans* did not survive much past its writer's death and few contemporaries commented on it. St. Jerome was disparaging, mentioning it in a letter to a friend ("were I to try to confute him with the doctrines of philosophers and stoics you would doubtless forbid me to strike a mad dog with the club of Hercules"[15]); two Christian writers wrote essays against it, which have not survived; and there was the Cyril account mentioned above. But when pagan books were proscribed in the early fourth century *Against the Galileans* was not even deemed worth banning.

The trap for anyone looking at Julian's religious policy today is that it is easy to see what his aims were. He wanted to unpick the

Constantinian religious reforms. His counter-reformation would see a pagan empire with an institutionalized state religion of paganism. The difficulty is that it is virtually impossible to see any coherent pattern or logical structure in his manner of doing so. Julian was never to develop his own explicit theological doctrine or creed and remained stuck in the metaphysical and mystical. The emperor knew where he wanted to go, but not how to get there. This means that while each law in itself can now clearly be seen as part of this overarching strategy, it could have appeared as though Julian was passing legislation as the thought struck him. Part of the reason of course is that Julian died in media res. We simply have no idea of what else the emperor was planning and what he might have done had he returned from Persia. More than anything else, these policies and laws allow speculation free rein.

Generally, however, it is possible to distinguish three strands in Julian's pagan revivalism: his reorganization of paganism; his maginal-ization of Christians within society; and finally his attempt at unifying the beliefs of the empire with his approach to the Jews. Julian's open-ing salvo within weeks of becoming emperor left little doubt about his longer-term plans and must have seemed like a bolt out of the blue. While the emperor's personal beliefs had been known to his intimate circle for some time, he had only come out of the religious closet to the army in November after the death of Constantius. His two reforms will have caused as much confusion as they inspired joy or alarm.

First, Julian announced that the temples must be reopened or built. The bedlam that this law caused can be only dimly appreciated.[16] Statues, columns and bricks that had been appropriated had to be returned, and if a temple had been completely destroyed, it had to be rebuilt by the culprit at his own expense.

Libanius gives all too vivid a picture of the realities of the law. Urging clemency for his young cousins who had converted a couple of temples into a house he wrote to the governor of Phoenicia: "Please show concern for my relatives. . . . Though we are bound to rejoice at the restoration of the temples, we must not surround the reform with an atmosphere of bit-terness in case we in turn hear similar accusations made against us (this is the sort of thing that is happening at present). The sons of Thalassius converted temples into a house. They acted in conformity with the policy approved by the emperor of the day. I do not approve of it, but this was legal at the time."[17] This is a problem that has rather been glossed over by modern commentators. It should not, however, be underestimated how difficult a bureaucratic challenge it must have been.

It is not true to say that Constantinople had been constructed without any temples—there were at least four[18]—but it is worth questioning what condition they were in. Certainly the emperor had a Mithraeum built in the middle of the imperial palace, but it was at the temple to Fortuna, while sacrificing, that Julian had a famous run-in with Maris, the blind bishop of Chalcedon. Various versions of the following exchange survived. Perhaps the most entertaining is in a Renaissance joke book from the seventeenth century. "When Julian the Apostate in a mocke demanded of blinde [Maris], why he went not to Galilee to recover his eyesight, hee made him this answer, no, I am contented with my blindenesse, because I may not see such a tyrant as thou art."[19] Amused, Julian did not pursue the matter.

This was followed by an edict of universal religious tolerance. Julian summoned Christian bishops to the palace, asked them to put their differences aside and allow anyone to worship in any way they pleased. To a friend, Julian wrote: "I have remitted their sentence of exile for all in common who were banished in whatever fashion by Constantius of blessed memory, on account of the folly of the Galileans."[20] It was an astute political move. In one fell swoop, Julian made clear the distinction between the aims for his reign and those of his cousin and uncle. At the same time, even if Ammianus's now famous comment that no wild beasts are as dangerous to man as one Christian to another[21] is overly cynical, the edict certainly did have the divide and conquer effect that he wanted, as the various Christian splinter groups all fell to arguing among themselves.

His decrees of universal tolerance were significant for their emphasis that no persecution would be tolerated. Although his stance at times has been seen as the blindness of the intellectual, Julian appears genuinely proud when he writes: "I have behaved with such kindness and benevolence to all the Galileans that none of them has suffered violence anywhere or been dragged into a temple or threatened into anything else of the sort against his own will."[22] The emperor was certainly adamant that there should be no physical persecution of Christians. "It is by reason that we ought to persuade and instruct men, not by blows or insults or physical violence,"[23] was how Julian believed people should behave and there was no consistent or state-sponsored policy of persecution. He had learned well and did not want to create any martyrs.

This is not to say, however, that there was no violence. In a letter written to the administrator of a district in the East, it is apparent that some towns took the emperor's laws as carte blanche to settle old scores. This was not part of Julian's grand plan. In the tone of a disappointed schoolmaster he had to reiterate that he didn't want Christians "to be put to death, beaten up, or to suffer any injury."[24]

The hostility appears to have operated both ways. Julian was driven to write an official reprimand after a pagan priest had been assaulted. What it was that the priest had done to excite the wrath of the town is not clear, but Julian's note is unmistakably irritated. "What sort of self-control can you have when you mistreat one at whose approach you ought to have risen from your seat?" he writes. His punishment is typically prissy: "Since by the laws of our fathers I am supreme pontiff . . . I forbid you to interfere with anything that concerns a priest for three months. If during that time you appear to be worthy, and the high priest of the city so writes to me, I will take counsel with the gods whether you may be received once more."[25]

Clearly, these two events are isolated incidents, and to what extent widespread violence was caused as a result of the law is debatable. Even though the Christian writers fall over themselves to give examples, it is worth looking carefully at the incidents that have come down to us. They fall into two definite categories. First are those that are patently nonsense. The stories of the sacrifice of children, anthropophagy, stripping nuns, and feeding them to the pigs remain in the same class as anecdotes about German soldiers bayoneting Belgian babies in the First World War.[26]

In the other cases that have come down to us, it is clear that there were usually specific local reasons for the violence. In Lebanon, near modern Balbec, a deacon was killed by a mob—but it was a revenge attack. In his religious zeal, during the reign of Constantine, the deacon had smashed up statues in temples. The same thing happened further north, in western Asia Minor, and three louts were then put to death after they refused to sacrifice. Again in Lebanon, Mark, the bishop of Arethusa, was as much of a liability as a martyr. He had taken Constantine's laws as an opportunity to demolish a popular local shrine. On Julian's restitution he was asked to restore the shrine or pay up. He refused to pay a single penny. He was stabbed with metal styluses by his pupils, then smeared with honey and fish sauce and hung out to die.[27]

By far the best-known case to come down to us is that of the lynching of George of Cappadocia along with two other notables. The murder of the man who had supervised Julian's early education had little to do with either the emperor directly or his laws. In fact this "human snake who had often made the people of Alexandria suffer from his poisonous fangs"[28] was lynched on December 24, 361, soon after news of Julian's accession had broken, and his mutilated body was paraded through the streets on a camel. While hardly justifiable, it was not without provocation—during his almost four years in the city George had managed to alienate not only the pagans and most of the local clergy with his religious intolerance, he had also irritated the populace at large with his heavy-handed policing and public profiteering. Religious factionalism ran deep in the city. Libanius was to refer later to "outrages" in the city[29] and in June the following year Julian had to have the military prefect of Egypt executed.

The emperor was placed in a difficult position. Civil disobedience could not be countenanced, but news must already have reached the city about where Julian's sympathies lay. He had already written, for example, to the former head of the city's medical faculty, a friend of Libanius who had been exiled by George, restoring him to his position.[30] But a public statement was necessary, and Julian's open letter to the city in January is notable in that it treads the line between sympathy for the city's problems and disapproval of its actions. "Though I wish to praise you, I cannot, because you have broken the law. Your citizens dared to tear a human being in pieces as dogs tear a wolf, and then are not ashamed to lift hands still dripping with blood to the gods," he writes. Even though, he concedes, George may have deserved it, they should not have taken the law into their own hands. In the end he does not even punish the city.[31]

Preoccupied with matters of state, Julian's next legal move against the Christians did not occur until after he had left the capital. He had, however, already begun to politicize the issue by holding audiences in sanctuaries, naturally favoring those who took part, refusing to receive embassies from complaining Christians, and he had already suggested that for all administrative positions "the god-fearing must be preferred"[32] to Christians. But on June 17, he passed the first of his educational laws. The wording of the law is simplicity itself. It asserted merely that all teachers held their positions at the pleasure of the emperor, not just the town council.[33] That in itself alarmed few. An educationalist on the throne was a novelty, not something to fear. Then followed the law for which the emperor has had opprobrium heaped upon him: the edict that banned Christians from teaching the classics. It was the single event for which he became notorious.

The exact wording of the law has not survived. Fortunately a letter, probably a memo to teachers in the East, does survive in which Julian explains his thinking on the law. Julian was at heart in many ways an academic. Not only did he see education and religion as inseparable, but also, unlike virtually every leader since, the emperor thought about it, encouraged it (Libanius comments that on his march from Constantinople to Antioch the emperor "was easy of access to teachers"[34]), and wrote about it. But Julian went as far as to state explicitly that the brighter and better educated are more useful members of society. It was a view he held consistently throughout his life. Elsewhere he wrote: "Every man would become better than before by studying the classics, even if he were altogether not the brightest. But when a man is naturally well-endowed with brains and receives a true classical education, he becomes a gift of the gods to mankind, by kindling the light of knowledge, by founding some kind of political constitution, by routing numbers of his country's enemies or even by traveling far over the earth and sea."[35] Julian may have sugar-coated the pill by reiterating that no one would be forced to recant, but he was adamant that Christians, who did not convert, were banned from teaching the three pillars of Roman education: grammar, rhetoric, and philosophy.[36]

In one fell swoop, Julian had cut Christians off from potential converts and from the classical tradition, from Homer and from Hesiod.

Let them keep their St. Paul if they wanted. It is an explicit statement that Hellenism equals paganism. Commentator after commentator ever since has spluttered his disapproval. "How did it come into your head, to deprive Christians of words, you silliest and greediest of mortals? . . . Where did the idea come from and for what reason? What oracular Hermes put this idea into your head? What Telchines did it, those mischievous and envious demons?"[37] screams Gregory of Nazianzus. Even Ammianus called it a "harsh act" that should be buried in "lasting oblivion."[38]

And this is precisely why the law was a masterstroke. Julian had marginalized Christianity to the point where it could potentially have vanished within a generation or two, and without the need for physical coercion. The choice for a parent was stark—either conform, or commit your son to being an outsider. The abuse Julian received is an indication that Christians realized what he had done. "We are shot with shafts feathered from our own wing,"[39] writes one. The irony, of course, is that the monk Theodoret is citing Aeschylus, one of the greatest of classical authors.

More legal restrictions were to follow. In the middle of January, he banned Christians from practicing law and a month later Julian passed his edict on funerals, banning burial during the daytime. "Death is rest and night harmonizes with rest,"[40] writes the emperor. For many pagans, it was bad luck to see a corpse during daylight hours, as the sight of it contaminated the bystander.

It is hard not to see this as a move toward the hard line, possibly as a response to the furor caused by the Babylas incident and certainly to do with his irritation with Antioch. There was a reaction throughout the empire. Bodies of martyrs were removed from Delphi in Greece, burned in Didyma, on the southwest Aegean coast of Turkey, and at Emesa, near modern Damascus. According to legend, Julian went so far as to burn the remains of John the Baptist.

Traditionally buried in the Church of John in Samaria, now a mosque in Sebastiyeh on the West Bank, several accounts report that Julian had the coffin opened, the bones burned and the ashes scattered abroad. The story emerged fairly soon after Julian's death[41] and was highly popular in the Middle Ages. The fourteenth-century traveler and teller of tall tales Sir John Mandeville relates just one version: "There [Samaria] Julian the Apostate when he was emperor had his bones exhumed and burned and the ashes were scattered to the wind. But the finger with which Saint John indicated our Lord, saying, *Ecce Agnus Dei* etc. could not be burned."[42] It is a tradition that was celebrated in several paintings; one by the Dutch artist Geertgen tot Sint Jans in the fifteenth century and another in the sixteenth century by the Master of the St. Johns Retable.[43]

But imperial patronage of paganism and marginalization of Christians was not enough for a full-scale pagan revival. Julian's masterplan was no less than the creation of a religious infrastructure that would counter the Christian model at the grassroots level. He understood its success and appeal and knew the difficulties in going against what was a tight-knit organization. "Why have we not noticed that it is their benevolence toward strangers, their care for the graves of the dead and the pseudo-holiness of their lives that has done most to increase atheism [i.e., Christianity]?"[44] he asked. Julian recognized that paganism had to be given the tools to fight back and turned his attention to the pagan priests who would be his frontline troops in the battle for the souls of the Roman Empire. With himself as head of the Church, he saw high priests as counterparts to the archbishops, who in turn appointed and managed their own priests.

As always, Julian had a strong vision of what he expected: he wanted the pagans to out-Christian the Christians. "The qualities that are appropriate for one in this high office are, in the first place, fairness, and next goodness and benevolence toward those who deserve to be treated like this. Any priest who behaves unjustly to his fellow men and impiously toward the gods or is arrogant, must either be given a warning, or be rebuked with great severity," he writes.[45]

He certainly had high expectations. As a supplement to the civic charitable ventures and as a counterbalance to Christian aid that was already in place, the priests at a parish level were to help the old, the poor and the sick, and provide charity.[46] Elsewhere more specifically, after detailing arrangements for the imperial distribution of corn to one high priest, Julian writes: "I order that one-fifth of this be used for the poor who serve the priests and the remainder be distributed by us to strangers and beggars. It is disgraceful that when no Jew ever has to beg and the impious Galileans support not only their own poor but ours as well, all men see that our people lack aid from us."[47]

The difficulty is that he was starting from such a low level. The position of pagan priests had at best become ceremonial in recent years and at worst a social liability. The priest who turned up with a goose at Daphne was symptomatic, the rot having set in with the decline of state funding since the reign of Constantine. And seeing the dearth of public money allocated for pagan rites, private individuals were less keen to contribute, preferring to put their money toward more secular spectacles such as games. No wonder, then, that pagan priests felt neglected and grew lax. To a chief priest the emperor writes: "Warn them that no priest may enter a theater, drink in a pub, trade or run a business that is improper and not respectable."[48] That he had to do so gives a fair indication of what most of them were up to. That he had to articulate that he expected prayers three times a day, sacrifice twice a day, and ritual purity is a further sign of how far things had degenerated.

And this was the problem. Julian wanted his priests to fulfill the same role that Constantine had assigned to Christians; pagan priests were to be agents of social change and also of social control. Not only did Christians have a thirty-year head start, the pagans were handicapped in that they were not taken seriously. Rather poignantly in retrospect, at the end of a letter to an unnamed priest Julian writes: "we should be ministers of prayers, not curses."[49]

The final strand to Julian's religious policy was that of the Jewish question. The emperor saw pagans and Jews standing side by side with arms linked against the Christian menace. The emperor's letter to the community of Jews from Antioch in January 363 is an extraordinary document.[50] In a remarkably placatory and friendly tone in which he addresses the patriarch, Hillel II, as his brother, Julian calls the fiscal burden on the Jewish community "impious" and the people who had enforced it "barbarians in mind, godless in soul." But the letter's real bombshell is dropped at the end. After asking the Jewish community to pray for his reign, he concludes: "This you ought to do, so that when I have successfully concluded the war with Persia, I may rebuild by my own efforts the sacred city of Jerusalem which for so many years you have longed to see inhabited, and bring settlers there and together with you, may glorify the Most High God therein."

This promise had huge significance. Much as Julian had betrayed his intimate knowledge of the Bible by referring to Christians as Galileans, so too here he was showing his detailed acquaintance with the Christian scriptures, specifically Jesus's prophecy with regard to the Temple in Jerusalem. "There shall not be left one stone upon another, that shall not be thrown down," Christ had said.[51] An attempt to rebuild the temple would stun Christians into submission. More to the point, it would show Jesus up as a liar.

The reasons for Julian's desire to court the Jewish community may seem slightly baffling, but become clear when seen as a reaction to his domestic policy against the Christians and his foreign policy against Persia. The emperor was no Zionist and had no natural feelings toward the Jews; indeed it is apparent that Julian's knowledge of Judaism was limited to the study of the Septuagint as a child. Insofar as they shared a common heritage, Julian was as dismissive of the Jewish past as he was of the Christian one. "Though God cared for all nations, he bestowed on the Hebrews nothing considerable or of great value," he writes at one point.[52]

His Jewish contemporaries, however, could help him and counterbalance this young religion. As a result, the emperor could describe them as "far superior to the Galileans"[53] because he was always going to look favorably on a religion that emphasized its forefathers and, even though it was monotheistic, one that had a tradition of sacrifice. Indeed, the reason given by ancient authors for Julian's offer to rebuild the Temple is that when he asked them why they had not sacrificed, they replied that it was not permitted them to do this in any other place than Jerusalem. He immediately ordered them to rebuild Solomon's temple. In fact, since the time of the emperor Hadrian, Jews had been forbidden to enter Jerusalem.

Julian had no problems with their monotheism. As a nation-state, the Jews were entitled to their own ethnic beliefs, but more importantly they were perceived as tolerant of other religions—something that stood in sharp relief to the bigoted zeal of the Christians.

In turn, the Jews appear to have looked sympathetically on Julian and his support had the effect that he wanted. Various inscriptions have been found: "God is one; victory to Julian" in Ascalon and one from the upper Jordan valley describing Julian as the "restorer of the temples."[54]

In the more immediate short term, a significant reason was geopolitical. Since the capture and destruction of Jerusalem almost 300 years previously by Titus, son of the emperor Vespasian, relations between the Romans and the Jews had been civil at best. In more recent times, Constantius's rule had not been the most sensitive; various revolts around Diocaesarea—now Zippori—in 353 had been put down with extreme prejudice by Gallus. Any sympathetic gesture toward the Jews would generate instant favor. A temple was a small price to pay for the goodwill that it would foster. Julian was not only hoping for a powerbase of support in Palestine. The entire region was densely settled with Jews, along the route Julian intended to follow against Shapur. On top of the natural enmity toward Rome, Constantine's Christianization would have made them even more anti-Rome. It was a calculated political gamble that Julian's olive branch would ensure if not support then at least neutrality among the Jews of Mesopotamia.

Although there is some confusion about timings—Julian indicates both that he had planned to start rebuilding the Temple after his return from Persia and that he hadn't quite got round to it—it seems that work started before his death under the supervision of a former governor of Britain. It is strange but not completely puzzling that Jewish sources are almost entirely silent on the matter—we find a reason in Julian's short reign and a subsequent desire not to offend his successors.

When the clearing of existing foundations in the area—now called Solomon's Stables on the Temple Mount—started in early 363, the project did not go entirely as planned. Although this was a high priority work and funded by the imperial treasury (some idea of the expense may be gauged from the fact that one commentator notes that the Romans made mattocks, shovels, and baskets of silver as this was specified by Jewish law[55]), everything about the project seems to have been doomed. Knowing none of this Julian remarked: "I am rebuilding with all zeal the new Temple of the Most High God."[56] But Julian was in Persia. Reading between the lines, we get a picture of accidents on the construction site that ended with an earthquake and mysterious balls of fire in the second half of May[57] that caused many fatalities and destroyed much of the surrounding area. The builders had never got further than the foundations and the project was abandoned without Julian ever hearing the news. "Even today, if you go into Jerusalem, you will see the bare foundation," gloats John Chrysostom in one of his homilies against the Jews, remarkably unpleasant to the modern ear, written a few years later.[58]

The three essays which Julian wrote in early 362—*To the uneducated Cynics,* the reply to the Cynic Heracleios and *To the Mother of the Gods*—show an emperor groping his way toward a unified set of beliefs. They were all written in haste and Julian admits that he had been "writing on such a great subject so rapidly and without taking breath" and that he was "only able to give it two days as the Muses, or rather you yourselves will bear witness."[59] Their importance lies in that they are a snapshot of the emperor's mindset rather than extended policy documents; editorials rather than academic papers. And although they cover different topics, all three emphasize the asceticism and the behavior that he expected. "Let no one divide philosophy into many kinds or cut it into many parts. Let no one suggest that it is many rather than one. Just as there is one truth, so too there is one philosophy," writes Julian.[60] Only if they pulled together could they defeat the enemy.

In the end, the difficulty is not that Christianity succeeded, it is that paganism failed. It was not a case of bringing the empire back to the fold; rather, Julian was faced with having to create an entirely new organization. While Christianity by its very exclusivity was unified, pagans worshipped a multiplicity of gods in a variety of ways and there simply wasn't anything that could be called a systemized pagan theology. Julian's attempts at creating a pagan doctrine betray his Christian upbringing. His law against teachers shows that he recognized the threat, but in a real sense Julian could never truly apostatise. By the very fact of his early education, he was already, as he would have put it, polluted.

At the start of the new year it is difficult to see why the thirty-year-old emperor would have been in anything other than optimistic mood. After a year in power, Julian had much to be proud of. The western half of the empire was essentially at peace, his plans were well under way to achieve the same in the East, he had cut out the deadwood from Constantius's inner circle and, from his point of view, his reforms were beginning to take hold. The immediate administrative and social issue facing him, the famine, is one that many had grappled with and survived. His track record must have led him to believe that he would soon have the people of Syria on side, and if the removal of the bones of St. Babylas had been a public-relations disaster, Julian had no reason to doubt that long-term he could not win them over.

His general buoyancy is reflected in the entertaining satire on the emperors called *The Caesars* that Julian wrote in mid-December. It is a work often criticized as a pale pastiche of the satires of the great classical humorist Lucian of Samosata, and for being unfunny. This is unfair for so witty and lively a read.

It was soon time to turn from works of fiction to matters of state. On January 1, 363, Julian and Salutius were inaugurated as the new consuls. Julian, wearing a purple toga decorated with precious stones, was carried through the town, while Salutius—the first nonroyal to receive such an honor in almost three-quarters of a century—also wore a ceremonial purple toga decorated with astrological signs and images of emperors. In a carnival atmosphere, the two threw money into cheering crowds. The official celebrations lasted the whole day. Libanius was the official orator and he spoke at length.

The philosopher's speech, which has survived, would have been one of the high spots of the day for the emperor. It is a bombastic piece of rhetoric and provocatively pagan. It praises Julian for his devotion to philosophy and learning, criticizes Constantius, and congratulates the emperor for bringing the empire back to the pagan fold "like a son reproving his mother."[61] The speech certainly raised eyebrows. Julian was so pleased with it that he jumped up from his seat and shook his cloak—as partisan and as subtle a gesture as raising the Black Panther salute at the Mexico City Olympics.

The celebrations continued two days later. On the morning of the third, the emperor conducted a public sacrifice at Antioch's gilded temple of Jupiter Capitolinus. The soldiers then took their annual oath of loyalty to the emperor and Julian handed out the expected donative, though this year he refused to do so to the Christians. The rest of the day was spent in games after the march through the city to the circus.

It was here that the humor and generally good-natured ribbing of the leaders that was traditional at this time of year seemed to turn sour. Julian, not a fan of the circus in the first place, had to put in an appearance and pay for the event, so it is fair to assume that he was not in the best of moods. Jokes turned into heckling and although the exact nature of what happened has not survived, it must have been offensive. Julian soon left and a couple of months later, Libanius was still apologizing for what had happened. "As for the misconduct in the hippodrome, you have long scorned that, but we shall exact punishment for it for we have spared no effort in tracking the scoundrels down and we are very near to arresting them," he writes, far too tantalizingly for the modern reader.[62] But it was to get worse. Julian was further humiliated on the way back to the palace. "We are held to have put on a shocking dance and turned a religious holiday into an excuse for a disreputable racing entertainment and in consequence I must plead for a people involved in such accusations," writes Libanius, ever the apologist for his fellow citizens.[63]

It was Julian's final break with the city. Oppression and violence were rarely Julian's style. Just as he had learned with the Christians, the most effective form of revenge was to turn the tables on them and treat them in precisely the same manner as they had treated him. One morning in late January 363 the citizens of Antioch found the satire known today as *The Beard Hater* posted up on the Tetrapylon of the Elephants. It is a curious document. Within the framework of a parody of himself he abuses the city in a quite extraordinary way. It is often regarded as a faux pas and is passed over in disapproving silence, rather like the aberration of an uncle who misbehaves at a family wedding.

Despite the way it has been seen since, *The Beard Hater* was not regarded as peculiar at the time. It was a response to Antioch's New Year celebrations, which were marked by behavior recognizable to this day: all night drinking and partying. The people also took the opportunity to satirize the emperor in ways that could be quite vicious. Constantius, for example, had been quite crudely treated in Edessa. In response to some slight, the inhabitants had pulled down a bronze statue of the emperor, turned it face down, and thrashed it soundly.[64] Julian's cousin had wisely chosen to ignore this distinct affront to his dignity.

Julian was savaged personally and politically. His famous beard, homage to Marcus Aurelius, was sent up and his coins were ridiculed. In preparation for his campaign, he had re-formed the empire's coinage with a new bronze issue that showed a standing bull facing right with two stars above its head on the obverse (only the Jews approved of this move; for them it recalled the Golden Calf of the Exodus rather than the Mithraic bull). They mocked his religious policy in general and specifically his addiction to blood sacrifice. He was nicknamed Victimarius, "the Slaughterer," and Causitaurus, "the Bull-Burner."[65] Admittedly even some pagans were put off, regarding his practices as a touch outré. In an uncharacteristically snide aside, Ammianus suggests that a win in Persia for Julian would have meant a shortage of imperial cattle.[66]

In one sense, Julian's response was appropriate in that it hit the Antiochenes where it hurt. The bullies weren't beaten, imprisoned, or made to suffer under the law—all of which would have been grist to the mill—Julian merely laughed at them. If he had left it at that, then face could have been saved on both sides. But a note of acrimony creeps into *The Beard Hater* and the latter half is a tart, two-fingered riposte to the city that had annoyed him. It shows Julian at his worst, petulant and bitter: "I thought it was my duty to help the people who were being wronged and the visitors who kept arriving in the city both because I was here and because of the senior officials who were with me. But since it is now the case, I think, that the latter have departed and the city is of one mind with regards to me—some of you hate me and the others whom I fed are ungrateful—I leave the whole matter in the hands of Nemesis. I will take myself off to another nation and to citizens of another sort."[67] After he returned from Persia, he was never going to darken the town's doors again.

8

WHERE KING NEBUCHADNEZZAR GRAZED

"I believe that river is the Euphrates," I said. "So," he said, acutely interested. "Then that's the waters of Babylon. Great snakes that I should have lived to see the fields where King Nebuchadnezzar grazed!"

JOHN BUCHAN, MR. STANDFAST

More than half a century before Julian planned his excursion into Persia, the still unborn Shapur II was crowned king. When his father, Hormisdas II, died in 309 after a seven-year reign, the nobles approached the magi and, according to legend, while his mother was still pregnant asked whether she was carrying a boy or a girl. When told it was a boy they held a crown over his mother's stomach and the embryo was proclaimed king.

At the time of Julian's invasion Shapur was fifty-four years old; a king, an absolute ruler and a god at the height of his powers. He was imposing physically—taller than average, with his black hair and beard long and curled, he looked like nothing so much as the heir to the great Achaemenid dynasty, the ruling dynasty of Persia founded by Cyrus the Great and destroyed by Alexander the Great. All in all, he was to reign for seventy years, making him the regal contemporary of ten Roman emperors and, at its peak, his empire stretched from Syria to northwest India. But even though Shapur was arguably the greatest of the Sassanid monarchs, the natural pro-Julian bias of Western historians has left the king a shadowy, distant figure, the amorphous depersonalized bogeyman of Western propagandists.

It is, admittedly, hard to draw up any kind of real picture of the man. If seeing the world through Julian's eyes is at times difficult, it is virtually impossible to do so with Shapur. We have few eyewitness descriptions of him. One of the few comes from Ammianus, who describes him wearing a gold helmet in the shape of a ram's head studded with precious stones, on his horse at the head of his army.[1] The problem is apparent—given that Ammianus was an enemy, protecting the city that Shapur was about to take, he is hardly the closest or most objective of eyewitnesses.

There are no portrayals of him per se, despite the many coins that have survived. The two most famous representations that we have not only fall under the category of official portrait but also are attributed rather than definitely him. The first is a royal head, hammered from a single sheet of silver, almost sixteen inches high, now in the Metropolitan Museum in New York. Even though the bust has some distinctive features—ovoid earrings for example—the majestic face and the arrogant stare suggest that this is a stylized, rather than a personal likeness. Similarly, the famous dish in the Hermitage depicting Shapur hunting lions, while an outstanding example of Sassanian silverware, gives little insight into the man.

Can we tell anything about him? Little is known of Shapur's youth. He was brought up in the palace along the left bank of the Tigris in the Sassanid capital of Ctesiphon. It must have been an impressive city: the administrative heart of the empire, the crossroads of trade routes from all four points of the compass and in the center of the empire's agricultural heartland. Less than a hundred and fifty years later it claimed a population of almost half a million, making it the largest city in the world. If that is the case, it is unlikely to have been that much smaller in the fourth century.[2] Nowadays, the site lies around twenty miles southeast of Baghdad in what is effectively a suburb of Iraq's capital called Taq-i-Kesra. Sadly, little of the palace remains. When the Tigris flooded in 1987 it destroyed many of the remaining buildings, but the surviving east-facing doorway arch of the gigantic vaulted hall (at a span of more than 78 feet and a height of 118 feet it is the largest intact brick arch in existence) gives some idea of the scope and grandeur of Shapur's palace.

An amusing vignette of the young king's early life is preserved in the Annales of the ninth-century Arab historian al-Tabari. One night, Shapur was woken up by a noise outside the palace. When Shapur asked what the disturbance was, he was told that it was people crossing backward and forward over the Tigris. His town-planning innovation was to have another bridge built, near the first one, so that "people now no longer needed to endanger their lives when they crossed the bridge"[3] and presumably with the added advantage that nothing would disturb the precocious monarch's beauty sleep.

At first Shapur's reign was dominated by the nobility and clergy, who had held power during his father's reign. With no real king and aging leaders, it was little surprise that surrounding countries had started to think of picking off bits of the Sassanid empire. They had taken advantage of thirty years of inconsequential rulers since Shapur I had died to occupy chunks of Mesopotamia and had even briefly captured Ctesiphon. Territory was lost to the east and the west and Arab raiders from the south—modern Bahrain—seem to have regarded Persian produce as a "help yourself" affair.

Shapur came of age in 325 at the age of sixteen and for the next twelve years, before he came into direct conflict with Rome, his domestic policy was one of consolidation. Two events in his early reign give significant insights into the mind of the new monarch. The first is another story related by al-Tabari. The monarch's viziers reported the depressed state of soldiers facing an unspecified enemy. Shapur ordered that letters be written to the soldiers to tell them that he had heard how long they had been at their posts, what they had achieved and that this was appreciated back home. Then he added that anyone who wanted to come home on leave was free to do so, but if they finished their tours of duty, it would not be forgotten. Needless to say, they all stayed.

Balanced with this thoughtfulness is the cruelty he exhibited in his first action against the brigands from Bahrain, which was breathtaking even for a Persian monarch. In an innovative lightning campaign that included the first naval detachments used in the Persian Gulf in centuries, Shapur led his troops in person. He attacked with 1,000 hand-picked soldiers and with the order that no quarter be given. Many were massacred and to make sure that this never happened again, he blocked up every well and every spring that he passed. The campaign was an outstanding success and the region was then secured by a series of forts—a military outpost which commanded the shipping through the Strait of Hormuz has been discovered in northern Oman while, more recently, an ancient Sassanian castle was found in the summer of 2001 at Julphar, now Al Koush in the United Arab Emirates.[4] The campaign also won Shapur his nickname "Lord of Shoulders." In revenge for their behavior—depending on which detail you believe—he either had the shoulder blades of his Arab captives ripped out, or their shoulders pierced and strung together with rope.

It was inevitable, however, that Shapur would eventually come into conflict with Rome. A delicate and sometimes not so delicate pas de deux had taken place between the two empires since the time of the Roman republic. It is perhaps easiest to think of it in terms similar to the Cold War. The antagonism, the language and the incredible importance attached to relatively unimportant events is reminiscent of that period.

There was rarely a reason needed for a fight. Rome didn't need an excuse to make war in Asia. As opponents like the Carthaginians had found out to their cost, Rome did not play well with others and their very existence was sometimes the only trigger necessary. It should come as no surprise that the world's two military superpowers, facing each other along a frontier that was several hundred miles long, should come into regular conflict. They were, as the Greek historian Herodian had written in the third century, the two greatest empires in the world, divided only by a river.[5]

Their enmity goes beyond a simple clash of civilizations. Antipathy ran deep. From the myths of the rape of Europa to ancient stories of Leonidas and Themistocles defending the civilized Western world against the Persians, an antipathy toward and a dehumanization of the East was bred into Romans from childhood. It is telling that Julian's default term for the entire nation was *barbaroi*—the Greek term that encompasses a sneer at their language, culture, and personal hygiene.

Although we know less about what the Sassanids thought, it was not that much different. The significance that the Persians put on beating Rome was huge even if the propagandist element so apparent in Roman coinage is lacking. A number of reliefs at Sassanid centers show humiliated Romans with all of the subtlety of the British media celebrating the defeat of Germany in a football match. At sites in modern Iran such as Bishapur and Naqsh-i Rustam a representation commemorating Shapur I's defeat of Rome has survived. The two Roman emperors submit to Shapur on horseback. Philip the Arab sues for peace on his knees, but although Valerian is portrayed standing up, his hands are held by Shapur, a reference to the fact he was taken prisoner. At Darab, a similar scene is shown—a Sassanid shah on horseback receiving the submission of two Roman leaders while a third lies on the ground. The point is made.

The Sassanid monarchs exhibited greater subtlety in some of their other propaganda, in the city of Bishapur, for instance, one of the main Sassanian administrative centers built by Shapur I in southwest Iran, but not much. For a start it says much about a Persian inferiority complex that the city in later times was known as Gundeshapur, a corruption of Antiuk Shapour—"more beautiful than Antioch." But a distinct case of knife twisting is evident in the discovery by archaeologists working in the remains of the palace of beautiful and distinctly Roman mosaics, showing nobles, musicians, and garland bearers. It may be presumed that these works of art were laid by Roman prisoners of war and, if this is the case, then it is something that will not have gone unnoticed by visiting diplomats.

In one sense the question of why Julian invaded Persia is a meaningless one. The emperor did not have an option. His invasion of Persia was the continuation of a frontier policy that he had inherited from Constantine and Constantius. It had a momentum all of its own and if in Julian's writings we find that he gives no reason for the war in Persia, it is because he didn't need one. Any more immediate or personal reasons for Julian's invasion must be seen through that prism.

There had been diplomatic niggling between the two rulers since 323, when Shapur's elder brother Hormisdas (the natural heir, who had been sidelined and imprisoned because of his Philhellenism) had taken refuge with the Emperor Constantine. Hormisdas escaped Persian imprisonment, as in the best fairy stories, with the help of a file that his wife had hidden in a large fish, and was treated by the Romans like a visiting monarch. By the time that Julian had become emperor, Hormisdas was a slightly pathetic figure after his years in exile—not unlike some of the émigrés in London and Paris after the Russian Revolution. Nonetheless Julian was to see his political potential as a pro-Roman Sassanid monarch.[6] But Hormisdas's escape and exile in 323, just like the inevitable raiding parties and frontier violations, was part and parcel of East-West *Machtpolitik*.

War between Shapur and the Roman Empire became inevitable after Constantine's conversion. Just as it was for Julian, it was in the context of their espousal of Christianity that we see Shapur's breach with Constantine's family. Constantine had thrown down the gauntlet in a particularly nasty letter to Shapur written in October 324, composed with the subtlety of a classical Metternich. In it, Constantine claimed to speak for all the Christians in the world.[7]

The letter was greeted with little enthusiasm by Shapur. If the Roman emperor thought that he was overlord of all Christians, who was not to say that the Christians did not think the same? Although the state religion of his empire was Zoroastrianism, the official line of the Persian Empire had been one of laissez-faire. Christianity was happily tolerated. If Constantine was right, then Shapur realized that he had a hefty population of fifth columnists within his borders, all potentially loyal to another ruler. The result was a persecution that began properly in the late summer of 344 and would last, with varying degrees of severity, for almost the next eighty years.

There is no doubt that Constantine's letter was a declaration of war.

He was planning what was to all intents and purposes a crusade against Shapur in the run-up to 337. His favored son Constantius had been in charge of defense of the East based out of Antioch since 335. The emperor had spoken of his intention to take bishops with him and he wanted to be baptized in the River Jordan before the invasion.[8] Those who preached in favor of the early Crusades would have approved wholeheartedly.

The first move in the war went to Shapur when he attacked Nisibis on around June 16, 337, for the first of what would be three futile attempts to take the city.[9] He had been gathering his forces on the border when news of Constantine's death reached him and the news of his rival's demise must have hastened his invasion. The loss of the city would be a huge embarrassment for the Romans and a great victory for the Persians: it would make control of Armenia that much easier and avenge the loss of the city almost forty years previously.

Now the rather dusty and insignificant Turkish town of Nusaybin, then the city was the lynchpin of Roman control in the East. It was a crucial military stronghold controlling the entrance to the upper Syrian plains from the mountain passes of Asia Minor. It was the capital of the province of Mesopotamia as well as the headquarters of the senior military and probably housed a legion. But it was more than just a military town. Although there has been little archaeological work carried out there, it is likely that it had all the attributes of a civilian city; we certainly know of a governor's palace. This was not a backward little town.

Shapur's tactics should then have won him the city; indeed, what is most surprising of all about the Persian king's war with Rome is that he did not win. Although he showed himself a military innovator par excellence with an enviable ability to think on his feet and grasp solutions out of thin air, fate always stopped Shapur winning. Frustrated by two months of getting nowhere, worn down by exposure to the elements, and with disease rife in the Persian camp, he withdrew on around August 17.

It is now that Arsak II, also known as Arsaces Tiranus, enters the story.[10] Whoever controlled Armenia controlled a clear route between Roman Cappadocia and Persia along the Aras valley. Any friendly power on the throne could dramatically reduce the costs of imperial defense; hence the king of the buffer state was regularly waltzed around the diplomatic floor by both Romans and Persians at times of tension. News of the death of Constantine had caused friction in Armenia. Even though the pro-Roman faction managed to get Arsak on the throne, opposition was such that he had to run to the Romans for help. By 339 some (unknown) accord was inked and Arsak was restored. Constantius cannot be blamed for thinking that Armenia was secure under Roman influence, but Arsak was to be one of the most untrustworthy allies of the Romans.

It was apparent what the aims of the two sides were. Shapur's grandfather had signed away northern Mesopotamia and interests in Armenia to the emperor Galerius in 299. Shapur wanted them back. Constantius wanted to concede nothing. Any perspective on Constantius's policy is made difficult by the bias of the Romans toward their ruler. A skim through the writings of Ammianus and Libanius would leave you with the idea that he was a wimp emperor. The former wrote "whenever Constantius took the field against Persia, bad luck always followed him," while the latter commented, "it was as if he had sworn to act in league with his opponents."[11] Nothing could be further from the truth. His policy of containment and diplomacy may not have sat well with traditional Roman ideals of aggression, but it worked for at least twenty years, despite Shapur's sorties over the border. For all Constantius's faults, he didn't secede any Roman territory and he didn't lose his life.

Shapur's strategy was different in 359, the year that everything started to come together for him. Intelligence from a Roman defector had provided the information that most of the imperial forces were in Illyricum. Rather than throw himself at Nisibis for a fourth time, Shapur attacked Roman defenses further north. He targeted Amida, a city situated at the limit of navigation of the Tigris. It was the fallout from this battle that was to give Julian the excuse to break with Constantius once and for all.

From the banks of the Tigris, the modern town of Diyarbakir does not look very different from the sight that would have greeted Shapur. The black basalt walls interrupted by sixteen keeps and five gates are as impressive now as they would have been then. Although the four miles of walls that you see now date from the eleventh century, they follow the plan of Constantius's walls and are the best-preserved ancient walls in the world after the Great Wall of China.

When Shapur and his 100,000-strong force arrived, the Sassanid king was in no mood to delay. The Persians threw themselves at the city, defended as it was by seven legions and auxiliary troops, for seventy-two days. Eventually, Shapur's siege efforts paid off. Ammianus, who had been posted to the eastern front from Gaul almost three years previously, gives us a vivid eyewitness account of the end of the siege on the night of October 6. In fact, he only just escaped with his life, through an unguarded postern in the dead of night.[12]

Shapur had won at Amida, but at what cost? It was a marvelous victory, but despite his triumph, the Roman defensive system held and there was no general collapse. The sieges over the last few years had depleted his armies and for all of the Roman losses, Shapur too had not escaped unscathed—losses as high as 30,000 men, a third of his army, are mentioned. Even the following year's sieges, which gave Shapur the two towns of Singara, now the Iraqi town of Sinjar, and the hilltop town of Bezabde, a strategically useful fort on the banks of the Tigris, which has recently been rediscovered north of Cizre at Eski Hendek, did not cause more than superficial damage. Despite the continual back and forth for much of the century, the genuine gains were as insignificant as those on the Western Front in the First World War.

The Persian king should have struck now. Shapur was in the stronger tactical position, as Constantius had been unable to boost the numbers in the army of the East, a result of Julian's revolt. The summer of 361 could have determined the war if not once and for all, then at least for a few years. The sources are, however, tantalizingly vague about what happened. Constantius had spent almost all of the winter mobilizing, and had deployed scouts up and down the Tigris to warn of any Persian advance. He had clearly decided on a pitched battle. The difficulty is that it is impossible to understand what Shapur was up to. He and his forces refused to cross the Tigris, yet Roman spies could give no reason why. Soon Shapur was to withdraw entirely, giving the excuse of bad omens.[13]

Was it fear of the Roman army that made Shapur withdraw? If so, then it is a sign that Constantius's policy was working. That argument has merit, especially in the light of Shapur's peace offering to Julian in early 362, but there is no getting away from the fact that however nervous the Sassanid king might have been that the throne was now occupied by a Hotspur, Shapur had the stronger military position—he had the experience and was already mobilized.

So why did Julian need to launch a campaign so soon into his rule? The primary reason is the need for some morale boosting PR. Although the Persian king's actual gains over the previous two years had been minor in the grand scheme of things—the destruction of Amida and Singara, and the capture of Bezabde—they had had a disproportionate effect on the Roman psyche. In the West, Julian could still count on the wave of goodwill following the German wars. He now needed something similar in the East, whose armies had always been loyal to Constantius. After the loss of Amida and then the upheaval caused by even the brief civil war a short, sharp success against the Persian bogeyman would have done much to legitimize his position, restore discipline, and put a stop to some of the factioneering.

Certainly, the picture we have of the Eastern armies is one of disillusionment. "If a dust cloud rose in the distance, such as horses would make, it did not spur [the Roman soldiers] to the fight, but turned them in flight," writes Libanius. He goes so far as to claim that a picture of the Persians was enough to scare them and if a joker shouted out, "The Persians are coming!" the soldiers would blanch and run away.[14] The old philosopher's description is obviously a caricature, but it is hard not to believe that there is an element of truth in the description of their morale.

Next, the omens were right. Julian's adherence to the mystical was well-known and as well as military intelligence and planning, the emperor asked advice from numerous oracles. One replied. "Now we gods all started to get trophies of victory by the river beast and of them I, Ares, bold raiser of the din of war, will be leader."[15] The "river beast" is obviously the River Tigris. But it is altogether more difficult to disentangle the legend surrounding the message of the best-known oracle of all, that of Delphi.

According to the famous story, Oribasius was sent to Delphi in late 362 to hear directly from the Pythia herself about Julian's chances in Persia. It is not too difficult to see Oribasius as an old man waxing lyrical about how he brought the news to Julian. The message was particularly popular as a dramatic theme in the nineteenth century; indeed you can buy tiles with the words inscribed on them even today in the gift shops that surround the modern site. It was perceived to have been the Delphic oracle's last utterance and came to be inextricably linked with images of the twilight of the gods. Swinburne's translation is the best known:

> *Tell the king, on earth has fallen the glorious dwelling,*
> *And the water-springs that spake are quenched and*
>   *dead.*
> *Not a cell is left the god, no roof, no cover,*
> *In his hand the prophet laurel flowers no more.*[16]

But Oribasius's trip never happened. Delphi had not yet closed for predictions. Even though Constantine had looted the site to decorate his new capital, he did put up a statue of himself there and it was joined by ones of Constans and Julian. The Pythia was still active, if arthritic. If Julian himself complains: "We see that the indigenous oracles of Greece have also fallen silent and yielded to the course of time,"[17] it is as much of a theme as complaints about declining educational standards in schools or a lack of attendance at church are today. It is a poignant story, but not true. It has neither the style of Julian, nor that of the oracle. Delphi was to close, but not for another twenty-one years.

Finally, while Julian's personal reasons have often unfairly been given too much prominence, they should not be rejected out of hand. Returning with the epithet "Parthicus" was of interest personally to Julian and would have given a unifying focus of pride for the empire with all the overtones of Trajan's campaign that it carried. One myth, however, must be dismissed. Much was made by Julian's critics after the emperor's death that an invasion of the East was an attempt to replicate the achievements of Alexander the Great. While Julian, like almost every Roman emperor, undoubtedly admired the Macedonian king, he was bright enough to see him with some sense of perspective and to distinguish the man from the myth. In one letter alone he refers to Alexander as "more cruel and more insolent" than the Persian rulers, before later asking rhetorically: "Who, I ask, ever found salvation through the conquests of Alexander? What city was ever more wisely governed because of them, what individual improved?"[18] He was indeed a hero, but not seen through rose-tinted spectacles and certainly not one to emulate.

The decision to invade was clearly taken early on in Julian's reign and the planning and organization of the campaign was not a slap-dash affair. The emperor had already given orders for a fleet to be built and research had been done—Julian would have had access to two works, sadly no longer extant, both of which were practical guides on how to defeat Persians.[19] The first, *The Parthian War*, was by Cornelius Celsus, but the latter was by Constantine, who had fought in Persia as part of Galerius's army.[20]

If Julian himself did not read them (though for a literary-minded man not to have read his uncle's book, however much he may have disliked him, is inconceivable), his advisers certainly took heed of many of their messages. Both books emphasized that the only successful stratagem was speed. Early spring was a good time to attack. The Roman army, made up primarily of Germans and soldiers trained on the western front, was inured to the cold and would have an advantage against an enemy, which traditionally did not fight spring campaigns. It had become a proverb that "a Mede will not then draw his hand from underneath his cloak."[21]

Julian had arranged help, indeed was confident enough to turn down all other offers of assistance from Georgia and various desert tribes at this moment, though he changed his mind later. Julian had pinned his hopes on support from Armenia's Arsak, now in his early fifties.

Arsak had not proved to be the most reliable of allies. In 359 he had taken the side of the Persians and his troops had acted as a diversionary force around Nisibis as Shapur advanced on Amida. But the turncoat had seen the error of his ways the following year almost certainly due to Constantius's enthusiastic efforts to keep him amenable. A law was passed in January 360 exempting him from all taxes in kind[22] while the emperor entertained him lavishly, showered him with presents and even offered him the hand of Olympias—previously Constans's fiancée. It was a move worthy of the Hapsburg monarchs, even if some thought it appalling to treat royalty in such an "unholy manner" and deliver her into the hands of a "barbarian."[23]

It is in this light that we should judge the letter that Julian wrote to Arsak in the spring of 363 from Antioch ordering him to mobilize as rapidly as possible, reminding him that he had been well treated by Rome in the past. Later writers accuse the emperor of "unbounded arrogance"[24] and of an overly harsh tone—certainly he calls the Armenian a coward and a rascal—but if Julian's tone seems threatening, it is less surprising given the king's predilection for changing sides.[25]

In spite of all the planning, it is noticeable that in the run-up to the campaign, indeed to the war itself, Julian appears to have had no coherent war aims. Everything points to the fact that it was always Julian's intention to be back on Roman soil by the autumn, but what did he want to do? Did he want to put Shapur's brother Hormisdas on the throne? Did he want to sack Ctesiphon? Did he really, as Libanius suggests, expect an unconditional surrender?[26] We simply do not know.

It is hard not to come to the conclusion that the end for Julian was the invasion itself. The issue of how strong Shapur was is almost an irrelevance. Julian simply had too much to lose at home by not invading. Only a man who had never known military defeat could have met Shapur's diplomats with no real demands. When the Persian ambassadors arrived in Antioch bearing heralds' wands and a letter from Shapur, wrapped, as was traditional, in white linen, Julian theatrically ripped the peace offering up in front of them. "You shall very shortly see me in person, so that there will be no need of an embassy," he said.[27] He needed no other excuse.

9
PRESENT OPPORTUNITY

*It seems to me therefore that there are an
overwhelming number of inducements in favor
of this war and chief among them the present
opportunity, which ought not to be left pass. It
would be contemptible to neglect it when it is here
and regret it when it is gone by. There is nothing
more that we could need for an attack on Persia
beyond what is ours already.*

ISOCRATES, *PANEGYRICUS*

The atmosphere was strained on the morning of March 5,
as Julian marched out of Antioch through the Eastern
Gate. The emperor may have paused at the pool on his
left, before passing under the gate's two arches on the
road to Beroea. For the citizens and city fathers who came to
see Julian and his retinue off, it was a moment of tension and worry. The
city had come to realize that it had completely burned its bridges with
the emperor. At the beginning of February there had been a conspiracy
to assassinate him, which had been discovered when the conspirators

got drunk and blurted out their plans. Strictly speaking, this rather amateur affair had nothing to do with Antioch—all of these revolutionaries were in the army—but it will have done nothing to endear the city to its emperor.

A couple of days before Julian left the city for the last time, Libanius had been sent to effect the first of several attempts at an imperial reconciliation. Although Julian received the old philosopher kindly, he told Libanius not to bother again because he "did not deserve to emerge unsuccessful."[1] The emperor was as stubborn as the Antiochenes and events had moved far beyond any chance of reconciliation.

As a goodbye present for the city, Julian had appointed a new prefect of Syria. It was an act both vindictive and childish. Alexander from Phoenicia was known for his violence and cruelty. Julian reckoned that he was the best that the city deserved and it proved to be the case. After Julian's death, Alexander was prosecuted for his harsh administration and although eventually acquitted, it is impossible to see him as anything other than unsympathetic.[2] All of this made what must have been the hastily arranged—and possibly even civically encouraged—crowd of citizens who lined the streets out of the city loudly praying for a successful campaign, appear both desperate and pathetic.

But if the people of Antioch were nervous, the imperial retinue and the departing emperor astride his favorite horse, Babylonius, were in a carnival mood. Relief at leaving the city will have been mixed with the anticipation of battle. Even if Julian's confidence now seems misplaced, those like Libanius, who watched Julian ride east, had few reasons to think the campaign would be anything other than a success. Libanius even composed two orations—one to mollify the emperor and the other berating his fellow citizens, based on the presumption that Julian had won—although for obvious reasons they were never presented.

Five days later, on March 10, Julian wrote to the philosopher from Hierapolis, the rendezvous point for his army (he was not planning to meet the navy until Callinicum). These are the final words of Julian that have come down to us and this is his last authenticated letter. From here on in, we are in the hands of others. Ammianus Marcellinus is the only substantial eyewitness we have and he did not join the campaign until the beginning of April. Every other writer is at least once removed from the events, which makes attempts to chronicle the campaign rather difficult. It is inevitable, therefore, that small events assume a disproportionate importance and, naturally enough, the journey into the heart of Asia takes on the flavor of a travelogue. But for the next five days we have an account of the emperor in minute detail.

By the time he wrote to Libanius, the emperor had clearly had a trying week, full of minor irritations. When he left Antioch, the sixty-mile ride to Litarba, now the town of el-Athareb, should have been a fairly straightforward two-day trip. The average day's journey for the Roman army was twenty miles, but given how unencumbered he was at this point, Julian certainly wasn't taxing their strength. The conditions of the road, however, did little for his blood pressure. He writes: "I must say that the road was partly swamp, part hill but the whole of it was rough and there were stones in the swamp which looked as though they had been thrown there on purpose. They lay there without any art in the manner of those who build main public roads. Instead of cement they make a deep layer of soil and then lay the stones close together as if making a boundary wall."[3] Most probably this was an indication of previous political uncertainty in the region, but Julian saw it as yet more negligence on the part of Antioch's council.

In the early afternoon of March 6, the party called a halt at a former winter camp, which has tentatively been identified with modern El-'Amk. There Julian made his final break with Antioch. He writes: "At my headquarters I received most of your Senate from Antioch. You have maybe heard what we said to each other." There is no doubt that Libanius will have heard of the conversation in considerable detail. Julian dropped his bombshell and told the Senate in no uncertain terms that he had no intention of ever returning to the city. He planned to make Tarsus his base that winter—in fact he had already written to the city's governor to let him know. It was a proposed move that had potentially serious and long-term economic and social repercussions for Antioch.

Libanius had been one of the delegates of the embassy and should have been present at that meeting, but had turned back for reasons unknown before they reached the emperor. He wrote an emotional and a none too subtle letter to the emperor attempting reconciliation, though for once, given the circumstances, he can perhaps be forgiven.[4] Again it had little effect. By the time that Julian received the letter he will have been in Beroea, the city he entered on March 7. By the period that Julian passed through, the city had been northern Syria's main trading center, on the route between the Mediterranean and the Euphrates for almost 1,700 years.[5] It is easy to see Beroea's attraction for merchants and travelers. A glance at a map shows the modern town of Aleppo at the center of a spider's web of rail links that connect Istanbul, Baghdad, Damascus, and Beirut.

Julian's two days in the city were less than entertaining although they started off well enough. When he arrived, "Zeus declared all things auspicious by showing a manifest sign from heaven. I stayed there for a day: saw the acropolis and sacrificed a white bull to Zeus in the imperial manner," he wrote.[6] Then, however, he came up against a Christianity that, while it may have been expressed more tactfully than that of Antioch, was just as intractable.

As always, the emperor raised the issue of paganism and the slipping of pagan standards. "I talked briefly to the Senate too about the worship of the gods," he writes. "Although they all applauded my arguments, very few were converted by them. Those few that were, were men who seemed to have sound views before I spoke," he continued.[7]

As Julian left the city on the morning of March 9, he was truly leaving behind the West he had known for most of his adult life. "If there be a better gate to Asia than Aleppo, I do not know it," wrote the British archaeologist and inveterate traveler Gertrude Bell in her 1911 classic travelogue *Amurath to Amurath*. You can still get a sense of what it was like for Julian as you pass along the main road to the northeast of the city. The city of Beroea and its valley vanished behind Julian and his party almost immediately as they went over the lip of the hill and then, as now, they were faced with a red, dusty, and barren countryside that stretches for miles.

The emperor was obviously relieved and delighted to reach the oasis of Batnae, now Tell Botnan. "[It is] a place like nothing that I have ever seen in your country," he writes. Even if "the imperial lodging was by no means sumptuous" he enjoyed the town's gardens and groves. The locals may have made more of an effort with the emperor than had the citizens of either Antioch or Beroea, but Julian was not especially convinced by their attempts to ingratiate themselves and sounds a note of skepticism. "The place maintains the pagan cults. I say this because the smell of frankincense rose on all sides through the country round about and I saw victims ready for sacrifice everywhere. Although this gave me great pleasure, it looked like overheated zeal and alien to proper reverence for the gods."

He did not have long to enjoy the pleasures of the gardens. By March 10, Julian had reached Hierapolis, one of the great towns of Syria and the province's breadbasket. Both Julian and his brother had used the city to alleviate Antioch's famines. The town was where he was to meet the rest of his army that at its peak now was 65,000 strong, not counting the various Scythian and, later, Arab auxiliaries.[8] The town is now called Manbij, a linguistic echo of its original Greek name Bambyce, but in 363 it was just Hierapolis, literally "the holy city" in Greek.

Hierapolis's importance for Julian at this point was primarily strategic—the city stood almost exactly halfway between Antioch and Seleucia-on-Tigris—but the town's economy was not just based on corn. It was one of the most important cult centers in Asia Minor, the center for the worship of the Syrian fertility goddess Atargatis, referred to simply as "The Syrian Goddess." In the much underrated account of his pilgrimage to Atargatis's temple, the first-century writer Lucian of Samosata calls it the greatest and the holiest sanctuary in Syria.[9] By the time that Julian came to the city the goddess had become conflated with both Aphrodite and Cybele, whose temple Julian had been so keen to visit in Pessinus.

Although it is inconceivable that Julian did not spend some time at the sanctuary, his few days in the city appear to have been taken up with the minutiae of administration and worries about security. Either because of the crush of people or as a result of poor construction—we don't know which—as the emperor entered the city a colonnade collapsed killing fifty soldiers and injuring many others. Some hint of the emperor's weariness and frustration comes through in his letter to Libanius. "As regards the military or political arrangements, you ought, I think, to have been present to observe and pay attention to them yourself. For, as you know, the matter is too long for a letter. In fact it is so vast that if one considered it in detail it would not be easy to confine it to a letter even three times as long as this." He does, however, give a brief summary:

I sent diplomats to the Arabs and suggested that they could come if they wished. That is one affair of the sort that I mentioned. For another, I despatched men as alert as I could obtain, that they might guard against anyone leaving here to go to the enemy and inform them that we are on the move. After that I held a court martial and, I am convinced, showed in my decision the utmost clemency and justice. I have got hold of excellent horses and mules and have mustered all my forces together. The boats to be used on the river are laden with corn, or rather with baked bread and sour wine. You can understand at what length I should have to write to describe how every detail of this business was worked out and what discussions arose over every one of them. As for the number of letters I have signed and papers—for these too follow me everywhere like my shadow—why should I take the trouble to enumerate them now?[10]

The overtures to the Saracens and the detailed provisions for his boats make absolutely clear that Julian had always intended to attack southward along the length of the Euphrates, but for reasons of subterfuge and false information—a crucial pin in Julian's strategy, as he mentions—the emperor and his army feinted toward northern Mesopotamia. Gleefully Libanius notes that this stratagem worked. "As soon as the emperor invaded early in the spring by a route which surprised them, the Assyrians were taken in straightaway,"[11] he wrote to a friend, soon after news of the first successes began to filter back to Antioch. It took Julian and his army just three days to cross the Euphrates on a pontoon bridge near modern Tell al Ahmar.

This was not a light undertaking. Writing twenty years after the campaign, Egeria was to note on her pilgrimage that the Euphrates here was "huge and really rather frightening," comparing it to the River Rhône, "only the Euphrates is still greater."[12] On March 15, the emperor reached Bathnae Anthemusias, a famous market town, now Sürüc in Turkey, some forty-one miles beyond the river. Here he was greeted by another accident. Perhaps it was a rush job, maybe it was just organizational laziness, but a hayrick collapsed killing fifty stable boys. It did not auger well for things to come.

Through a series of forced marches, it took another couple of days for the army to reach Carrhae, a base for Julian and his army for the next few days. Now a rather tatty town with an economy split fairly equally between farming and smuggling, Harran is one of the region's oldest trading cities, indeed the word "harran" is the Assyrian for "road." For the Romans, however, the city had a more immediate and depressing resonance. It had been the site in 53 BC of one of Rome's most abject defeats—20,000 men were lost under the command of Crassus, colleague of Julius Caesar and Pompey and financier extraordinaire of the classical world. He became holed up in the city and was eventually murdered. The ignominy did not end there. His head was thrown onto a stage at the Parthian court where a theatrical troupe were performing Euripides' *Bacchae*.[13]

Julian's knowledge of history would have been enough to put him on edge, and the current situation did nothing to ease this. Persian spies appear to have been a permanent irritant, making an already security-conscious operation even more jittery. Julian even had fake supply dumps set up to throw the enemy off the scent. At the same time he had a number of major decisions to make. First and foremost he had to work out his route. If the plan was to take Shapur's capital at Ctesiphon, two paths lay open to him, both of them resonant with history. The former entailed marching toward Persia's other great river the Tigris and following the route taken by Alexander the Great. The latter meant marching down the Euphrates, the route of Xenophon and his Ten Thousand. Julian will have known and studied both options carefully. The former had the advantage of ease, the latter of surprise.

While he and his war cabinet were formulating strategy, news reached him of a lightning attack by raiding enemy cavalry across the frontier. That was the spark. The enemy was closer and more aggressive than Roman intelligence had suggested. To confuse any other enemy units Julian made as if toward the Tigris but as soon as it was dark he wheeled round and headed south. The military planning now appears a mirror image of Trajan's successful strategy 205 years previously—a pincer attack along the two great rivers. The emperor himself headed down the Euphrates and sent his second force (there is no way of resolving the widely diverging figures we have for this force, though it was probably less than 20,000 men strong[14]) down the near side of the Tigris under the joint command of Procopius and Sebastian, the former commander in Egypt known for his good nature, honesty, and, most important of all, successful command.

Procopius, a relative on his mother's side, five or six years older than him, is one of the more curious characters in Julian's circle. He served for a long time as a notary and a tribune and seems to have had the bearing of a bureaucrat—tall and austere, he stooped and kept his eyes to the ground as he walked. The consummate politician, he is described as reserved and silent but was certainly successful in hanging on to his famous relative's coat tails.

The reason for the question mark that now hangs over Procopius's character is the tradition that after sacrificing at Carrhae, Julian had handed him his purple cloak and appointed him successor if he were to fall in battle. In itself, the event is not impossible. The city was a major cultic center—it was home to the great temple of Sin, the Mesopotamian god of the moon, by now linked with Zeus—and Julian is known to have sacrificed there. Yet there is a sense of implausibility about the story. Not only were there no witnesses to this imperial anointment but also Procopius's subsequent coup gives it an air of fiction. In fact, that it was given any credence at all is rather an indication of the chaos that followed Julian's death.

At the very least, this force could buy Julian some time. Its immediate role was to act as bait for Shapur, who might be misled into thinking that this was the main force, thereby allowing it to tie up as many Persian units as possible. But the second force had three other objectives too: it was to act as a buffer to the left flank of Julian's army, protecting it from surprise attacks; next, it was to liaise with Arsak; and, finally, to link up with Julian in Assyria. In their first two aims Procopius and Sebastian were successful, in the latter two not only were they abject failures, but they even managed to fall out with each other in the process as the command descended into petty bickering.

Not all the blame, however, rests with them. The biggest disaster, both militarily and psychologically, was that Arsak failed to get the promised army to Julian on time. There are hints of what happened in the *History of the Armenians,* by the eighth-century writer Moses Khorenats'i. Although it is a source that needs to be handled extremely carefully—there are questions of chronology and, at the most basic level

Khorenats'i is even muddled about which king was on the Armenian throne at the time—some light can be distinguished through the fog.

It appears that a force was sent, but then either turned back or ran away. Khorenats'i excuses the Armenian army's action by suggesting that the commander of the Armenian forces was disgusted by Julian's impiety, and he preserves what appears to be a version of a letter from Julian to the king in which the emperor orders Arsak to execute the general and his family or he would invade Armenia on his return. Its authenticity is questionable, but even if Julian's words are not wholly genuine, there is no reason to doubt their general tenor, and certainly the account accords with the common perception of Arsak as a traitor.[15]

Heading south down the Euphrates, Julian soon reached the city of Callinicum—Alexander the Great's Nicephorion. The emperor had traveled one hundred eighteen miles since leaving Beroea and sixty-two miles since Carrhae. To begin with, Julian had a couple of days of consolidation in front of him. He even found time to celebrate the festival of the Mother of the Gods (the ritual washing of Cybele's image on March 27), though it is to be imagined that it was under very different circumstances to the relaxed environment in which Julian had participated the previous year at Pessinus on his way to Antioch.

But this was just a diversion. It was here, on March 28, that the emperor welcomed his fleet of 1,100 transport ships with 50 armed galleys accompanied by an equal number of flat-bottomed boats, the last of which could double as pontoons when needed. The role of the navy under the command of Constantianus, which had sailed down from Samosata on the upper Euphrates,[16] bringing Lucillianus and some 1,500 shock troops, was massively undervalued and misunderstood by Julian's contemporaries. In fact it was central to the emperor's strategy. It is not too much of an exaggeration to suggest that the role of the navy was similar to that played by the Huey helicopter in Vietnam in shipping equipment and provisions and providing transport for Lucillianus's elite marines.

With the combined forces now at full battle strength—at Callinicum Julian had also assimilated a force of experienced Arab guerrillas into the army—it was a dull and flat hundred-mile march along the Euphrates to Circesium, now Busayrah in Syria. The calm before the storm.

Julian had little reason to feel anything but optimism. The sight of the Roman army at full strength—stretching ten miles from van to rear—was an impressive and, for the emperor, reassuring one. By now, presuming that Sebastian and Procopius were carrying out their orders, the emperor believed that they were harassing Persian forces—buying him time—and were soon due to rendezvous with the Armenian allies.

When he arrived at the beginning of April, Circesium was a "teeming city"[17] with all the hubbub of a frontier station of the Roman Empire. The flotsam and jetsam that collected at the boundaries of civilized society meant that traders of all races will have mixed with soldiers. Security was clearly uppermost in Julian's mind. The town controlled the confluence of the Euphrates and Khabur rivers, but even though Circesium had been strengthened only sixty years previously and there was already a garrison here, Julian bolstered it with another 4,000 troops. It was a deliberate move by the emperor to secure his lines of communication.

Although the campaign seems to have been as slickly orchestrated as it had been earlier, for the first time a sense of nervousness comes through in the actions of the high command, almost as if they were on edge. It was at Circesium that Julian received a letter from his commander in Gaul advising him to delay the campaign—not a missive that will have left him in a good mood—and this unease seems to have transmitted itself to his lieutenants. The normally sanguine Salutius, for example, had one of his quartermasters executed for failing to deliver provisions on time. Certainly the army began to have its first doubts. The newly arrived fleet was put to use building a pontoon bridge for the army to cross the Khabur, which was then inexplicably—to the infantry—ordered to be destroyed. Undoubtedly Julian would have claimed that it was a practical measure. The army would be coming back in glory by another route so it was sensible to disable a resource that could be used against the empire, but Ammianus preserves what must have been camp gossip: that the bridge was destroyed so that "no one should lag behind his unit in the belief that he could go back."[18]

It is difficult to follow what happened over the next few days, indeed to get much of an idea of the army's state of mind. The problem is that Ammianus trips over himself to signal portents of doom and it is impossible to untangle fact from dramatic fiction. He evokes the ghost of Gordian III who unsuccessfully led the campaign into Asia;

a thunderstorm breaks and a soldier called Jovian is struck dead by a thunderbolt; and Julian is presented with the dead body of a lion—"The death of a king was foreshadowed, but it was not clear which king," writes Ammianus portentously.[19] What we can say for certain is that by April 7, Julian had traveled the thirty-one miles from Circesium and passed the city of Dura Europos, the final outpost of the Roman Empire. Whatever the state of mind of the Roman army over the previous week, the sight across the plains of the sturdy remains of the city walls will have reminded them exactly what it was that they were fighting for.

When the emperor passed by, the city had been destroyed just over a hundred years previously by the Persians. Julian will have been able to see the huge walls and towers of mud of the city from miles away, just as the modern traveler to Syria can today. Little has changed in the intervening centuries.

From here on it becomes even more difficult to trace Julian's route as he continues into what is now modern Iraq. International politics has made it difficult to verify the condition of sites for much of the past two decades. Since the U.S.-led invasion of Iraq in 2003, the task has become even more fraught. Some of the archaeological sites that are discussed have suffered considerable war damage and it will be many years before a full assessment is possible. It is a problem that is not at all alleviated by confusion in the ancient sources over the names of the towns through which the Roman army passed. Not even Julian's contemporaries agree. In some cases they are clearly transliterations of similar names, but in others they are totally different.[20]

When it passed Dura Europus, the army had left what even the most excitable hawk might call the Roman Empire—it had definitely crossed the boundary between the olive and the date. Up to now the army's march had been through terra cognita. It could now presume that it would be under immediate attack too and, recognizing this, Julian started to march in battle order. By April 11, he had reached Anatha, just south of the modern town of 'Ana, a fortified island on the Euphrates, linked by a natural causeway and several bridges to the mainland.

The city had been an important trading hub on the Euphrates route since at least 2200 BC. In more recent times, it had been briefly in Roman hands, but the city had virtually always been Persian. Here Julian dealt with his first real military action on the campaign easily. The emperor ordered a marine attack on the fortress under the command of Lucillianus. The commander was soon persuaded to surrender and, although the fort was burned down and the surrounding countryside laid waste, the lives of the defenders were spared—they were sent into exile.

Rather more poignantly, after the city was relieved Julian came face to face with the past. It is easy to think of the imperial campaigns in Persia in isolation, but among the locals was a soldier who had been left behind, sick or injured, after the emperor Galerius's campaigns sixty-six years previously. Now, presumably over eighty, the man had gone native and had acquired several wives, but he maintained enough loyalty to the eagle to be one of the leaders of the surrender.

It took Julian the rest of the month to reach Pirisabora, the next major obstacle, and it was two weeks of the continual danger that is war. By April 13, the army had marched the nine miles south to Thilutha, the modern town of Telbes. The town decided to remain neutral and as it would have been impossible to take without a lengthy siege, Julian passed by. The same thing happened two days and thirty-one miles later, when they reached the fortress of Achaiacala, probably but not definitely the modern oil town of Hadithah. The army crossed the Euphrates on April 17, continuing with what was becoming its policy of capturing, then destroying any forts it passed. On April 22, the army was given two days rest and relaxation, but on the second day a reconnaissance unit was ambushed by a unit of Persians with Saracen auxiliaries. The Romans beat them off and on April 25, reached the small town of Macepracta, situated near the modern Ummu-r-Rus.

Two days later, Julian arrived before Pirisabora. This heavily protected city could not simply be passed by—it was too important both as a military depot and as a strategic stronghold. Shapur had garrisoned the city, which guarded an important ford where the Euphrates enters the alluvial plain, with perhaps as many as 2,500 men. In fact its modern name of Al-Anbar still reflects its ancient importance—"anbar" is the Persian for granary.

The emperor devoted three days to taking Pirisabora, and it was eventually subdued by siege towers called "city takers," the ancient world's Chieftain tanks. Julian was an expert in siege machinery, in fact had written a book called *Military Engines* on the subject.[21] After the surrender, the Romans found the supplies of barley fodder and straw they needed and the pattern of burning followed.

The success was marred by a sour note. The next day, April 30, three squadrons of Roman cavalry on a reconnaissance mission were ambushed. A few soldiers, including a tribune, were killed and a standard was captured. In terms of military defeat it was negligible, indeed Julian himself commanded the force that routed the enemy, which was done efficiently and rapidly, but the episode is worthy of mention for the emperor's extreme reaction to it. The two surviving tribunes were cashiered and, even more surprisingly, Julian ordered decimation on the survivors.

Decimation had long been considered an archaic practice and his order thus raises questions about Julian's thought processes. Certainly the event was worthy enough of comment to be raised disapprovingly by the sixteenth-century French essayist Michel de Montaigne in his essay on the punishment of cowardice.[22] Decimation was normally used only as a last resort for treason. Was it that the emperor believed that the squadrons had betrayed the Roman positions, which he interpreted as treason? Was it a sign of increasing nervousness on the part of the high command? Was it that the troops were beginning to make rumbling noises of discontent? Was Julian losing his hold? It is impossible to say. There is no doubt that the troops were becoming disillusioned with the campaign. Certainly when Julian publicly thanked them for their work so far and promised them a donative of 100 pieces of silver each, they reacted almost mutinously at what they saw as a pitiful amount and it took all of the emperor's powers of persuasion to bring them round. In the end his speech boiled down to: "I'm broke, but the Persians have got lots of cash—let's go get it."

Over the next few days, the march proved both time-consuming and dangerous. The Euphrates was in spate and the Persians had flooded the plain by breaking the sluice gates—any dreams that the Romans might have had about an element of surprise vanished. The army appears to have half floated, half waded across the plain as Persian archers periodically took pot shots at them. The only mitigating factor was that the army had all the dates it could eat. Not much of a consolation.

The army approached Maiozamalcha around May 10. It was only some twelve miles from Ctesiphon, but the troops had to prepare themselves for yet another siege as, left untouched, it could have posed a serious security threat. A more daunting prospect would be hard to imagine. A naturally protected site, the city was high up on a rocky projection, further defended by the few paths that wound their way up the hill where any attackers could be picked off at leisure. Calls to surrender were met with predictable scorn. Initial attacks were not helped by the fact that the ground was too uneven for the tortoise formation to work with any degree of success, losses were rising and time was of the essence if they wanted to take the city before reinforcements arrived. A vignette, made more tragic by Ammianus's apparently cursory mention of it, shows daily life before the town: "In the course of these operations one of our engineers, whose name escapes me, happened to be standing behind a scorpion [siege engine] when a stone, carelessly fitted to its sling by the artillerymen, was hurled backward. His breast was crushed and he was thrown on his back and killed. His whole body was so mangled as to defy recognition."[23]

The physical and psychological discomforts of the campaign are hard to imagine. Julian had heard all about the heat, for example, and presumably had read about it in his uncle's reports, but there was a difference in experiencing it first hand. In the summer, the heat of the plains near Baghdad can regularly top 40°C while nights are freezing.[24] There are no surviving contemporary accounts of what it was like to be a soldier on that campaign, but it is possible to gain some insights into the dangers and discomforts by looking at the British experience on the same plain in Iraq during the First World War. The medical officer's report to the parliamentary commission investigating the debacle before the Turkish troops in 1915 makes chilling reading. "I doubt whether there was a single person equal to a five mile march carrying his equipment," he concludes.[25]

In the end it was sappers who took the city. During the day a battering ram had succeeded in taking down one of the towers, but the Romans had been fought off. All this time, sappers had been tunneling under the walls and in the early hours of the third day, Julian was informed that they were almost through. Two fake assaults were launched to distract the defenders and hide the noise the sappers were making. It was down to three men to leap out of the tunnel, clear the nearby buildings and open the gates. The city was savaged and it was only when Julian intervened that the commander and eighty of his men were spared. The three heroes who had tunneled their way in were honored with a siege crown and publicly commended the next day. If Julian's actions on the day following the siege of Pirisabora had shown the emperor at his worst, he now showed himself at his best. In the division of spoils he made sure that his men knew how little he took: only three gold pieces and a mute boy. Julian was remarkably proud of this and wrote to Libanius that he had given him "something to talk about."[26]

Nothing now stood between the Roman army and Ctesiphon. By May 15, Julian was within sight of Milton's "royal towers of great Seleucia, built by Grecian kings,"[27] then an abandoned ruin. As the army edged ever closer toward its goal a note of cruelty begins to come through in the accounts. The cavalry discovered the hunting park of the Persian king, filled with lions, boars, and bears, all of which the Romans slaughtered and then, because of an unexplained dispute, the commander of Maiozamalcha, who had surrendered, was burned for insolence. If this is a sign of nervousness it was not eased by assaults on the Roman baggage train and, especially grisly, the sight of the remains of the entire family of the man who had surrendered Pirisabora—corpses hung on gibbets.

Julian and his command still had the problem of how to attack Ctesiphon. He needed his ships—Ctesiphon sits on the east bank of the Tigris, faced by Coche, much in the same way that Buda and Pest face each other across the Danube. The obvious move would have been to follow the Euphrates down to where it met the Tigris, and then sail up the latter river. The inescapable flaw in this plan, as Julian realized, is that any ships would have been caught, exposed to fire from both cities simultaneously.

Julian's solution was ingenious, but it is difficult to track in detail not just because of confused historical accounts, but because of the topography too. This whole area is a patchwork of canals and the shifting of river patterns since the fourth century has made it virtually impossible to follow.

The army reached an old and blocked up channel of the Royal Canal—the twenty-five-mile-long, man-made canal that linked the

Euphrates and Tigris. It was not just silted up, but hidden, as it was being cultivated. The benefits of a literary disposition and the time spent with his books in Macellum proved their worth. Julian, who knew his Herodotus inside out, had read of this channel and tricked an old man into showing him where it was. In what was to be one of the most significant actions of the entire campaign—though its effects would not become apparent for another month—the channel was opened and the fleet was able to sail the few miles to the Tigris and appeared a little in front of the cities while the army marched in parallel to the canal, by around May 17, to encamp just outside Coche.

The army had come far, but was not only no nearer to taking Ctesiphon, but also was still in a vulnerable position. The Romans were on the wrong side of the river and by now the Persians had a fair idea of what they were planning. Ammianus's fear, facing as he did the opposite banks of the Tigris swarming with the assembled ranks of the Persian army, is palpable. He refers to the Persian cavalry's armor that "dazzled the eyes" and speaks of elephants "looking like moving hills."[28] The fear that elephants evoked in the hearts of the Romans cannot be underestimated—every source mentions them. Since the time of Alexander the Great the so-called civilized world had been terrified by what these huge beasts could do. But if they scared Julian's eastern army, one can only imagine what horror the Germanic soldiers were experiencing.

But now, Julian's last great military maneuver, a frontal assault on Shapur's troops before Ctesiphon was clearly impossible, so Julian delivered a brilliant subterfuge. Before the eyes of the watching and increasingly baffled Persians, he had a racecourse leveled out and invited the cavalry to race in his birthday games, offering prizes for the victors. One can only surmise what the Persians thought of this, or indeed what the Romans did too for that matter. During the day he had also begun to unload food and artillery from the ships. To the spies it would have seemed that Julian was intending to camp down for a while.

The distraction worked. Julian had decided on a nighttime commando-style raid on the eastern bank on the Tigris, similar to the ones that had worked in Germany. Only one of Julian's commanders thought these orders were insane—the one who would have to carry them out. Lucillianus cited both the difficulty of the terrain and the number of enemy soldiers facing his, but the emperor overruled and dismissed him. The topography would be the same tomorrow, but the number of soldiers would merely increase, he said.[29]

A bridgehead was established—but only just. Persian lookouts gave the alarm and the Roman ships with the advance squadron of men were attacked with a salvo of firebombs. Showing impressive presence of mind, Julian told his men that the fires were the agreed signal that the commandos had landed and the rest of the army started to follow. Despite the reinforcements, it was a difficult assault. The Persians were encamped at the top of an escarpment, while the Romans were trudging up hill, in full armor, in the dead of night. With the rest of the army crossing the Tigris by daylight, the second part of the battle continued well into the next day, Julian rallying his front-line troops and encouraging those at the back. It was beginning to turn into a massacre and the Persian withdrawal into Ctesiphon itself was turning into a rout.

Julian could have won now, but the Romans did not follow up what was an undoubted advantage and failed to attack Ctesiphon at once. It was not that they had suffered huge fatalities. Despite the danger of taking any Roman battle figures at face value, there were clearly few Roman casualties. The figures we have agree that 70 Romans died to 2,500 Persians.[30] The official version is that the commando leader, who had been wounded in the shoulder, was scared of a trap. He thought his men could too easily have become cut off within the walls of the large city with no retreat. Unofficially, rumors circulated that it might have been possible for the commando unit to take the city if they had been a little quicker off the mark and a little less keen on plundering the Persian dead. It does not require too much reading between the lines to see elements of truth in both accounts.

Why didn't Julian try to take Ctesiphon? The Roman command met just to the north of the city to decide what to do. Details of the meeting are sadly lacking, but two points of consensus emerged. First, that a siege of Ctesiphon was impossible. Although Trajan and three subsequent emperors had reduced the city, the Sassanids had learned from experience and had strengthened the city beyond Roman expectations. Second, Shapur was en route with his soldiers, and it was far from ideal to be caught between the city and the Persian army.

It is difficult to believe the first reason. The Romans had not shied away from sieges in the past. Even more pertinently, it is clear that Julian had access to spies and used them a great deal. Is it really possible to believe of a man whose strategy so far had been based on subterfuge and misinformation, indeed who had been in touch with the commander of Maiozamalcha before its surrender, that he was lacking information about something as basic as the reinforcement of Ctesiphon?

This is normally cited as the moment at which Julian begins to lose his grip. Critics suggest that the emperor's decision not to besiege the city throws the lack of coherency and confusion of Julian's long-term strategy into sharp relief. "Like sand slipping from beneath the feet or a great storm bursting upon a ship, things begin to go black for him," writes the ever-unsympathetic Gregory.[31]

In fact the opposite is true. Our view of Julian's decision has been colored by such adverse comments. Portents of doom come thick and fast but facts are even thinner on the ground than usual—a considerable lacuna in Ammianus's text means we have little insight into the emperor's mind-set. But if we step back for a moment, we see an unwillingness to commit to a siege and face Shapur there and then as neither cowardice nor a lack of command; rather it was the most sensible decision. The emperor's army was untested in pitched battle. It had proved itself successful at guerrilla fighting, but a set battle was an unknown quantity. When the nonappearance of Procopius and Arsak is also considered, avoiding the fight becomes even more reasonable.

These points are fairly convincing by themselves, but one does not need to look far for the overriding cause, which can be traced back to the opening of the Royal Canal. Flooding was one of the original reasons that the canal had been blocked off; it was a perennial problem in the region, indeed that was the reason for the abandonment of Seleucia in the first place. Julian's impromptu engineering work had had a brilliant psychologically damaging effect on the Persians. The fear of flooding, writes Libanius, caused great panic in the cities,[32] but it also had the side effect of creating an actual flood. Ammianus speaks of so many mosquitoes and flies that they "veiled the light of day and the twinkling stars at night."[33] Stagnant water meant malaria. Assuring the health of his soldiers meant that waiting it out was not an option. In a prequinine era, one cannot exaggerate just how much of a problem malaria was right up until modern times. It was certainly endemic throughout Iraq, especially in the Baghdad area, until the late 1950s with March to November renowned for being especially difficult periods—precisely the time when Julian was on campaign.[34]

Julian's next move, at the beginning of the second week of June, has also been heavily criticized, and certainly it caused much disquiet among the army. He decided literally to burn his boats, with the exception of twelve which were to be kept for pontoon bridges and could be transported by land. It is an action that has been much misunderstood and mythologized—not helped by the fact that Alexander the Great had famously got rid of his fleet, making the emperor's soldiers think that either they were bound for India or their commander had delusions of grandeur. Julian's contemporaries have complicated matters with fictions of Persian spies misleading the emperor and tricking him into what was regarded as a rash move.[35]

The most obvious explanation is also the most plausible. The boats had been consigned to the flames—"better that than the enemy," adds Libanius[36]—and there is little reason to doubt this. It would have proved impossible to sail the ships upstream, especially given that the Tigris was swollen with water from the Royal Canal. As long as the ships had a useful role to play, it was worth tying up a large proportion of his force to look after them. When that use was gone, these troops could be better deployed elsewhere.

A second war council was called at the end of the second week in June. With siege plans abandoned, Julian's thoughts were now on how to get home. It was rightly decided that the army could not retreat the way it had come. The flooding and the various towns that the Romans hadn't bothered to take on their way south made it too difficult and too dangerous to attempt to return that way. A secondary consideration must have been that it would have been demoralizing and uncomfortable to march the same way in the heat, only this time without the fleet. The only way was north, up the Tigris. They would soon be safely within striking range of the borders of Armenia, and might even rendezvous with Procopius.

If, with all the benefits that hindsight affords us, we are looking for a moment from which the expedition was doomed, it was here, as the army headed north toward the Roman province of Cordene. It is a feeling that is heightened not just by the doom-laden prose of our witnesses, but by the fact that we can only dimly see the final ten days of Julian's life—names are barely identifiable on a map and dates and times have to be guessed. From now on the Romans began to encounter real difficulties. The early church fathers had Julian marching through a desert and, although not literally true, it was to all intents and purposes an accurate description. The Persians carried out a very successful scorched earth campaign, burning all food that the floods had not destroyed, as well as harrying the Romans at every opportunity.

In the early hours of June 16, Roman outriders saw a huge dust cloud in the distance. In a cliffhanger worthy of a Saturday matinée, Ammianus finishes Book 24 at this moment, with the army debating whether it was the sign of a herd of asses or even of Arsak and Procopius. The army set itself up in a defensive position and waited until the next day.

When it woke up on the morning of June 17, the army found itself encamped in front of the assembled Persian army. This is, curiously, our first sight of Shapur, remarkable in the campaign up to now by his absence. In its favor was that the army was in a reasonable position. To its left was the Tigris, to its right a desert from which the Romans could not be surprised, while in front was what is now the River Diayala, one of the Tigris's main tributaries.

By now, the army was itching for a fight, though uncharacteristically Julian urged caution. This was probably a mistake. It meant that Shapur could avoid the pitched battle he had continuously been evading since Amida, and it gave the Persians time to practice their lightning attacks. They mounted one serious raid on the Roman encampment, killing a senior commander before vanishing, leaving heat and frustration to do the rest.

It was a slow day's march to the modern town of Baquba.[37] The army had traveled only thirty-one miles in two weeks. Here they rested for a much needed two days (Ammianus calls it an "unhoped-for relief"[38]), before continuing north on the 20th. It was all too brief a respite. The psychological effects of the war, the heat and the scorched earth policy now become apparent. The Persians carried on their raids, picking off high-ranking officers and depressing the whole army. Regiments began to squabble. Infantry and cavalry regiments accused each other of cowardice; one cavalry corps was stripped of its ranks while four infantrymen were cashiered. Another major engagement which the Romans nominally won at an unidentified place called Maranga[39] was followed by a three-day truce. The army seemed to be settling into a routine as, hungry and tired, it crawled toward Samarra.

On the night of June 25—the night before his fatal encounter, the omens had deserted Julian, as had his luck. In the middle of the night, troubled by sleeplessness, the emperor sat alone in his tent writing. Lost in thought—reading one of the philosophers, according to the story he told his intimates the following morning—he saw for the second time in his life the shape of the Genius of the Roman people in the gloom of his tent. Did it really happen like this? It almost doesn't matter. No story sums up the atmosphere toward the end of the campaign as well as this. The real question is whether Julian believed that it happened. For him, interaction between divine and human was natural. He stood at the end of a line of Roman emperors and he had a sense of history. While he had little else in common with Mark Antony, it is even possible that he was reminded of Antony's god deserting him after his rout by Octavian at the battle of Actium.[40]

The first time he had such an experience had been in France the night before he had been proclaimed Augustus, an eternity ago. Then the shade had steeled his heart: "For a long time Julian, I have been watching in secret at your door, desiring to place you in a higher position, but more than once I have departed feeling myself rebuffed. If I find no admission even now, when public opinion is unanimous, I shall go away dejected and sorrowful. Do not forget that I shall then dwell with you no longer."[41] This time, however, the shade said nothing. With its head veiled, it departed in sadness through the curtains of his tent.[42] The emperor went outside and saw a blazing light like a falling star. It flashed through the air and then vanished. It was a sign from Mars, the god of war, that he too was leaving.

10

TOWARD THE ISLANDS OF THE BLEST

The Scian and the Teian muse,
The hero's harp, the lover's lute
Have found the fame your shores refuse:
Their place of birth alone is mute
To sounds which echo further west
Than your sires' Islands of the Blest

GEORGE GORDON, LORD BYRON,
THE ISLES OF GREECE

If it is always hard to look into the past and get a satisfactory answer to the questions of where people were and when, let alone why they were there; it is doubly difficult to do so for battle scenes. Your eyewitnesses are invariably preoccupied, trying not to succumb to one of the many invitations to death that combat offers, rather than taking accurate notes for future historians. If this makes any firsthand accounts of a battle of dubious reliability, it holds particularly true for accounts by contemporaries who relied on those eyewitnesses. The hero returning from the military is hardly likely to confess to the prodding questions of would-be historians that he spent the battle hiding behind auxiliary wagons, for example, and inevitably an element of fictionalization creeps in.

When one has to add misinformed speculation, deliberate propaganda, and pure fiction into the mix, it gives some idea of the near-impossibility of the task of deducing what happened on that dusty plain in Persia on June 26. We can never know for certain what occurred unless new evidence comes to light, but because of the mass of misinformation and the way some tried to use their versions for political gain, it is important to try and give plausible answers to the three questions: Who killed Julian?[1] How did he die? And when did he die?

The natural place to start looking for who killed the emperor is on the battlefield and the obvious person to turn to is Ammianus. Hungry, thirsty, probably confused, certainly scared and demoralized, his account of the battlefield is one of the more honest ones. It is all the more poignant, because you do not need to read too far between the lines to realize that Ammianus was too busy staying alive to pay much attention to what was happening around him. His silence as to his own movements that day is a bit of a giveaway. Nevertheless, Ammianus's account is probably the most useful to have survived. He did not publish his history until 390, which would have given him time to talk to other survivors and read other accounts, both official and unofficial, and as a result is as objective an account as any:

> Our flanks were strongly guarded and the army was moving in battle formation, though with some raggedness owing to the nature of the ground, when the emperor, who had gone on ahead, unarmed to reconnoiter, was told that our rearguard had been suddenly attacked from behind. Shocked by this disaster he forgot his breastplate and in his hurry simply laid hold of a shield, but as he was rushing to bring support to those in the rear he was recalled by the fearful news that the van, which he had just left, was in a similar plight. He was hastening to restore the position there, regardless of danger to himself, when in another quarter a troop of Parthian cuirassiers attacked our center, overran its left wing, which gave

way because our men could not stand the smell and noise of the elephants, and tried to force a decision with pikes and showers of missiles.

The emperor flew from one danger spot to another and our lightly armed troops took the offensive, hacking at the backs and legs of the Persians and their monstrous beasts as they turned tail. Julian, throwing caution to the winds, thrust himself boldly into the fight, shouting and waving his arms to make it clear that the enemy had been routed and to encourage his men to a furious pursuit. His escort of guards, who had been scattered in the mêlée, were crying out to him from all sides to avoid the mass of fugitives as he would the collapse of a badly built roof, when suddenly a cavalry spear—directed no one knows by whom—grazed his arm, pierced his ribs, and lodged in the lower part of his liver. He tried to pull it out with his right hand, but both sides of the spear were sharp and he felt his fingers cut to the bone. He fell from his horse, there was a rush to the spot, and he was carried to the camp where he received medical attention.[2]

He says that he had no idea who threw the spear that killed the emperor and there is no nuance in the language that suggests that he is even prepared to hazard a guess. Even the phrase that Ammianus uses for the spear—in the original Latin it is *equestris hasta*—is neutral, meaning simply the spear or lance of a cavalryman. What gives Ammianus's account weight is that another soldier who was there comes to the same conclusion. We know next to nothing about Magnus of Carrhae other than he wrote a book about the campaign and that although he is usually credited with a commanding role in the siege of Maiozamalcha, he probably didn't play one. But in the few lines of his account to have survived, he writes: "Julian was wounded by someone unknown."[3] The view from the battlefield, therefore, was that they did not know.

After those in the military, chronologically the first people to hear what had happened would have been the inhabitants of the towns the Roman army passed on its way back to civilization. Julian's funeral procession went through Nisibis in early autumn and Ephrem Syrus watched its progress and even saw the body. Ephrem had lived on the Persian front line for years—his mother was from Amida—and had survived three sieges of his city. Now in his fifties or sixties, he was later to be one of those directly affected by the treaty that the emperor Jovian signed with the Persians and by the end of the year he would be forced to flee the city. But that was still a few months off. As one of the city's leading lights, he would have known survivors of the campaign, indeed have heard some of the freshest reports. His account helps little; his version is more poetic than factual:

> *Because he [Julian] dishonored Him who had removed*
> > *the spear of Paradise,*
> *the spear of justice passed through his belly.*
> *They tore open that which was pregnant with the oracle*
> > *of the diviners,*
> *And God scourged him and he groaned and*
> > *remembered*
> *What he wrote and published that he would do to the*
> > *churches.*
> *The finger of justice had blotted out his memory. . . .*
>
> *When he saw that his gods were refuted and exposed*
> *and that he was unable to conquer and unable to*
> > *escape,*
> *he was prostrated and torn between fear and shame.*
> *Death he chose so that he might escape in Sheol*
> *and cunningly he took off his armor in order to be*
> > *wounded*
> *so that he might die without the Galileans seeing his*
> > *shame.*[4]

Ascribing the death to a suicide wish is fanciful in the extreme. Ephrem clearly did not know who threw the spear either.

The only other person who could have heard a great number of eyewitness reports by the end of the year is Libanius. His *Funeral Oration for Julian*, written the following year, was the first version to be published. It should have been a straightforward affair. Antioch, the military center of the East, would have been full of returning soldiers, but in this age of instant communication it is easy to dismiss the length of time that it took to get reliable information. Toward the end of 363, Libanius mentions in a letter that he has been trying to find out what happened from anyone who will tell him. "I have been requesting an account of the actions from my friends out of those who have returned and from people who are likely not to have been neglectful of a written account of such matters. But though everyone says he can and will provide the material, no one has done so—in fact has not even informed by word of mouth. Our dead hero is slighted—everyone's concern is for himself,"[5] he moans, adding that some soldiers he had cornered had given him an itinerary and the broad outline of the campaign but it was "a shapeless, shadowy tale, unsuited to the lips of a historian."

The philosopher complains on several further occasions how difficult it was to find out exactly what happened. He wrote to one friend asking for his campaign diary (rather pompously he adds: "you give me the words, and I shall clothe them in the robes of rhetoric"[6]). Finally he wrote to another urging him to hurry up and publish his own account of the war. "You may be quite sure that by writing your account, you will oblige all mankind. You and many more saw the events—you alone of the eyewitnesses have an eloquence equal to the events."[7] It is questionable, therefore, whether he had even talked to any of the protagonists by the time he had finished writing his speech. But in spite of this, he will have been party to city gossip, which is reflected in these rapid conclusions:

> The emperor was riding in haste with only one attendant as escort to repair the gap in the ranks when a cavalryman's spear pierced him. He was without armor—apparently confident in his success— he had taken no precautions and the spear passed through his arm and penetrated his side. Our noble emperor fell to the ground and seeing the blood gushing out, he wanted to conceal what had occurred. He remounted straightaway, but when the bloodstains showed that he was wounded, he called out to everyone he met not to be afraid about his wound for it was not fatal. That was what he said, but he was already beginning to succumb. He was carried to his soft bed and the lion skin and straw of which it was made.[8]

Can we be sure of any of the elements of the story from Julian's contemporaries? Certain points do come across. First, that Julian was not wearing a breastplate. Second, that his guards were scattered and that he was either unguarded, or poorly guarded. Third, that he was on horseback. And fourth, that he was killed by a spear that went through or grazed his arm and ended up in his lower abdomen.

Enemy sources only confirm the confusion. Al-Tabari, in the ninth century, is the earliest eastern written source we have and comments only that "an arrow, shot by an invisible hand, hit him fatally in the heart."[9] The two other medieval historians to mention the emperor's death provide rather muddled evidence. One writes that while Julian was on a horse in front of his tent "an arrow came from Shapur's camp, hit Julian in the liver and he fell off and died," while the other is even more vague, noting simply that Julian was hit by an arrow. The only contemporary evidence is a bas-relief at the Sassanid site of Taq-i Bustan. It purports to show Julian, on the ground, his head resting on his left arm, while Shapur stands on the emperor's legs facing the supreme god Ahura-Mazda, who stands on Julian's head. The god Mithras stands behind Shapur. The fact that it is Ahura-Mazda, and not the Sassanid monarch, who stands over the emperor's head, suggests that Julian's death is the result of divine intervention. In other words, the Persian army had no idea who killed Julian either.

This is where the historical waters become increasingly opaque. It is easy to forget that (*pace* Antioch) Julian had been a popular emperor, especially among the populace at large. The West had not been particularly affected by his anti-Christian legislation as it had always been broadly pagan, while many still cherished the memory of the victories of their Caesar—the battle of Strasbourg had occurred only six years previously. The army was desolate at his death. Emotions reached their bloody climax in the lynching of Lucillianus, the father-in-law of Jovian, and of a tribune who accompanied him, by troops at Reims who did not believe what they saw as slander about the death of their beloved Julian.[10] Within this climate, people wanted to know what happened to him and many writers were only too happy to fulfil this demand.

While Ammianus and Libanius saw a chance to mythologize the memory of the emperor, others were mere opportunists. Where there was a lacuna in the story, they were only too happy to plug it and as the person who killed Julian was unknown, it gave people a tabula rasa on which to scrawl graffiti. One of Julian's bodyguards, a certain Callistus, in depressingly contemporary mode cashed in with memoirs of his time with the emperor. Although they have not survived, we do know that Callistus celebrated the emperor's deeds in heroic verse, and, showing a disregard for reality that is also all too familiar in royal biographies, concluded that the wound which killed Julian was inflicted by a demon. The memoirs of the infantryman Eutychianus took a similarly supernatural turn—they claimed Julian was killed in his sleep. In his dream a man wearing a cuirass at his side, came into the emperor's tent at night and stabbed him with a spear. The eunuchs of the bedchamber and his guards appeared, but Julian was fatally wounded.

The best known and most enduring of the supernatural stories about the death of Julian is that of St. Mercurius. The earliest surviving version, dating from the early-sixth century, has Basil of Caesarea witness the death of the emperor in a dream. He saw Jesus Christ sitting on a throne and ordering Mercurius who stood beside him, identified by his protective iron breast plate, to kill Julian. The saint soon reappeared before Christ saying that the deed had been done.[11] There is no mention of the weapon used in the legend and the earliest frescos that have survived—there is a particularly fine one in the Pillared Church in Cappadocia—show Mercurius with a short sword instead of a lance. The legend was soon amended. By the ninth century we see Mercurius pictured with a lance in a manuscript of Gregory of Nazianzus's speeches in the Bibliothèque Nationale in Paris. The panel of a beautiful thirteenth-century Italian encaustic wooden triptych in the Jarves Collection at Yale shows Mercurius spearing the emperor with a javelin while Julian lies there breathing fire and Christ sits above the action in the attitude of benediction. It is the same in Gautier de Coinci's medieval bestseller *Miracles of the Virgin;* Mercurius kills the emperor with a "very great and mighty spear."[12]

With a sense of confusion surrounding Julian's end established, it is a short step to mystery and from there to conspiracy. So it was with the emperor's death. The word "murder" was bandied around and a whispering campaign appears to have started that the weapon that killed Julian was a Roman one.

It is a story that Ammianus had heard, but didn't believe. He tries to distance himself from it as much as possible; indeed he seems to go out of his way to discredit it. He says that he had heard, from the enemy, who had heard it from deserters, that Julian had been killed by a Roman weapon.[13] But of course, by the time Ammianus's history was published, the story had a life of its own and was difficult to stop.

It is Libanius, however, who, probably more than anyone else, can be blamed for stirring things up and starting this game of Chinese whispers. In the autumn of 363 he was still saying that no one knew: "That spear, the bloodshed, and death. The omniscient gods know where that came from."[14] By early 364 he is referring in correspondence to "the murder of the emperor."[15] And by the time he had finished the *Funeral Oration* he had come up with a guilty party.

> You would like to know who it was that killed him. I do not know his name, but that his murderer did not belong to the enemy is clearly proved by the fact that none of the enemy received any award for killing him. But the Persian king issued a proclamation and invited his killer to claim a reward and if he had come forward he could have obtained a great prize. Yet nobody boasted of doing it, not even in his desire for the reward. We should be very grateful to the enemy for not claiming credit for what they had not done and for allowing us to seek his murderer from among ourselves. For those fellows, who found his existence detrimental to themselves and whose whole manner of life was contrary to the law, these had long conspired against him and then, at last, seized their chance and acted.[16]

It is a quite remarkable syllogism—Libanius is arguing that because no one collected Shapur's prize, the killer had to be a Roman. The story had rapidly gone from a Roman spear, to a Roman soldier, and Libanius points a finger at the Christians. That suggestion was to cause a great deal of confusion, but taken in context sounds like nothing so much as a sideswipe at the people of Antioch who had made the emperor's life miserable earlier. But the urban myth was born. By the time that Gregory, the first Christian to comment extensively on Julian's death, picked it up, there were at least four different stories circulating. With almost too much glee for comfort he mentions a randomly thrown Persian missile; a Roman officer frustrated about the management of the campaign; a barbarian auxiliary or hanger on; or a Saracen. There is no hint at all in Gregory's work of anything approaching a Christian plot—and if such a version had been in general circulation, he of all people would have mentioned it.[17]

But none of that matters. It was too late. By then Julian's death had acquired a life of its own—it had become a folk myth. Other details started to become part of the canon and were accepted as fact. The most famous tradition of all is the detail of Julian lying on the ground, thrown from his horse, filling his hand with the blood that was dripping at his side and shouting in defiance and rage: "Thou hast won, O Galilean." Although it is the Christian version that is best known, in fact there are two distinct accounts of the same story. In both, Julian lies there with blood pouring from his side. In both, he fills his hand with the blood and offers it up. In one, however, Julian berates Christ for having beaten him, and in the other, he blames the Sun or the gods for having deserted him.[18]

It is easy to see why the tradition took off—it is a powerful story that manages to encapsulate the character and history of the emperor in one sentence. What raises doubts about its veracity, however, is that similar stories were already in circulation long before Julian was born. It is hardly coincidence that during the murder of Domitian, an early emperor who rivaled Nero and Caligula in the popularity stakes, a certain Apollonius of Tyana climbed a rock at Ephesus at the very moment that the emperor's freedman Stephanus struck the first blow. Apollonius is said to have shouted: "Good, Stephanus. Bravo, Stephanus. Smite the bloodthirsty wretch. You have struck, you have wounded, you have slain."[19]

With myth and history blending seamlessly, is it at all possible to work out what might have happened? Cautiously, yes. If it is Libanius who either unwittingly or wittingly caused much of the confusion surrounding the emperor's death, it is also Libanius who gives us at least a plausible suggestion of what might have happened. Between the *Funeral Oration* that he had finished by the very latest in 365 and his speech *On Avenging Julian,* written fifteen years after the emperor's death, the details of the old philosopher's story have changed. Now he writes: "Our renowned Julian received that blow in the side as he strove to unite part of his line that had broken, spurring his horse toward them, cheering and threatening. The assailant was a Taiene acting in obedience to their leader's command. This action, indeed, would probably secure for the chief a reward from the people who were keen to have him killed. So he made the most of the opportunity offered by the prevailing confusion and the winds and swirling dust to strike him and retire."[20] Why had Libanius's story changed? The simplest explanation is that he had information by the time that he was writing this oration in 378, that he did not have in 364. The word he uses to describe the killer is "Taienos"—remarkable because it is not a Greek word at all, but a Syriac word used to describe the Saracens. Certainly they had been the subject of one of the earlier rumors and it is worthy of note in all the fuss that surrounds the death of the emperor in being an explanation that is at the very least plausible. What gives the story credibility is that it is backed up by two other pieces of evidence. John Lydus, a sixth-century civil servant based in Constantinople, seems to corroborate the story. In his account of Julian's death, he writes: "One man from the Persian division of the so-called Saracens guessed the identity of the emperor from his purple robe and cried out in his own language *malchan.*"[21] The stray word *malchan* is Syriac and means "king." It is little enough evidence, but could suggest that there was a Syriac version doing the rounds.

Most convincingly of all, however, there is a version with even more detail preserved by a writer called Philostorgius, born around five years after Julian's death.[22] In his account,

> The Persians rushed upon the Romans, having joined to their forces
> as allies some Saracen horsemen who were armed with spears. One
> of them thrust a spear at Julian, which struck him forcefully on the
> thigh near the groin and when the spear was drawn out, it was fol-
> lowed by a quantity of feces and blood also. Subsequently, one of
> the bodyguards of the emperor immediately attacked the Saracen

who had wounded the king and cut off his head, while the Romans immediately placed the mortally wounded Julian on a shield and carried him off into a tent. Many even thought that the fatal blow was struck by Julian's own friends, so sudden and unexpected was it and so much at a loss were they to know [from] where it came.[23]

If we can say with as much certainty as is possible that Julian was killed by the lucky strike of a Persian ally, questions remain about precisely how he died. In the orthodox account, Julian was wounded some time in the mid-afternoon. The emperor was carried back to the Roman camp and laid out on the lion skin and straw bed in his tent where he received medical attention from Oribasius.

In his last hours, the emperor supposedly turned into a latter-day Socrates, a philosopher-king engaging his companions in musings on the soul as he prepared to die. Libanius draws the parallel with the Greek philosopher directly, while Ammianus goes so far as to compose a final speech.[24] Suddenly, the wound in his side gaped wide and the veins in his throat swelled up and obstructed his breath. He asked for, and drank, some cold water. Then, at around midnight, Julian lost consciousness and passed away peacefully.

In itself, this account is not implausible. If a deathbed scene sounds contrived, it was certainly well in accord with Julian's character to have staged such theatricals in his moments of lucidity, playing the philosopher in the face of history. Two points, however, cast doubt on this scenario. First is Julian's refusal to name a successor. Even though the Roman army, his men, many of whom had followed him faithfully all the way from Gaul, was in enemy territory, harried on all sides and about to become leaderless Julian does not name an heir. Apart from bearing suspicious similarities to the death of Alexander the Great (in Arrian's account of the Macedonian king's death, his lieutenants ask him to name a successor, to which Alexander replied, "the best man"[25]), it is a remarkably selfish act. Much more significantly, the medical evidence tells a different story. The difficulty is that the wound, the symptoms described and the time of death do not correlate.[26]

Frustratingly, Oribasius's memoirs, which covered the thirteen years the doctor was in Julian's service,[27] have not survived. But even if we have no access to the doctor's own words, his account was read by many of the other commentators on the emperor's reign. By piecing together these accounts, it is possible to reconstruct to some extent how Julian was wounded.

The spear grazed the emperor's arm, pierced his ribs, and ended up in the lower part of his liver. When Julian tried to pull the spear out from his side, he cut himself as the head of the spear was long and sharp on both sides. When the spear did come out, it was followed by a quantity of blood and fecal matter,[28] which suggests that it had clipped the wall of the gut. Julian then fainted ("Weakness, enervation, weak pulse, a dull voice, coldness of the extremities, and some cold sweat"[29] is Oribasius's description of a faint, one of only two classical descriptions that have come down to us), before the emperor recovered consciousness enough to climb on his horse, then passed out again. He was rapidly taken to his tent to be treated by Oribasius where some attempt at surgery appears to have taken place.[30]

The study of classical war wounds and field surgery is in its infancy, but it is possible to make some educated guesses, primarily from other writings of Oribasius that have survived, about how someone would have been treated after an abdominal wound. Liver wounds were, unsurprisingly, regarded as difficult throughout the ancient world. The number of instructions that ancient medical authors give on having the patient bound during such an operation provides an unpleasant insight into contemporary surgical practices; uneasiness is heightened when you realize that it is also unlikely that Julian was given any analgesics. Opium was known, but it was regarded as a drug too dangerous to use. At most, as Oribasius recommends several times in his writings, the emperor would have been given a drink of pomegranate in wine.[31]

The general technique would not have been very different from the procedure today. First of all, the prolapsed organs would have been replaced. In the first instance Oribasius would simply have pressed the coils of the intestine back into the bowel, but if that had failed, he would have extended the original wound with a lancet and then, with the patient's legs in the air and head back, have attempted again. All the while, the entire area would have been drenched in various solutions, most probably a high alcohol wine. The antiseptic qualities of wine had long been known—the Good Samaritan treated the man he found on the road to Jericho in this way.[32] Finally, Oribasius would have had to suture the abdominal walls together. Suturing was certainly undertaken for a variety of injuries, but it was a procedure known to be tricky, as indeed it still is for abdominal wounds.

It is questionable, however, whether Oribasius would have closed the wound at all, given that there appears to have been some damage to the gut. The doctor was in the field, away from civilization and with the emperor's life in his hands. He was not going to risk difficult techniques. More pertinently, both Galen and the first-century doctor Celsus recommended cleaning wounds like this, then leaving them open.

We know that when Julian received a spear to his right side it hit his liver. Bleeding from the liver is often heavy, but may have been moderate and may have sealed itself off. It is plausible that Julian initially lost consciousness, regained it, and then continued to lose blood for hours, to die that evening.

It is the further details—of the blood and feces flowing when Julian pulled out the spear—that cast some doubt on Ammianus's time of death as midnight that evening. With this type of injury it is certainly possible that blood and fluid from the gut would have flowed, perhaps partially slowed and then restarted as infection took hold—relatively rapidly, as it might, in a time before antibiotics. This points to Julian dying as a result of peritonitis. In this case, the emperor's abdomen would have swollen up, and there would have been an increase in discharge from his wound. In a pre-antibiotic era it would have been common for a wound like this to have become infected with gas gangrene, which would also have led to swelling as the muscles and subcutaneous tissue surrounding the wound became filled with gas. This type of infection also tallies with Ammianus's account that at the moment of death, the wound in Julian's side gaped wide and the veins in his throat swelled up and obstructed his breath.[33]

A similar case is seen in the other instance of abdominal injury that has come down to us from the early Byzantine period, that of Basil I, who ruled toward the end of the ninth century. Wounded across the stomach in a hunting accident, doctors in this case also decided not to suture and the emperor died nine days later with many of the symptoms that Julian displayed. That Basil survived for six days longer than Julian says more for the locations in which they found themselves—an imperial palace rather than a tent in Persia—than their relative fitness. For a young, healthy commander, as Julian undoubtedly was, death from peritonitis and perhaps gas gangrene is likely to follow in three days. Only one account gives this, that of Philostorgius who does write that Julian did not die that evening, rather that he succumbed "after three days of suffering."[34] That would put his death at June 28, if we count, as the Romans did, inclusively.

This is a case of the dog that didn't bark. Julian did not name a successor, because there was no need for him to appoint one. He was not going to die. A patient in the ancient world who survived the first night was likely to survive. By the morning of June 27, most of the senior commanders would have believed that the emperor would pull through. Even if Julian did believe that his time had come, it is unlikely that he was in much of a position to select anyone to succeed him. The symptoms of peritonitis are fever, vomiting, and extreme weakness; and patients often also suffer mental confusion, prostration, or shock. Stories, therefore, that Julian was leaving the decision up to the army are pure bunkum and editorializing after the fact. Julian spent two days semiconscious, before dying on the third day.

Despite the historical white noise distorting what happened, Julian was killed by a lucky strike from a Saracen auxiliary who was fighting on the side of the Persians. The blow would have been a difficult one— one man on a moving horse stabbing another man also on horseback and neither with stirrups—but while certainly a fluke, it is no more of one than a lucky shot out of a book store repository window. While the emperor fell off his horse in agony, Julian's bodyguards went after, attacked, and killed the guilty party. Three days later, Julian died.

Ammianus was able to hide behind this historical fog. Confusion on his part is hardly plausible. The answer lies both in the soldier's desire to mythologize the emperor and his dissatisfaction with Julian's successor. There was no state conspiracy to hide details of Julian's death but it was not the death that people wanted to believe, so they ignored it or rejected it. A lucky shot was not what either pagans or Christians wanted—it gave the former nothing to eulogize and the latter nothing to rail against. A murder or a conspiracy was something that everyone could get their teeth into, but a spearman who took a chance and then paid for his success with his own life has none of the narrative excitement that people crave. We demand, of course, that our heroes die with a bang, not a whimper—to die like Julius Caesar stabbed on the steps of the forum; in glorious battle like Leonidas and his 300 Spartans facing the entire Persian army; or even by their own hand and on their sword like Mark Antony when backed into a corner. Julian's was not a glamorous death. It was not the way an emperor was supposed to die.

EPILOGUE

BY THE
SILVERY KYDNOS

*By the silvery Kydnos, coming from the streams
of the Euphrates and the land of Persia, after
launching his army on a task it did not complete,
Julian found this tomb. He was a good king and a
brave warrior.*

ZONARES, *ANNALES*

What the Roman army needed now, above all else, was leadership. It was east of the Tigris, in the heart of enemy territory and surrounded by Persians. The death of the emperor meant the death of the campaign and the army just wanted to get out of Persia in one piece.

Julian had not named a successor. As he had no reason to presume that his wound was fatal, why would he? Nonetheless, this failure inevitably led to some jostling for power when the senior command met formally on June 28, as each faction wanted its own candidate on the throne. In one corner were Julian's two Gaulish generals and in the other, two of

197

Constantius's old generals. One person was immediately offered the job. Salutius, however, realizing what a poisoned chalice it could be, turned it down, hiding behind the excuses of old age and infirmity.

In the end, the job fell to Flavius Jovianus, better known as Jovian, the ultimate compromise candidate. Accounts disagree whether it was the soldiers that forced him on the commanders or the other way round, but either way the necessary unanimity was achieved.

Jovian was unencumbered by any obvious talents. All who knew him agree that his main interests were wine, women, and song—indeed, if you look at his coins, his profile is distinctly jowly. Up to now his career moves had been unspectacular other than marrying into rather a good family. Now thirty-two (he had been born in Belgrade in 331) he had served in the household guard under Constantius, and Julian had promoted him to chief of guards, the gossip went, because he was remarkably tall. It was said that one of the difficulties of his appointment was that his staff could not find a royal cloak to fit him. Nonetheless Jovian was a senior enough figure to be taken seriously as emperor and certainly his role in escorting Constantius's remains back to Constantinople gave him a high public profile. Indeed, there are whispers that he had been mentioned in connection with the throne once before in the brief time there was for maneuverings between Constantius's death and Julian's accession. But he had several points in his favor now, and one, which should not be discounted, is that he was acceptable to all parties.

Jovian himself may have come across as more acceptable than brilliant, but his father and his father-in-law were anything but, and probably the underlying reason for the choice. Jovian's father, Varronianus had held high military command and been a senior cavalry officer under Constantius. Although now retired, he remained in touch with the empire's decision makers. Jovian's father-in-law, Lucillianus, had had an even more stellar career. Diplomat and commander, he had been retired after coming up against Julian in Sirmium, but again had the right connections. Both of them had enough status and enough influence to know the people who mattered and to ensure a smooth transition of power.

Jovian's other outstanding feature, as far as the high command were concerned, is that he appears to have been untroubled by too many thoughts of the afterlife. Although personally favorably inclined toward

Christianity, he refused to be drawn into Christian factionalism and he was not above using sacrifice publicly when it was useful to do so. There was no suggestion of a purge of pagans. His credo was: "I abominate contentiousness; but I love and honor those who exert themselves to promote unanimity."[1] Toleration was the order of the day—crucial given the damage limitation needed to the purple after the confusion of the previous years.

Getting home in one piece was the more immediate priority. The army marched on but it became rapidly apparent that the Romans were completely outgunned. The Persians kept up the pressure, especially after news of Julian's death had been leaked, and on one occasion broke into the Roman camp and almost reached Jovian's tent. The Romans continued their march along the Tigris but progress was painfully slow. On July 1, when the army reached Dura-on-the-Tigris they had managed to travel fewer than four miles. A fighting retreat was obviously out of the question. Here the army was forced to retrench for three days, unable to move for the Persian assault.

It was becoming obvious that the tight disciplinary grip that had been maintained on the troops was starting to evaporate. When rumors—falsely or perhaps optimistically—began to circulate that the army was only a few days' march from Roman territory, some of the Western troops that had been brought up next to the fast-flowing rivers of Germany and Gaul, swam across the Tigris. To prevent the rest of the army deserting, engineers made vain placatory promises of pontoon bridges, while the rest of the troops remained pinned down for another couple of days.

There was nothing for it other than to negotiate. Jovian picked Salutius to head the team of underexperienced negotiators and talks went on for four days as the Roman soldiers sweated and died in the heat. The brevity of the talks suggest that the Persians to all intents and purposes dictated terms and it is hard to see the treaty as anything other than a total Roman capitulation. The Romans ended up conceding five territories on the Upper Tigris and the fortress towns of Nisibis, Singara, and Castra Maurorum (recently identified as the town of Seh Qubba[2]). This not only destroyed the Roman defensive military system in eastern Mesopotamia, the loss of Nisibis meant the loss of the Roman monopoly of income from the trans-border trade in the town. Finally, Salutius and his team appear to have agreed to terms, which debarred Rome from both military and political intervention in Armenia.

Jovian was now placed in an extraordinarily difficult position. He had to minimize the bad publicity for signing away Roman territory that could dog his reign. The natural solution of politicians throughout the ages—to blame their predecessor—was not an option. First, people simply would not have believed it. Julian was known and loved as a successful military leader. It would have taken a great deal of persuasion to convince them of Julian's feet of clay. Second, total capitulation to Rome's greatest enemy was hardly the best way for a new emperor to stamp his authority on the empire.

Jovian's answer was to present the campaign as a victory. This can be seen especially clearly in his coinage. Even before the army reached Nisibis, emissaries were sent round the empire and the mints were ordered to change the coinage. First of all, the emperor's image was as different as possible from that of Julian. A clean-shaven profile not only was a radically different picture, but also suggested a return to Christianity. On the obverse, the imagery is even more blunt. Phrases like "restorer of the state," "victory of the empire" and "victory of the Romans" were stamped on his coins and, most obviously of all, there is the image of a chained prisoner—clearly a Persian from his dress—under a standard with the symbol of Christ on the banner.

However audacious, these moves were not a total success. Although the modern world is kinder to Jovian, he was soon reviled by contemporaries for his cowardice. Many started to believe that the army could have fought its way out of Persia and that Rome had been sold out by its politicians. It was the old story of the lions led by donkeys. When Jovian finally reached Antioch, the emperor found himself lambasted by the city's ever-subtle inhabitants. Anonymous pamphlets declared: "You came back from the war, you should have died there," and the emperor was heckled in the hippodrome.[3]

It is clear that even after the treaty had been signed and the Romans had been given free passage, their withdrawal resembled nothing so much as Napoleon's retreat from Moscow—a long, dangerous and hungry trek. It was almost two hundred miles to civilization—Ammianus's one hundred miles is little more than wishful thinking and political cant to minimize the need for a treaty—and certain parts of the route were completely barren of any water and food. The army cannot be said to have been safe until it reached Nisibis.

Not that the army was welcomed by the city. Sold out by the accord, there is one report that the messenger was lynched when he appeared with news of the terms of the treaty and the locals were not comforted by the fact that Jovian had passed through with what they thought was unseemly haste. Again this is a little unfair on Jovian. The Persians were keen to take control of the city under the terms of the agreement and the new governor even hoisted the Persian flag before the emperor had left. No surprise, then, that he had little inclination to dally. But this is where we meet Julian again. His body, preserved in honey and spices against the heat, just like Alexander the Great's, was carried there by his soldiers. Ephrem mentions "the corpse of that accursed one which passed by the wall."[4]

By October at the latest, Julian's body had been brought via Antioch to Cilicia first by a Gaul called Merobaudes and then by Procopius who had liaised with Jovian just south of Nisibis.[5] Even his death had done little to mollify the Antiochenes. There were street parties when the news broke and Libanius wrote sadly: "A couple of cities even danced for joy at the event and for one of them I am ashamed."[6] By the end of the month Julian had been laid to rest just north of Tarsus along the road that led toward the Taurus Mountains. Following the emperor's break with Antioch, he had always envisaged resting in the city after his eastern campaign.

Tarsus has been eclipsed by the glory of Antioch, but it could so easily have been the other way round. St. Paul's home commanded the southern end of the Cilician Gates, the only pass in the Taurus Mountains that links Anatolia with the Mediterranean coast. The muscatel-style wine that the region produced was famed throughout the ancient world while its merchants sold the city's linen across the Mediterranean via the now landlocked harbor of Rhegma. And its university rivaled those of Athens and Alexandria. By the time that the emperor Septimius Severus passed through the Cilician Gates at the end of the first century, the emperor could describe the city in an inscription on the rock face of the Gates as "first, greatest, and most beautiful."

We do not know whether Julian had ever specified where he wanted to be buried. Both Ammianus and Libanius disapproved of Tarsus, however. Rather pompously Libanius reckoned that it would have been more proper for the emperor to have been buried near the tomb of Plato in the Academy in Athens—all philosophers together.[7] Ammianus, on the other hand, pedantically states that "if proper consideration had then been given to the matter, Julian's ashes should not lie within sight of the River Kydnos, beautiful and limpid though it is. To perpetuate the memory of his exploits, they should have been laid where they might be lapped by the Tiber which intersects the Eternal City and skirts the monuments of earlier deified emperors."[8]

It is, however, appropriate that he was buried in Tarsus. Julian's tomb lay near that of Maximianus Daia, buried almost exactly fifty years previously, another passionate pagan emperor who had lost out in Constantine's rapid rise to the top. By all accounts the tomb was a minimalist affair, in keeping with his ascetic nature if we are being charitable or, if we are not, swiftly done so that those in charge of the burial could make it back to Constantinople as rapidly as possible and secure their own political futures. The funeral too was simple, just like the great Roman funerals of old.

Passing through on his rapid march to Constantinople, Jovian took time to embellish Julian's tomb. It was perhaps Jovian who gave the order for the following epitaph to be inscribed on his predecessor's tomb several months later:

> Here lies Julian, who fell by the strong-flowing Tigris.
> He was a good king and a mighty warrior.[9]

Julian would have approved of the epitaph. He would have recognized the second line not only as a description of Agamemnon but as Alexander the Great's favorite phrase too.[10]

Within a few years there was a plan to transport Julian's remains to Constantinople. Valentinian and Valens had contemplated such a move, but it came to nothing. So his bones rested in Tarsus until the seventh century. Then, Julian was laid to rest in the Church of the Holy Apostles—the very place in which he had said goodbye to Constantius—the Roman equivalent of the Hapsburg's Kapuzinergruft in Vienna. There is some confusion as to exactly where he was buried, but most likely it was in a free-standing stoa to the north of the church, a separate building enclosed by pillars supporting a roof. He was laid to rest in a new cylindrical sarcophagus, cut from reddish stone. An expanded epigram of the one at Tarsus—the one that heads this chapter—identified his final resting place. Julian's sarcophagus survived until the eighteenth century, the last person to see it a French manufacturer called Jean-Claude Flachat, then resident in the city. Today, one similar to that—simple and elegant—lies outside the Archaeological Museum in Istanbul, but here we lose track of it and the physical remains of Julian.

Julian is difficult to categorize—idealists and thinkers always are. If we are looking at physical remnants of what he was as emperor, then he is an ephemeral irrelevance. In terms of architecture, we can visit the Santa Costanza, the church in Rome that he finished for his wife, but virtually everything else has vanished. He didn't even leave any cities named after him.[11] Admittedly a disproportionately large number of inscriptions have survived, but they give little spirit of place. Of his monumental building works in Constantinople, nothing remains, and of those elsewhere inspired by his reforms we can guess at little more than outlines.

There is only one contemporary work of art that can arguably be connected to him—a silver platter called the Corbridge Lanx in the British Museum. But it causes considerable debate. Found in the River Tyne in the eighteenth century, it is engraved with five figures that have been identified as Greek gods associated with Delos and is traditionally said to commemorate Julian's visit there. The emperor, however, never set foot on the island; indeed there is nothing whatsoever to connect Julian to the work other than its obviously pagan theme and late Roman origin.

As for his legacy as a ruler, by almost every standard, Julian left nothing behind. There is no Julianic equivalent of the Code Napoleon. His foreign policy ended in disaster, fatally for him, and resulted in total Roman capitulation. The gains Julian had made militarily in the West were soon forgotten. Indeed, the "mighty warrior's" only real victory was cleaning up the tax system.

The religious reforms, for which he is best known, died with him. Like other rulers who tried to swim against the religious flow of the time—the Pharaoh Akhenaten with his worship of the sun Aten before him, or the Mughal emperor Akbar and his regicentric creed Din Ilahi after him—the tide turned even before his body was cold. Indeed, the following year Libanius was able to acknowledge that the battle was over. "[Christianity] has quenched the sacred flame; it has stopped the joyful sacrifices, it has set them on to spurn and overthrow your altars; it has closed, demolished, or profaned your temples and sanctuaries are given to harlots to live in. It has utterly undone the reverence that was yours and has established in your inheritance a dead man's tomb," he weeps.[12]

Nonetheless, despite (or perhaps even because of) the fact he was a failure, it is his personality as a man that comes through. His impulsive nature that made him attempt anything and everything as and when it came to his attention, while a flaw in an emperor, is a human failing. For all of his defects, his impatience, his credulity and his arrogance, power did not corrupt him. He listened to other people, whether or not he took their advice. From Oribasius who told him he needed more self-control and his praetorian prefect in Gaul who advised him not to invade Persia, to Salutius Secundus who told him not to persecute the Christians in Antioch, Julian was never the unapproachable despot.

So how should we remember Julian?

Until the late Middle Ages, Julian was a caricature, a cipher used in literature and art that was instantly recognizable. Two anecdotes in particular dominated. The first is that of Julian's death at the hands of St. Mercurius, mentioned above. The other is that of his martyrdom of Saints John and Paul.[13] The best-known version of the latter story is preserved in the medieval bestseller *The Golden Legend*. So the story goes, John and Paul were eunuchs in the service of Constantina, daughter of Constantine; the one her steward, the other the master of her household. The emperor sent them to serve under his general Gallicanus, who was then defending Thrace against the Scythians. John and Paul told the general that victory would be his if he converted to Christianity. He did so and the Scythians were routed. When Julian came to the throne, the two refused to serve under him, were placed under house arrest, then executed in Rome.

The story has a far older heritage. It reflects the martyrdom of Juventinus and Maximinus, two soldiers in the emperor's guard, overheard criticizing Julian on the eve of the Persian campaign.[14] Nonetheless, Saints Paul and John soon found themselves in the Christian canon. A church, the Santi Giovanni e Paolo, was erected over their home, where they had been buried and, underneath its twelfth-century structure, the rooms of an early fifth-century building have been found, decorated with early Christian frescos.

We see this version of the story in the play *Gallicanus* by the German nun Hrotsvitha (occasionally still referred to as Roswitha) of Gandersheim. Written toward the end of the tenth century in rough and ready, intermittently rhymed Latin prose, it was meant to be read aloud rather than performed. When he appears at the beginning of Act II, Julian is a catalyst for evil rather than an active participant, indeed at one point he is referred to as the "devil's chaplain." Julian argues that the cause of unrest in the empire is Christianity and orders his soldiers to take Gallicanus's property. "Soldiers, arm yourselves and strip the Christians of all they possess. Remind them of these words of their Christ: 'He who does not renounce all that he possesses for my sake cannot be my disciple'," he says.[15] Gallicanus, John, and Paul are all put to death, while redemption is manifested when the executioner and his son seek forgiveness for their crimes and are baptized.

Even in art, Julian is a shorthand for evil. One of the earliest and most detailed representations of the emperor appears in two of the ten frescos from the life of St. Martin of Tours, the patron saint of France and the first great leader of monasticism in the West, which Simone Martini painted in the chapel of San Martino in the lower Church of San Francesco in Assisi. Martini was one of the outstanding European artists of the fourteenth century, revered as much during his lifetime as afterward. His close friend Petrarch (the painter even completed a portrait of Laura, now sadly lost) wrote that only the "impediments of the earth"[16] restricted Simone's vision, and the Assisi frescos display Simone's skill as a great narrative painter with a sense of drama. *The Knighting of St. Martin* and *St. Martin's Renunciation of Arms* both refer to incidents in the saint's life, and in each picture Julian is the pagan foil to the saint's Christian holiness.

From both paintings, it must be admitted, we get a greater sense of the Anjou court in Italy than of fourth-century Gaul; the protagonists are accompanied by medieval-looking knights and tents. In *The Knighting of St. Martin,* the emperor is shown bending down to attach a sword to Martin's belt as courtiers and minstrels look on. In *St. Martin's Renunciation of Arms,* a seated figure of Julian, surrounded by soldiers and a monkish-looking treasurer counting out money into a soldier's palm, faces the barbarian enemy peeking out from behind a hill. Martin stands between the two sides holding a cross, looking back toward his emperor but holding his cross as a defense toward the enemy. In both pictures Julian is shown in profile and it is popularly thought that Simone used a Roman coin as a model.

What is intriguing about the way that Julian was seen in the Middle Ages is less how he was represented than quite how far afield stories of his reign had traveled. We should not be surprised that Julian was a recognizable term of abuse at royal and Vatican levels, but that both Julian and the manner of his death were clearly well known to people for whom the Roman Empire must have been unimaginably alien. He is even mentioned in one of the Old Norse sagas.[17]

It was not until the sixteenth century and Hans Sachs's five-act play *Julian the Emperor while Bathing,*[18] published on September 22, 1556, that we begin to see Julian as anything other than purely evil. Idealized in Richard Wagner's opera *Die Meistersinger von Nürnberg,* Sachs remains one of the most prolific and influential of German poets. Although his verse sounds odd to the modern ear—it is mostly written in rhyming couplets—Sachs's play has a peculiar charm all of its own.

The play is very strange indeed, not helped by the fact that Sachs is vague on any details of Julian's life. After a long boar hunt, the emperor goes for a swim. His clothes are stolen by a doppelganger angel—the *engel-kayser*—who then rides off with the court. As in all the best folk stories, the naked Julian is then not recognized by anyone. Humbled and miserable, the emperor eventually acknowledges his pride: "O lord I now recognize that I have sinned greatly. That I through power, property and esteem, good fortune and all of the other gifts from heaven, in pride raised myself up. I haven't thanked you for your goodness but I elevated my own mind as if I myself were God and Lord. Therefore you have thrown me out of my empire. You have made my people and land not recognize me. I will knock on this door again and shall confess my sins and see if God will show me mercy," he says. In the end he gets back his empire.

Julian remained, if not a popular theme, then at least a recognized one throughout Europe. Plays were performed in Italy, Spain, Germany and Switzerland. In Britain, for example, the Admiral's Men, the Elizabethan theatrical company closely associated with Christopher Marlowe, under its manager Philip Henslowe performed an otherwise unknown play called *Julyan Apostata* at the Rose Theater in London three times in 1596.[19] As much as it is possible to gather, however, these all propagated the traditional view.

The first genuinely positive view of the emperor is that of Michel de Montaigne from the mid-sixteenth century. Editions of Ammianus Marcellinus's history had been around since its first printing in 1474 and by the end of 1533 there had been at least five editions of his history. In an essay that was to have tremendous significance entitled "On Freedom of Conscience," the French essayist compared Julian favorably to Alexander the Great and Scipio. "He was a truly great and outstanding person, appropriately enough for a man whose mind was steeped in the philosophical argument by which he claimed to order all his activities. And indeed he left behind examples of model behavior in every single field of virtue," he writes.[20]

By the end of the seventeenth century, Julian is to be found embroiled once more in a fight against the Church, but this time it was a battle he would win. The emperor came to the political foreground in the Britain of the 1680s as the specter of Catholicism appeared over the English throne following the death of Charles II. It is hard to think of a more appropriate figurehead for the social challenge to the power of the priests. Rather confusingly, however, the emperor was adopted by English Protestants both as a symbol of resistance and as a symbol of repression.

By far the most vociferous party were those who saw Julian as medieval thinkers had done and used the emperor as a stick with which to beat Catholics as Parliament argued whether it was possible to prevent James II, who had converted, from ascending the throne. The loudest clarion call was sounded by Samuel Johnson, rector of Corringham. His

1682 pamphlet *Julian the Apostate: being a short account of his life* is a direct and hugely inflated attack on Rome, as he put it, "a comparison of popery and paganism" in which Julian's apostasy is an allegory for the king who turns his back on the Protestant faith in favor of idolatry. It isn't a subtle tract. The Catholic Church is, among other things, "the Babylonical Beast and Whore," "a devilish drab," "a stinking strumpet" and the "seat of Satan." It was, however, a runaway bestseller, had run to at least three editions by 1689 and was widely translated, appearing in 1688 in French and Dutch.

This triggered a wave of pamphleteering. If Julian could be used against Rome, then other emperors could be recruited in favor of it, and of the many pamphlets that appeared, George Hickes's *Jovian, or an answer to Julian the Apostate,* and John Bennett's *Constantius the Apostate: being a short account of his life and the sense of the primitive Christians about his succession and their behavior toward him,* both of which were published the following year, are the best of the bunch.

This was all grist to Johnson's mill. He published at least two more pamphlets and was imprisoned for libel. Finally James II stripped him of his priesthood and sentenced him to be flogged from Newgate to Tyburn with the words: "Mr Johnson has the spirit of a martyr and it is fit that he should be one." Normality was not restored until William of Orange ascended the throne. Wisely the king paid off "Julian" Johnson, as he had become known, but refused to let him anywhere near a position of power.

Rather more subtly, at the same time, Julian was being reborn as a pagan witness to the truth of Protestantism. Rather than being perceived as an apostate from the Protestant faith, a cabal of thinkers who had been influenced by Montaigne's humanism saw Julian as a philosophical hero opposing the tyranny of the Church. In 1681, a pamphlet entitled *Some Seasonable Remarks on the Deplorable Fall of the Emperor Julian, with an Epistle of His to the Citizens of Bostra* appeared (editions of Julian's writings had been around since 1499). Written under a pseudonym, it portrays Julian as a charitable and intellectual man. The author of *Some seasonable remarks* has plausibly been identified as the philosopher John Locke. He is an appropriate champion of Julian: an establishment figure who had apostatized. But even if he is not the author, it was certainly Locke and his contemporaries who fashioned Julian as the mascot for the Age of Reason, a symbol of toleration.

This image of Julian as a symbol of emancipation reached its apotheosis in the largest, most ambitious, and most successful series of paintings about the emperor, which decorate the King's Staircase at Hampton Court. The Italian painter Antonio Verrio used themes from The Caesars to celebrate William of Orange's victory over the Stuarts. In the painting on the south wall Julian sits at a desk while Hermes dictates to him. "It was from him that I learned what I am going to tell you," explains Julian.[21] Several of the scenes from the satire are shown, notably the one near the beginning when Hercules, backed up by Silenus, forces Zeus to invite Alexander the Great to the dinner asking: "Let's see whether all these Romans can match up to this one Greek."[22] The imagery is not sophisticated. William, whose favorite images were the lion and the lion slayer, is clearly Alexander.

When it was finished in 1702 Verrio's work was not universally popular. Horace Walpole is rather rude about it. The author of *Anecdotes of Painting in England* suggests that it was "as ill as if he had spoiled it out of principle"—but then he didn't much like any of Verrio's work, calling him an artist "without much invention and with less taste." The paintings do have an impressive grandeur. More sympathetic to the artist is Thomas Tickell, one of the earliest contributors to the *Spectator*, who wrote, "Great Verrio's hand hath drawn / The gods in dwelling brighter than the air."[23]

The emperor's appearance center-stage in this political brouhaha at the beginning of the eighteenth century together with the Anglomania among continental intellectuals at the time, had been the breach in the wall of intolerance toward Julian.[24] Despite the often still fatal consequences of anything that smacked of atheism or blasphemy (the last man to be hanged in Britain for denying the Trinity was in 1697, while in Switzerland it was as late as 1782), by the mid-eighteenth century, some people went as far as to consider Julian's a success story. Influenced by the thinking of Locke and his colleagues, it is not that surprising that the French political philosopher Montesquieu was moved to write of Julian that "there has not been a prince since his reign more worthy to govern mankind," even if he did cover his bases with the aside "a commendation thus wrested from me will not render me an accomplice of his apostasy."[25]

But it was the French philosopher Voltaire who rehabilitated Julian as an ideal of toleration, the enlightened sovereign, and it is he who shaped how most Europeans saw Julian. The two make comfortable bedfellows. The emperor would have recognized many of the broader questions that Voltaire raised in *The Philosophical Dictionary* as those he himself had pondered in *Against the Galileans* (certainly their intentions were the same—to discredit the religion by pointing out inconsistencies), while *The Philosophical Dictionary* contains two entries, "Apostate" and "Julian," which are essentially *apologiae* for the emperor.

Following Voltaire's rehabilitation of the emperor's reputation, the English-speaking world went down a similar path. Edward Gibbon, the English language's greatest historian, was hugely influenced by Voltaire (whom he knew). Published only twelve years after *The Philosophical Dictionary*, in his *Decline and Fall of the Roman Empire* Julian's transformation to hero of the Enlightenment was complete and it is through Gibbon's eyes that the English-speaking world has come to understand the emperor.

Gibbon's view of "my friend Julian"[26] is shamelessly partisan. "The last of the sons of Constantine may be dismissed from the world with the remark that he inherited the defects, without the abilities, of his father" gets rid of Constantius, while Julian is the hero of *The Decline and Fall of the Roman Empire*: "Whatever had been his choice of life, by the force of intrepid courage, lively wit, and intense application, he would have obtained, or at least he would have deserved, the highest honors of his profession, and Julian might have raised himself to the rank of minister or general of the state in which he was born a private citizen. If the jealous caprice of power had disappointed his expectations; if he had prudently declined the paths of greatness, the employment of the same talents in studious solitude would have placed beyond the reach of kings his present happiness and his immortal fame."

It would be wrong, however, to infer that everyone was happy with this emancipation of Julian. As late as the mid-nineteenth century there was still a movement in schools to protect children from the evil influences of pagan authors. In France, Abbé Gaume's *The Woodworm of Modern Society* suggested that all pagan authors in the school curriculum be replaced by church fathers.[27] But his was a lone voice. Julian had now entered the popular imagination of Europe.

The nineteenth century became increasingly secular as science progressed (the infamous 1851 religious census in Britain uncovered the fact that just under 40 per cent of the population had attended church that Sunday). Proving Chesterton's maxim correct that when man stops believing in God he doesn't believe in nothing, he believes in anything, aesthetic paganism began to take hold, encouraged by recent bestsellers such as James Frazer's *The Golden Bough*. As a result, a much more sympathetic Julian begins to appear.

It is perhaps surprising that Julian has not attracted the attention of the visual arts. He avoided the gaze of Laurence Alma-Tadema, a painter who simultaneously encapsulates both the best and the worst of the Victorian obsession with the classics. And although he came to the attention of John Ruskin—in a letter to his father in October 1861 continuing their argument about his religious beliefs he writes: "The unbeliever may be taught to believe, but not Julian the Apostate to return"—nothing more came of it.

The sole Victorian painting of Julian came in 1874 in Edward Armitage's *Julian the Apostate Presiding at a Conference of Sectarians*. Now in the Walker Art Gallery in Liverpool, it was finished just after the Leeds-born student of Delaroche had been appointed a Royal Academician. A serene Julian is shown sitting back on a leopardskin-covered chair; he draws the eye, as all around him is chaos. It is a totally compassionate portrait, though artistically not especially satisfying. Even though two of his frescos decorate the House of Lords, Armitage never quite made it to the top rank of Victorian painters.

The most successful of all the nineteenth-century writers to approach the fourth century for inspiration was Algernon Swinburne—indeed, he was one of the first to refer to the emperor as "the last pagan."[28] Even though the emperor is never mentioned by name, two of Swinburne's poems refer to Julian, the "Hymn to Proserpine" from 1866 [cited in my Introduction] and "The Last Oracle" in 1878. His interpretation of the emperor was so influential that it gives the key to the character of Sue

Bridehead, Thomas Hardy's heroine in *Jude the Obscure,* who quotes from the former poem.

Both of Swinburne's poems dramatize the thoughts of a person experiencing the destruction of an entire culture and its beliefs using recognizable images from Julian's life without being tied to historical narrative. Swinburne is concerned with mankind's need for faith, but the new faith of Christianity comes across as barbarism washing the world of color. In "The Last Oracle," the focus is the final oracle of Delphi:

> *Years have risen and fallen in darkness or in twilight,*
> *Ages waxed and waned that knew not thee nor thine,*
> *While the world sought light by night and sought not*
>   *thy light,*
> *Since the sad last pilgrim left thy dark mid shrine.*

These two poems are, however, the highlights. For the rest of the century, the emperor was the victim of numerous novels and poems that played on the popularity of Edward Bulwer-Lytton's *The Last Days of Pompeii,* Henryk Sienkiewicz's *Quo Vadis,* and Lew Wallace's *Ben Hur.*[29]

In Germany, Felix Dahn published *Julian the Apostate* (*Julian der Abtrünnige*). It falls into a specific genre known in Germany as *Professorenromane,* and is full of precise antiquarian detail while being devoid of imagination or literary feeling. It was hugely popular when it appeared in 1893, following as it did the law professor's 1876 bestseller about Alaric the Goth called *A Struggle for Rome* (*Ein Kampf um Rom*).

In Scandinavia, few were satisfied by Ibsen's dire play *Emperor and Galilean* (1873). Quite rightly it has been described as "bad history and bad theater."[30] In fact every attempt to put Julian on the stage has been little short of disastrous—an excess of philosophy and too little sex seem the logical reasons. Richard Sheil's *The Apostate: A Tragedy in Five Acts* and Aubrey de Vere's *Julian, the Apostate* in 1818 and 1822 respectively, are not much better and it is to be lamented that Friedrich Schiller's intentions of writing a play on the subject came to nothing.[31]

Rather better was Viktor Rydberg's 1859 novel *The Last Athenian* (*Den Siste Athenaren*), which is still regarded as a landmark of Swedish literature. Unashamedly pro-pagan, he contrasts Hellenic tolerance with Christian bigotry. For the historian, the novel's interest lies in its portrayal of Chrysanthius of Sardis, Julian's teacher in Pergamum, who personifies the ancient world in the novel, versus Peter, the power-mad bishop of Athens, a runaway slave who tries to cheat his way to the papal throne.

In the English-speaking world, Julian was especially popular among American authors. While Eliza Buckminster Lee's *Parthenia,* which appeared in 1858, dealt solely with Julian's life, others set their stories just after the emperor's reign. Frederic Farrar's tale *Gathering Clouds* (1895) is set thirteen years after Julian's death. The novel's true hero is John Chrysostom, but the spirit of Julian lingers. His reign is a "lurid cloud," while Daphne is a "paradise of heathendom." If Julian himself does not appear, an aged Libanius does, and is presented as the voice of reason in the Antioch Senate.

Similar in theme is *The Lost Word, A Christmas Legend of Long Ago* by the Presbyterian minister Henry van Dyke, whose short stories, many of which originated as sermons for his New York congregation, were popular in the early decades of the twentieth century. Written in 1898 and set in the early 380s it tells the tale of a young disillusioned Antiochene called Hermas, a former playmate of Libanius's—fictional—daughter and the son of rich pagan called Demetrius. A walk-on part is given to "an old man with a long beard and a threadbare cloak" who turns out to be the last priest of Apollo at Daphne. Ruefully he reflects on the sacrifice that caused Julian's scorn. "You mean the goose? Well, per-haps it was not precisely what the emperor expected. But it was all that I had, and it seemed to me not inappropriate," he says. After Demetrius dies, Hermas briefly apostatizes but is redeemed on his deathbed by John Chrysostom.

Special mention needs to go to the thankfully little-known James Athearn Jones, the spiritual brother of William McGonagall. His poem *The Vision of Julian the Apostate,* published in the *Southern Literary Messenger* in November 1851, is gloriously dreadful and includes the immortal stanza:

> *The horsemen of King Sapor*
> *Mind not the summer heat;*
> *As the lion they are mettled,*
> *As the leopard they are fleet;*
> *The men of Rome are valiant*
> *No foe hath seen them run;*
> *But the Roman soldier fainteth*
> *In the hot Assyrian sun.*

One of the first of the new century was John Ayscough's *Faustula* (1912). Rather than feature Julian in person, the book is told from the perspective of the young Vestal Virgin Faustula and is set for the most part in and around Rome from the date of Constans's defeat of his brother to the death of Julian. Political and military events do not greatly impact on the action, but the clash between pagan and Christian societies is framed in the love story between the heroine and a Christian neighbor. The book is written in a very brittle style—the heroine's father is an atheist and an aesthete and would perhaps have been more comfortable in one of Saki's drawing rooms than fourth-century Rome—and Ayscough has considerable sympathy for paganism. "Those who desire excuse for hatred of a religion or of a system can usually find it in the faults of those who belong to it; and Julian's observations were made in the Court of Constantinople where such faults have seldom been conspicuously absent."

These are slight distractions; in the twentieth century Julian's reputation was propped up by the twin bookends of the poetry of Constantine Cavafy and the prose of Gore Vidal. "A gentleman in a straw hat, at a slight angle to the universe," is how E. M. Forster described Cavafy, the Alexandrian-born master of contemporary Greek verse. Little read in his own lifetime—he died in 1933—Cavafy spent most of his working life with the Egyptian Ministry of Public Works, publishing only privately. His reputation did not begin to grow until after the Second World War, when he was championed by such writers as the Greek Nobel laureate George Seferis and Lawrence Durrell.

It is hard to imagine a poet whose tone and style is more appropriate to the theme of Julian. Cavafy wrote seven poems on Julian. "Julian Seeing Contempt," "Julian in Nicomedia," "A Great Procession of

Priests and Laymen," "Julian and the Antiochenes" and "You Didn't Understand" were published between September 1923 and January 1928. "Julian at the Mysteries" from November 1896 and "On the Outskirts of Antioch," written just before he died, remained unpublished at his death.

A dry irony pervades these seven poems. Prefaced by an epigraph from the *The Beard Hater*,[32] "Julian and the Antiochenes" is one of Cavafy's most cynical works and is all the more effective for it. It deals with the collapse of the relationship between the emperor and the city. On the part of the Antiochenes he asks:

> *How could they ever give up*
> *their beautiful way of life, the range*
> *of their daily pleasures, their brilliant theater*
> *which consummated a union between Art*
> *and the erotic proclivities of the flesh?*

While Julian is flayed for

> *His hot air about the false gods,*
> *his boring self-advertisement,*
> *his childish fear of the theater,*
> *his graceless prudery, his ridiculous beard.*

What gives the poem such poignancy is the regretful sense of loss on both sides. Even though Cavafy, through the voice of the speaker, clearly sides with the Antiochenes, he does blur the matter somewhat by reversing the stereotypes to portray Christians as hedonistic sensualists and pagans as dull prudes.

It is understandable that Julian has always remained an underground hero in Greece, but despite the number of artists that he has inspired there, their work has had little impact on the outside world. The Cretan-born writer Nikos Kazantzakis, most famous for *Zorba the Greek* and *The Last Temptation of Christ*, wrote his play *Julian the Apostate* in the latter half of 1939 while living in Stratford-upon-Avon as a guest of the British Council. It has only been staged once, in

Paris in 1948. More recently, at the end of the 1990s, the Greek conceptual artist and sculptor Molfessis created a piece called the *Delphic Cube,* a large concrete box with a telex transcription of Delphi's reply to Julian.

Since the Second World War, there have been several major novels written about the emperor. By far the best known—and rightly the most successful—is Gore Vidal's *Julian* (1964). Presented in the form of a diary dictated by Julian during the Persian campaign with harmonies provided by comments from Priscus and Libanius in the form of letters to each other, in style it owes something to Thornton Wilder's novel about the end of the Roman Republic, *Ides of March.* It is a racy and entertaining account, the more so because Vidal's stance is unashamedly and provocatively pro-Julian. Nonetheless, its strength lies in Vidal's understanding of the conflicts within Julian's character. "At heart he was a Christian mystic gone wrong" is how he sums up the emperor.

But there have also been four others. By far the most entertaining is Somerset de Chair's *Bring Back the Gods* (1962). This is a *Boy's Own* adventure that owes something at least to G. H. Henty. Appropriately for someone who was an intelligence officer during the Second World War and later a Member of Parliament, de Chair describes Julian as "a sort of pagan Field Marshal Montgomery. No self-indulgences; and 100% fit," with all of the flaws of a great military commander. Louis de Wohl's *Imperial Renegade* (1950) is less successful. Best known for his series of saints' lives, de Wohl wrote the novel to combat growing disenchantment with the Vatican and it reads that way too. Then there is *Julian the Apostate* (*Haikyosha Yurianusu*), published by the Tokyo-born novelist Kunio Tsuji in 1972, which won the Mainichi Award for Art. Highly regarded in Japan, it is untranslated in English. Finally, there is Michael Curtis Ford's *Gods and Legions* (2002). Julian's story is told from the perspective of Gregory of Nazianzus's brother Caesarius, from 354 to the emperor's death. Ford's Julian is, at least at first, altogether more human than Vidal's, and his account of Julian's time in Gaul is especially vivid.

Apart from these odd flashes of light, for the most part Julian has almost slipped away from the arts and remains in the grip of historians. Unlike his uncle, he has not been embraced by Hollywood.[33] Since Cavafy, he has not been the subject of poetry either (the exception is "Julian the Apostate" in his 1957 collection *The Sense of Movement,* by the British-born poet Thom Gunn—but the poem is opaque to the point of incomprehensibility).

In modern fictional versions the story and myths of Julian have come full circle. Just as he was for Hrotsvitha, the emperor is an inspiration or a metaphor, but his actions all take place off stage. Gillian Bradshaw's *The Beacon at Alexandria* (1987) is set on the eve of the battle of Adrianople, eight years after Julian's death. Fleeing, dressed as a eunuch, from an arranged marriage in Ephesus, the lead character Charis, who wants to be a doctor, witnesses the execution of Maximus and ends up as physician to Athanasius. Then there is John M. Ford's fantasy novel *The Dragon Waiting* (1983). It is set in a fifteenth century in which Byzantium did not fall and in which Julian's religious reforms were successful. Brian Stableford's intriguing short story *The Mandrake Garden* takes Julian's letter to Callixeine as his inspiration in his support for paganism;[34] while in *From Hell,* Alan Moore's graphic novel about Jack the Ripper, the spirit of Julian is evoked as having inspired architects like Nicholas Hawksmoor.

It would be easy to imagine Julian as one of the soldier academics of the last two world wars. It is the direction in which Edward Gibbon, in his famous portrait of the man, pushes us and it would be easy to romanticize the emperor as a Patrick Leigh Fermor figure, or even more appositely, a John Pendlebury type. We should not fall into that trap. British army fatigues would have sat badly on Julian. If we are looking for a modern parallel it is almost easiest to see him as a Che Guevara figure. Not naturally a soldier, yet forced into that role; then a rebel and finally an undoubtedly charismatic leader for a system of beliefs whose resurrection we can now see as having been doomed to failure.

These renderings all force modern interpretations onto the classical mind. Looking back, only one classical writer appears to have had any sense of balance about Julian, and his approach remains one of the best. Prudentius was only fifteen when the emperor died (and writing a good forty years later), but he describes Julian almost fondly.

> *Of all the emperors, one there was*
> *Whom I recall from boyhood—bold in war,*
> *A lawgiver, far-famed in word and deed;*
> *He cared much for his country, but cared not*
> *For the true faith, and loved a host of gods,*
> *False to the Lord, although true to the world.*[35]

Prudentius gets us close to the emperor, but doesn't get us close to Julian. He fails both him and us. The best way to see Julian is to go to the ground floor of the Louvre, beyond the flashing bulbs that surround the Venus de Milo and past the vigilant *Victory of Samothrace* to the comparative calm of the late Roman section and look at the statue of Julian there. It stands both aloof and somehow lonely, looking over the room. Almost life-sized, Julian is dressed in the garb of a philosopher. The beard and the stance are those of a pagan thinker while the simple crown and the penetrating gaze do not let you forget that you are looking at a Constantinian emperor.

But these are merely the accoutrements of power, status, and image. Look instead at the face. The features are those of a real person. The shock of the image is on a par with looking at a painting such as Caravaggio's *Jesus at Emmaus*. It is the humanity above all that is portrayed. If we look at statues of Julian's contemporaries like Constantine and Constantius, or later representations of emperors such as the mosaics of Theodosius in Ravenna, we perceive a deliberate distance. We are there to worship, honor, or fear. This is different. This statue is not that of the emperor as a defender of the faith, a ruler of all things temporal and spiritual. It is a statue of a ruler as man.

NOTES

INTRODUCTION

1. Libanius, *Selected Works,* vol. 1, translated by A. F. Norman (Cambridge: Harvard Press, 1969), Oration 17.2.
2. Gregory of Nazianzus, *Julian the Emperor containing Gregory Nazianzen's Two Invectives and Libanius's Monody with Julian's Extant Theosophical Works,* translated by C. W. King (London: Bohn's Classical Library, 1888), Oration 4.1.
3. Ibid., Or. 5.13.
4. Socrates Scholasticus, *Church History,* 3.21, in *Nicene and Post-Nicene Fathers,* edited by Henry Wace and Philip Schaff, series 2, vol. 2 (Oxford: Parker & Co., 1900).
5. Notker the Stammerer, *Two Lives of Charlemagne,* translated by Lewis Thorpe (Harmondsworth: Penguin Books, 1969), 2.1.
6. Robert Liddell, *Cavafy: A Biography* (London: Gerald Duckworth & Co., 1974), 197.

CHAPTER ONE

1. Julian, *In Honor of the Emperor Constantius,* 37B. All translations of Julian's writings are based on the three volumes of the emperor's works in the Loeb Classical Library, translated by Wilmer Cave Wright (Cambridge, 1913–23) and I have followed her numbering of letters throughout.
2. Lactantius, *On the Deaths of the Persecutors,* 44, in *Anti-Nicene Fathers,* edited by Alexander Roberts and James Donaldson, vol. 7 (Edinburgh: WMB Eerdman's Publishing Co., 1989).
3. Eusebius, *Life of the Blessed Constantine,* 1.28–29, in *Nicene and Post-Nicene Fathers,* Wace and Schaff, series 2, vol. 1.

4. Zosimus, *Historia Nova*, 2.29.2. Translations are based on F. Paschoud's *Zosime: Histoire Nouvelle*, vols. 1 and 2 (Paris: Budé, 1971). For a considered overview of the career of the much-neglected Crispus, see Hans Pohlsander, "Crispus: Brilliant Career and Tragic End," *Historia* 33 (1984): 79–106; and for an analysis of Fausta see Jan Willem Drijvers, "Flavia Maxima Fausta: Some Remarks," *Historia* 41 (1992): 500–506.

5. Julian, *The Caesars*, 336A–B.

6. There is debate about Julian's date of birth. The traditional year given is 331, but see Frank Gillard, "The Birth Date of Julian the Apostate," *California Studies in Classical Antiquity* 4 (1971): 147–51 for a full discussion and a convincing case for 332. Following Gillard's argument for a date of birth of between the last week of April and the first three weeks of May, with my dating of the birthday games before Ctesiphon, I have suggested a date of the middle of May.

7. Julian, Ep. 25.

8. Julian, *Letter to the Athenians*, 270C.

9. Julian, *Panegyric in Honor of Constantius*, 9A.

10. Hilary of Poitiers, *Patrologia Latina* 10, edited by J. P. Migne (Paris: Migne, 1845), in *Constantium*, 11.

11. Julian, Ep. 13.

12. Athanasius, *History of the Arians*, 69, in *Nicene and Post-Nicene Fathers*, Wace and Schaff, series 2, vol. 4.

13. Julian, *Misopogon*, 352A–C.

14. Ibid., 351C–D.

15. Anne Hadjinicolaou discusses the most probable location of the palace in "Macellum, lieu d'exil de l'empereur Julien," *Byzantion* 21 (1951): 15–22.

16. Julian, *Letter to the Athenians*, 271C–D.

17. Ibid., 271B.

18. Ibid.

19. Julian, Ep. 23.

20. Ibid., 38.

21. Gregory of Nazianzus, Or. 4.30.

22. Ibid., Or. 4.25–27, gives one construction but no name; Sozomen, *Church History*, 5.2, in *Nicene and Post-Nicene Fathers*, Wace and Schaff, series 2, vol. 2, gives the church of St. Mamas; Theodoret, *Church History*, 3.1, in *Nicene and Post-Nicene Fathers*, Wace and Schaff, series 2, vol. 3, tells the story as two chapels.

23. Socrates Scholasticus, 3.13.

24. Timothy Barnes, "Himerius and the Fourth Century," *Classical Philology* 82 (1987): 206–25; Themistius, Or. 5.67D.

25. Julian, Ep. 2.
26. Despite the charge of pederasty, the exact nature of the disagreements is confused and it appears to have been professional. Libanius, Or. 1.44–47 and Eunapius, *Lives of the Sophists*, 495. Philostratus and Eunapius, *The Lives of the Sophists*, translated by Wilmer Cave Wright (Cambridge: Harvard University Press, 1921).
27. Libanius, Or. 18.12.
28. On Magnentius's background Julian, Or. 1.34A; Or. 2.95C; and Zosimus 2.54.1.
29. Themistius, Or. 2.36.
30. Zosimus 2.47.3; Aurelius Victor, *De Caesaribus*, translated by H. W. Bird (Liverpool: Liverpool University Press, 1994), 41; *Artemii Passio* 10 in *From Constantine to Julian: Pagan and Byzantine Views*, edited by Samuel Lieu and Domenic Monserrat (London: Routledge, 1996).
31. Zosimus 2.42.5 preserves Constans's place of death as Helena, on the Gallic side of the Pyrenees.
32. Himerius, Frag. 1.6, cited in Barnes, "Himerius and the Fourth Century," 206–25.
33. Ammianus, *The Later Roman Empire (AD 354–378)*, translated by Walter Hamilton (London: Penguin, 1986), 14.1.2.
34. Julian, Ep. 47.
35. Julian, *Hymn to King Helios*, 130C–131A.
36. John 7:52.
37. Julian, Ep. 2.
38. See J. Vanderspoel, "Correspondence and Correspondents of Julius Julianus," *Byzantion* 69 (1999): 396–478.
39. Eunapius, *Lives of the Philosophers*, 474.
40. Ibid.
41. Ibid., 475.
42. Gregory of Nazianzus, Or. 4.44.
43. Julian, *To the Cynic Heracleios*, 235B.
44. See for example the letter Libanius wrote to Maximus after Julian had become emperor (Libanius, Epistle 694), where he calls the philosopher Phoenix to Julian's Achilles. Libanius, *Autobiography and Selected Letters*, vols. 1 and 2. For consistency's sake I have followed the numbering of Foerster for the letters, as Loeb prints only a small percentage of Libanius's output. A concordance is in vol. 2, pp. 465–74.
45. Libanius, Or. 18.19.
46. Julian, *Letter to the Athenians*, 271D.
47. Philostorgius, *Ecclesiastical History*, 3.28, in Sozomen and Philostorgius,

History of the Church, translated by Edward Walford (London: H. G. Bohn, 1855).

48. The assassination attempt is traditionally taken to have been instigated by Magnentius, but see Robert Frakes, "Ammianus Marcellinus and Zonaras on a Late Roman Assassination Plot," *Historia* 46 (1997): 121–28.

49. Ammianus, 14.11.6–9; Socrates Scholasticus, 2.34; Philostorgius 4.1.

50. *The Artemii Passio,* 14, names the spot, "a lodging post in Bithynia called Gallicanus."

51. Julian, *Letter to the Athenians,* 272A.

52. Libanius, Ep. 19.

53. For an illustration and other images of Julian throughout his life see Andrew Alföldi, "Some Portraits of Julianus Apostata," *American Journal of Archaeology* 66 (1962): 403–5.

54. Gregory of Nazianzus, Or. 5.23.

55. Julian, *Letter to the Athenians,* 273A.

56. Anatole France, "The Emperor Julian," in *On Life and Letters,* vol. 4, translated by Bernard Miall (London: Bodley Head, 1924), 238–51.

57. Zosimus, 3.1.2–3.

58. Julian, *Panegyric in Honor of Eusebia,* 118C.

59. Ibid., 119A.

60. Horace, *Satires, Epistles and Ars Poetica,* translated by H. Rushton Fairclough (Cambridge: Loeb Classical Library, 1926), Ep. 2.2.45.

61. Libanius, Or. 18.31.

62. Julian, *Hymn to the Mother of the Gods,* 173C–D.

63. Julian, *Letter to the Athenians,* 274D–275B.

64. Ibid., 275D–276B.

65. Julian, *Panegyric in Honor of Eusebia,* 122A.

66. Julian, *Letter to the Athenians,* 274C–D.

CHAPTER TWO

1. Ammianus, 15.8.22.

2. Julian, *Panegyric in Honor of Constantius,* 48C.

3. Ammianus, 15.8.17. The line is from *The Iliad* 5.83. Julian was punning, as the word *porfureov* refers both to the color of blood and the color worn by the emperor.

4. Julian, *Panegyric in Honor of Eusebia,* 123D–124B.

5. Julian, *Letter to the Athenians,* 284C.

6. Julian, Ep. 29.

7. Vasari, *Lives of the Artists,* vol. 1 (Harmondsworth: Penguin Books, 1965), 34.

8. Ammianus, 16.10.18–19. The obvious question is that if the story was nonsense,

why did Ammianus mention it at all? As Shaun Tougher has pointed out in "Ammianus Marcellinus on the Empress Eusebia: A Split Personality," *Greece and Rome* 47 (2000): 94–101, it says considerably more about Ammianus than about Eusebia.

9. Libanius, Or. 18.40.

10. Horace, *Odes and Epodes,* translated by C. E. Bennett (Cambridge: Harvard University Press, 1914), Odes 2.20.

11. Libanius, Or. 18.42.

12. Ammianus, 16.5.3.

13. Julian, *Letter to the Athenians,* 277D.

14. Claudian, *Sexto Consulatu Honorii Augustii,* vol. 2, translated by Maurice Platnauer (Cambridge: Harvard University Press, 1922), 625–30.

15. Vegetius, *Epitome of Military Science,* translated by N. P. Milner (Liverpool: Liverpool University Press, 1996), 2.23.

16. Julian, Ep. 1.

17. Julian, *Panegyric in Honor of Eusebia,* 124B.

18. Julian, Or. 8.241C.

19. Julian, Ep. 4.

20. Julian, Or. 8.241C.

21. Sozomen, 5.2; Libanius, Or. 18.44–45.

22. Ammianus, 16.2.11.

23. Vegetius, *Epitome of Military Science,* 3.20.

24. Ammianus, 16.2.12.

25. Tacitus, *On Britain and Germany,* translated by H. Mattingly (Harmondsworth: Penguin Books, 1948), *Germania,* 16.

26. Libanius, Or. 18.48.

27. Julian, *Letter to the Athenians,* 278B.

28. Ammianus, 16.7.2.

29. Julian, *Letter to the Athenians,* 279A–B.

30. Ammianus, 18.3.6, "subagrestis arrogantisque."

31. Ammianus, 16.11.12.

CHAPTER THREE

1. Vegetius, *Epitome of Military Science,* 3.12.

2. Ammianus, 16.12.25.

3. Vegetius, *Epitome of Military Science,* 3.25.

4. Ammianus, 16.12.39.

5. Ibid., 16.12.51.

6. Ibid., 16.12.61.

7. Zosimus, 3.3.5.

8. Ammianus, 17.1.2.

9. Ibid., 17.1.8.

10. Pomponius Mela, *Chorographie,* translated by A. Silberman (Paris: Les Belles Lettres, 1988), *De Chorographia,* 3.24.

11. Julius Caesar, *The Conquest of Gaul,* translated by S. A. Handforth (Harmondsworth: Penguin Classics, 1951), 1.2.

12. Julian, Shorter Fragments, 2.

13. Ammianus, 17.1.11.

14. Julian, *Misopogon,* 340D.

15. Ibid., 340D–341B.

16. Julian, *Letter to the Athenians,* 279C–D.

17. Libanius, Ep. 370.

18. Julian, Ep. 4.

19. Zosimus, 3.5.2.

20. Julian, *Letter to the Athenians,* 279D.

21. Ibid., 280A–C.

22. Ibid.

23. Ammianus, 17.9.3: "Graeculum et fallacem et specie sapientiae stolidum."

24. Julian, *Letter to the Athenians,* 280C–D.

25. Ammianus 21.6.4 does not give a reason but Philostorgius 4.6 mentions "disease of the womb." The theory about anorexia is aired by Noel Aujoulat, "Eusébie, Hélène et Julien: Le Témoignage des historiens," *Historia* 53 (1983): 439–45.

26. Julian, *Heroic Deeds of Constantius,* 53A–B.

27. Ammianus, 18.1.4.

28. Julian, Ep. 1 and Ep. 2.

CHAPTER FOUR

1. Julian, *Letter to the Athenians,* 284A–285C.

2. Ibid., 282D.

3. Ammianus, 20.4.4, "ne ducerentur ad partes umquam transalpinas."

4. Ibid., 20.4.5.

5. Libanius, Or. 18.95.

6. Ammianus, 20.4.10; Zosimus, 3.9.1.

7. Ammianus, 20.4.13.

8. Eunapius, Fragment 21.3, in R. C. Blockley, *The Fragmentary Classicising Historians of the Later Roman Empire* (Liverpool: F. Cairns, 1983).

9. Julian, Ep. 4.

10. Ammianus, 20.9.2.

11. Ioannes Zonaras, *Corpus Scriptorum Historiae Byzantinae* 42/2, edited by Theodor Büttner-Wobst (Bonn: Weber, 1897), 13.10.

12. See K. S. Painter, "The Mildenhall Treasure: A Reconsideration," *British Museum Quarterly* 37 (1973): 154–80.

13. This is the last date it is possible to give in 361, up until Julian's entry into Constantinople on December 11, with absolute confidence. While it is possible to trace Julian's movements with a fair degree of accuracy, the same cannot be said of the chronology and depends to what extent you believe Ammianus's account. I have followed the arguments of C. E. V. Nixon, "Aurelius Victor and Julian," *Classical Philology* 86 (1991): 113–25.

14. Julian, Ep. 8.

15. Julian, *Misopogon,* 360C.

16. Ammianus, 21.2.2.

17. Ibid., 21.5.12.

18. Ibid., 21.9.6; Libanius, Or. 18.111; Mamertinus, *Speech of Thanks to Julian,* 6.2, in *The Emperor Julian: Panegyric and Polemic,* edited by Samuel Lieu (Liverpool: Liverpool University Press, 1986).

19. No one gives the number, but from the fourth-century longboats found at Mainz, thirty-two feet long and thirteen feet wide, we can guess that they carried around 100 men each. See O. Höckmann, "Late Roman Rhine Vessels from Mainz, Germany," *International Journal of Nautical Archaeology* 22, no. 2 (1993): 125–36.

20. Mamertinus, *Speech of Thanks to Julian,* 7.2.

21. Zosimus 3.10.3 says eleven days.

22. Libanius, Or. 12.63.

23. Ammianus, 21.9.8.

24. Ibid., 21.10.1.

25. Julian, *The Heroic Deeds of Constantius,* 71D.

26. Ibid., 274A and 282C.

27. Ammianus, 21.10.7.

28. Julian, Ep. 8.

CHAPTER FIVE

1. Ammianus, 22.2.5.

2. Vatican Greek MS 1162, fol. 2b.

3. Julian, Ep. 13.

4. Libanius, Or. 18.153.

5. Ibid., Or. 18.152; Ammianus, 14.5.6.

6. Jerome, *Select Letters,* translated by F. A. Wright (Cambridge: Harvard University Press, 1933), Ep. 1.

7. Ammianus, 20.11.5.

8. Ibid., 22.4.9.

9. Ibid., 16.10.10.
10. Libanius, Or. 18.129.
11. Ammianus, 22.4.6.
12. Socrates Scholasticus, 3.1.
13. Ibid.
14. Julian, Ep. 8.
15. Ibid., Ep. 43.
16. Ibid., Ep. 52.
17. Ibid., Ep. 15.
18. Sozomen, 5.4.
19. Julian, Ep. 26.
20. Ibid., Ep. 14.
21. Libanius, Or. 16.14.
22. Julian, *The Heroic Deeds of the Emperor Constantius,* 2.91C.
23. Julian, *Letter to Themistius,* 262A–C.
24. Ibid., 261D; see also *Panegyric in Honor of Constantius,* 45D and 48A.
25. Libanius, Or. 18.184.
26. Socrates Scholasticus, 3.1.
27. *The Theodosian Code and Novels and the Sirmondian Constitutions,* translated by Clyde Pharr (Princeton: Princeton University Press, 1952), Theodosian Code, 9.2.1.
28. Theodosian Code, 11.23.2.
29. Ibid., 12.1.50.
30. Julian, Ep. 39.
31. Theodosian Code, 10.3.1.
32. Ibid., 12.13.1; and Libanius, Or. 18.193.
33. Julian, *Misopogon,* 367D.
34. Ibid., 368A.
35. Ibid., 365B.
36. Theodosian Code, 8.5.12–16.
37. Libanius, Or. 18.143.
38. Theodosian Code, 8.5.16.
39. Ibid., 8.1.6.
40. Ibid., 2.29.1. For an explanation see T. E. Barnes, "A Law of Julian," *Classical Philology* 69 (1974): 288–91.
41. Ibid., 11.16.10.
42. Julian, Ep. 27.
43. Libanius, Or. 12.76–77 and Or. 17.19.
44. *Greek Anthology,* translated by W. R. Paton (Cambridge: Loeb Classic Library, 1916–18), 9.689.

45. Julian, Ep. 30.

46. Ibid., Ep. 29.

47. It is now in the Nationalbibliothek in Vienna. O. A. W. Dilke, *Greek and Roman Maps* (London: Thames & Hudson, 1985), chapter 7.

48. Libanius, Ep. 35. See also Ammianus, 22.9.4.

49. Ammianus, 17.7.2–5.

50. Julian, Ep. 42.

51. Catullus, *The Complete Poems,* translated by Guy Lee (Oxford: Oxford University Press, 1990), 63.

52. Julian, *Hymn to the Mother of the Gods,* 159C.

53. Ibid., 159D–161A.

54. For details see P. Wilson, ed., *Cataractonium: A Roman Town and its Hinterland* (York: York Publishing Services, 2002).

55. Lucian, vol. 4, translated by A. M. Harmon (Cambridge: Loeb Classic Library, 1925), *De dea Syria,* 50–51.

56. Julian, Ep. 22.

57. Ammianus, 22.9.14.

CHAPTER SIX

1. There is debate about the precise dating of the Adonea and Julian's entry into the city. See J. den Boeft, J. W. Drijvers, D. den Hengst, and H. C. Teitler, *Philological and Historical Commentary on Ammianus Marcellinus XXII* (Groningen: Egbert Forsten, 1995), 177–80. Given that there is no conclusion about the precise dating, other than it had to be before July 28, I have kept the traditional date.

2. Although the cult was localized around Byblus down the coast, now Jbail, north of Beirut in Lebanon, it was so popular throughout the Levant that the Biblical prophet Ezekiel damned the rites as "abominations"; Ezekiel 8:14–15.

3. Libanius, Or. 11.207, in *Antioch as a Center of Hellenic Culture as Observed by Libanius,* translated by A. F. Norman (Liverpool: Liverpool University Press, 2000), 3–65.

4. Libanius, Ep. 736.

5. Ibid., Or. 15.51.

6. Julian, Fragments 12.

7. Julian, *Misopogon,* 347A.

8. Ibid., 348B.

9. Julian, Ep. 29.

10. Julian, *Misopogon,* 361D–362B.

11. Ibid., 362D–363C.

12. Theodoret, 3.6; John Chrysostom, *On the Holy Martyr, St. Babylas,* 2.

13. Psalm 97: 7.

14. Ibid., 115: 4–8.

15. Ibid., 68: 1–2.

16. Theodoret, 3.7; Socrates Scholasticus, 3.19.

17. Several months later Libanius penned a memo to Heliodorus commenting on further problems for Vitalius, Ep. 1,376.

18. Theodoret, 3.8.

19. The most succinct and earthy version of the story is from an anonymous English fifteenth-century writer: "On the commandment of the emperor, he took this hallowed vessel and pissed in it and said: 'This vessel in which the Son of Mary was sacrificed, now I piss in it.' And with that suddenly his mouth was turned into his arse and ever after as long as he lived, all the filth and digestion of his body came out at his mouth and not his buttocks." Etienne de Besançon, *Alphabetum narrationum*, 696. *Alphabet of Tales: An English 15th Century Translation of the Alphabetum Narrationum of Etienne de Besançon, from additional MS. Add. 25719 of the British Museum,* edited by Mary Macleod Banks (London: Kegan Paul, 1905).

20. Ammianus, 22.13.3.

CHAPTER SEVEN

1. Julian, *Misopogon,* 368C. *"Panta gemei, panta pollou."*

2. Theodosian Code, 2.24.1.

3. Julian, *Misopogon,* 368C–370A.

4. Libanius, Or. 16.24.

5. Julian, *Misopogon,* 350C.

6. Libanius, Or. 16.15.

7. Continued by Constantius, Theodosian Code, 16.10.1–6.

8. John Wilkinson, *Egeria's Travels* (London: SPCK Publishing, 1971), Egeria, *Travels,* 20.8.

9. Augustine, Ep. 16 and Ep. 17, in *Nicene and Post-Nicene Fathers,* Wace and Schaff, series 1, vol. 1.

10. Ibid., Ep. 91.

11. Julian, Ep. 41.

12. Julian, *Against the Cynic Heracleios,* 229C–D.

13. Julian, *Against the Galileans,* 39A.

14. Ibid., 152A.

15. Jerome, Ep. 70.

16. Libanius, Or. 18.126.

17. Libanius, Ep. 1364.

18. Zosimus, 2.31.2. A temple to Castor and Pollux, one to Apollo, one to Rhea, and one to Fortuna.

19. Sozomen, 5.4; Socrates Scholasticus, 3.12. Gratiae Ludentes, or Jestes from the University 16. An edition has been published by the Department of English at the Memorial University of Newfoundland, www.mun.ca/alciato/jests/jest1.html.

20. Julian, Ep. 15.

21. Ammianus, 22.5.

22. Julian, Ep. 40.

23. Ibid., Ep. 41.

24. Ibid., Ep. 37.

25. Ibid., Ep. 17.

26. Gregory, Or. 4.87; Sozomen, 5.10; Theodoret, 3.3.

27. Theodoret, 3.3; Sozomen, 5.10–11; Socrates Scholasticus, 3.15; Gregory of Nazianzus, Or. 4.88–9.

28. Ammianus, 22.11.3.

29. Libanius, Ep. 964.

30. Julian, Ep. 17.

31. Ibid., Ep. 21.

32. Ibid., Ep. 37.

33. Theodosian Code, 13.3.5.

34. Libanius, Or. 18.161.

35. Julian, *Against the Galileans,* 229D–E.

36. Julian, Ep. 36.

37. Gregory of Nazianzus, Or. 4.101.

38. Ammianus, 22.10.7.

39. Theodoret, 3.4, citing Aristophanes, *Birds* 808, who in turn was citing Aeschylus, *Myrmidons,* frag. 139. Julian himself uses the same quotation writing about the Christians; Julian, Shorter Fragments, 7.

40. Julian, Ep. 56.

41. Philostorgius, 7.4.

42. Sir John Mandeville, *Travels,* translated by C. W. R. D. Moseley (Harmondsworth: Penguin Books, 1983), 12.

43. Geertgen tot Sint Jans' *Legend of the Relics of St. John the Baptist* is in the Kunsthistorisches Museum in Vienna and the Master of the St. John's Retable's *Emperor Julian the Apostate Burning the Bones of St. John the Baptist* is now in the Caylus Anticuario in Madrid.

44. Julian, Ep. 22.

45. Ibid., Ep. 20.

46. Julian, *Letter to a Priest,* 290D.

47. Julian, Ep. 22.

48. Ibid.

49. Ibid., Ep. 18.

50. Ibid., Ep. 51.
51. Mark 13:2.
52. Julian, *Against the Galileans,* 176AB; 218B–C.
53. Julian, Ep. 47.
54. See Michael Avi-Yonah, "Greek Inscriptions from Ascalon, Jerusalem, Beisan and Hebron," *Quarterly Review of the Department of Antiquities in Palestine* 10 (1944): 160–69; and Avraham Negev, "An Inscription of the Emperor Julian at Ma'ayan Barukh," *Israel Exploration Journal* 19 (1969): 170–73.
55. Theodoret 3.15; Deuteronomy 27:5; and 1 Kings 6:7.
56. Julian, Shorter Fragments, 11.
57. The exact date is a matter of some debate. For an overview see G. W. Bowersock, *Julian the Apostate* (London: Gerald Duckworth & Co., 1978), appendix 1.
58. John Chrysostom, *Patrologia Graeca,* 48, edited by J. P. Migne (Paris: Migne, 1862); *Adversus Judeaus,* 5.11.10.
59. Julian, *To the Uneducated Cynics,* 203B.
60. Ibid., 184C.
61. Libanius, Or. 12.69.
62. Ibid., Or. 15.75.
63. Ibid., Or. 15.19.
64. Ibid., Or. 19.48.
65. Ammianus, 22.14.3; Gregory of Nazianzus, Or. 4.77.
66. Ammianus, 25.4.17.
67. Julian, *Misopogon,* 370B–C.

CHAPTER EIGHT

1. Ammianus, 19.1.3.
2. Percy Sykes, *A History of Persia,* vol. 1 (London: Macmillan & Co., 1930), 447.
3. Al-Tabari, 290. The most accessible translation of al-Tabari is in *The Roman Eastern Frontier and the Persian Wars (AD 226–363), A Documentary History,* edited by Michael Dodgeon and Samuel Lieu (London: Routledge, 1991), 275–95.
4. See B. de Cardi, "A Sasanian Outpost in Northern Oman," *Antiquity* 46 (1972): 305–10 and report in the Dubai-based *Gulf News,* October 4, 2001.
5. Herodian, *History,* translated by C. R. Whittaker (London: Loeb Classical Library, 1970), 4.10.
6. Zosimus, 2.27.1–4.
7. Eusebius, *Life of Constantine,* 4.13.
8. Ibid., 4.56 and 4.62.
9. There has been some debate about whether the first siege of Nisibis took place

in 337 or 338. See R. W. Burgess, "The Date of the First Siege of Nisibis and the Death of James of Nisibis," *Byzantion* 69 (1999): 7–17.

10. The chronology of Armenian history at this time is confused; indeed it is impossible to say for certain whether the Arsak is the second or the third to hold the name. See R. H. Hewson, "The Successors of Tiradates the Great: A Contribution to the History of Armenia in the Fourth Century," *Revue des études arméniennes* 13 (1979): 99–126.

11. Ammianus, 20.11.32; Libanius, Or. 18.206.

12. Ammianus, 19.8.2–4.

13. Ibid., 21.13.8.

14. Libanius, Or. 18.211.

15. Theodoret, 3.16.

16. Cedrenus, 532. *The Last Oracle,* translated by Algernon Swinburne, cited in *Julian,* vol. 3, translated by Wilmer Cave Wright (Cambridge: Harvard University Press, 1923), lvii.

17. Julian, *Against the Galileans,* 198C.

18. Julian, *Letter to Themistius,* 257A and 264D. See also *Panegyric in Honor of Constantius,* 1.46A.

19. John Lydus, *De magistratibus populi Romani,* translated by Anastasius Bandy (Philadelphia: American Philosophical Society, 1983), 3.33–34 preserves accounts of these books.

20. Constantine, *To the Assembly of Saints,* in Wace and Schaff, *Nicene and Post-Nicene Fathers,* series 2, vol. 1, 16.

21. Socrates Scholasticus, 3.21.

22. Theodosian Code, 11.1.1.

23. Athanasius, *History of the Arians,* 69.

24. Sozomen, 6.2.

25. Julian, Ep. 57.

26 Libanius, Or. 18.282.

27. Socrates Scholasticus, 3.19.

CHAPTER NINE

1. Libanius, Or. 15.9.

2. See Libanius, Ep. 811 to Julian, trying to put a positive spin on events, then Libanius, Ep. 838, Ep. 1351 and Ep. 1411.

3. Julian, Ep. 58.

4. Libanius, Ep. 802.

5. Recent discoveries of a Byzantine coin excavated from a tomb in Qinghai province in northwestern China and dating from the reign of Theodosius II in the early fifth century—the second such discovery in recent years—together with

numerous silver Sassanid coins, indicate the closeness of such a route. Reported in Xinhua News Agency, July 3, 2002. For the connection with China, specifically the writings of Hou-han-shu and his comments on Antioch, see F. Hirth, *China and the Roman Orient: Researches into their Ancient and Medieval Relations as Represented in Old Chinese Records* (Shanghai and Hong Kong: Kelly & Walsh, 1885).

6. Julian, Ep. 58.
7. Ibid.
8. Zosimus, 3.13.1.
9. Lucian, *De dea Syria,* 10.
10. Julian, Ep. 58.
11. Libanius, Ep. 1,402.
12. Egeria, *Travels,* 18.1.2–3.
13. Plutarch, *Lives,* vol. 3, translated by Bernadotte Perrin (Cambridge: Harvard University Press, 1916); *Crassus* 33.
14. Magnus gives 16,000; Zosimus 18,000; Libanius 20,000 and Ammianus 30,000. This author tends toward a lower figure. If Procopius and Sebastian's force was intended initially as a diversion and then to join with Arsak, it seems unlikely that the higher figures are plausible.
15. Moses Khorenats'i, *History of the Armenians,* translated by Robert Thomson (Cambridge: Harvard University Press, 1978), 3.15; Libanius, Or. 18.260.
16. Nothing remains of Samosata, the city that was of such crucial strategic importance. In the early 1990s, the modern town of Samsat was one of the first victims of the lake that rose behind the Ataturk Dam—the price for progress in what had been the least developed region of Turkey. All 4,600 inhabitants were evacuated and resettled a couple of miles away.
17. Procopius, *The Secret History,* translated by G. A. Williamson (Harmondsworth: Penguin Books, 1966), 3.30.
18. Ammianus, 23.5.5.
19. Ibid., 23.5.8.
20. There is a useful table that gives the names of all towns and the variations in spellings in R. T. Ridley, "Three Notes on Julian's Persian Expedition," *Historia* 22 (1973): 327–29.
21. It does not survive. John Lydus, *De magistratibus populi Romani,* 1.47.
22. Michel de Montaigne, *Complete Essays,* translated by M. A. Screech (Harmondsworth: Penguin Books, 1993), 1.16.
23. Ammianus, 24.4.28.
24. Julian, Or. 1.26A; cf. Or. 1.13A.
25. *The Times,* June 27, 1917, pp. 7, 8, and 10.
26. Libanius, Or. 18.242.

27. Milton, *Paradise Lost*, BR 4, l.211.

28. Ammianus, 24.6.8.

29. Libanius, Or. 18.251.

30. The number of Persian casualties in both accounts is the same, but the Romans suffered 75 losses according to Zosimus 3.25.7 and only 70 according to Ammianus 24.6.15.

31. Gregory of Nazianzus, Or. 5.10.

32. Libanius, Or. 18.247.

33. Ammianus, 24.8.3.

34. Hassan Yahya, Khalid Khalel, Nasir Al-Allawi and Ferial Helmi, "Thalassaemia Genes in Baghdad, Iraq," *Eastern Mediterranean Health Journal* 2.2 (1996), 315–19.

35. It has been convincingly argued that the story of the spies seen in Ammianus 24.7.5, Magnus, Fr. 9–10, and Gregory of Nazianzus 5.11 is nonsense. Julian not only had read widely, he also had Hormisdas with him, so had little use for guides of any kind. See R. T. Ridley, "Three Notes on Julian's Persian Expedition," *Historia* 22 (1973): 322 and Johannes Geffcken, *Kaiser Julianus* (Leipzig: Teubner, 1914), 168.

36. Libanius, Or. 18.262.

37. Ammianus 25.1.4 calls the town Hucumbra; Zosimus 3.27.2 calls it Symbra.

38. Ibid., 25.1.4.

39. Zosimus 3.28.2 calls it Maronsa.

40. Plutarch, *Lives*, vol. 9, translated by Bernadotte Perrin (Cambridge: Harvard University Press, 1916), *Antony* 75.3.

41. Ammianus, 20.5.10.

42. Ibid., 25.2.3.

CHAPTER TEN

1. Since the groundbreaking article on the subject by Theodor Büttner-Wobst in 1892, there has been little serious questioning of the assumption that Julian was killed by a lucky strike from a Saracen auxiliary who was fighting on the side of the Persians. See "Der Tod des Kaisers Julian," *Philologus* 51 (1892): 561–80.

2. Ammianus, 25.3.1–7.

3. Magnus of Carrhae, FGrH 225 F. *The Roman Eastern Frontier and the Persian Wars (AD 226–363), A Documentary History* (Dodgeon and Lieu), 261.

4. Ephrem Syrus, *Hymns against Julian*, 3.14 and 16.

5. Libanius, Ep. 1220.

6. Ibid., Ep. 1434.

7. Ibid., Ep. 1508.

8. Libanius, Or. 18.268ff.

9. Al-Tabari, 293.

10. Ammianus, 25.10.7.

11. Ioannis Malalae, *Chronographia,* edited by Ioannes Thurn (Berlin: de Gruyter, 2000), 13.25.

12. Gautier de Coinci, *Miracles de la Vierge,* vol. 4 (Geneva: Slatkine, 1955), 483–96.

13. Ammianus, 25.6.6.

14. Libanius, Ep. 1187.

15. Ibid., Ep. 1264; cf. Ep. 1430.

16. Libanius, Or. 18.274–5.

17. Gregory of Nazianzus, Or. 5.13.

18. Cedrenus 1.23, Theodoret 3.25, Zonaras 13.13, *Artemii Passio* 69 have Julian berating Christ; Malalas/Magnus of Carrhae FGrH 225 F15, Philostorgius 7.15 have Julian blaming the sun. All cited in *The Roman Eastern Frontier and the Persian Wars,* chapter 9.

19. Cassius Dio, *Roman History,* vol. 8, translated by Earnest Cary (Cambridge: Harvard University Press, 1925), 67.18.

20. Libanius, Or. 24.6.

21. John Lydus, *De mensibus,* 4. *The Roman Eastern Frontier and the Persian Wars,* 253.

22. He is perhaps best known today in scientific circles for preserving the first report of a comet discovered during a solar eclipse on July 19, 418. Philostorgius, 3.8.

23. Philostorgius, 7.15.

24. Libanius, Or. 18.271; Ammianus, 25.3.15–20.

25. Arrian, *The Campaigns of Alexander,* translated by Aubrey de Sélincourt (Harmondsworth: Penguin Books, 1958), 7.27.

26. Thanks to Dr. John Kelt for his invaluable help in giving a medical perspective on Julian's death.

27. Eunapius, Fr. 15.

28. Philostorgius, 7.15.

29. The most significant study to date of Roman field medicine and wounds is to be found in Christine Salazar's invaluable *The Treatment of War Wounds in Graeco-Roman Antiquity* (Leiden: Brill, 2000); see p. 24. Oribasius Coll. Med. L50/4.68.

30. For details of the surgical procedures attempted see John Lascaratos and Dionysios Voros, "Fatal Wounding of the Byzantine Emperor Julian the Apostate: Approach to the Contribution of Ancient Surgery," *World Journal of Surgery* 24 (2000): 615–17.

31. Salazar, *Treatment of War Wounds,* 60.

32. Luke 10:34.
33. Ammianus, 25.3.23.
34. Philostorgius, 7.15.

EPILOGUE

1. Socrates Scholasticus, 3.25.
2. The most easterly excavated site in the Roman Empire is discussed in W. Ball, "Soundings at Seh Qubba, A Roman Frontier Station on the Tigris in Iraq," in *The Eastern Frontier of the Roman Empire,* edited by D. H. French and C. S. Lightfoot (Oxford: British Archaeological Reports, 1989), 7–18.
3. Eunapius, fr. 29.
4. Ephrem Syrus, *Hymns against Julian,* 3.1.
5. Procopius is normally named only as transferring Julian's body, Ammianus 25.9.12, but Philostorgius 8.1 gives the other name. It follows that the former was in charge of the body until the two parts of the army united.
6. Libanius, Ep. 1,220.
7. Libanius, Or. 18.306.
8. Ammianus, 25.10.5.
9. Zosimus 3.34.4 preserves this version, as does the *Greek Anthology* 7.747, which ascribes the epitaph to Libanius. Zonaras 13.13.24 and Cedrenus 1.539.6–9 the one at the head of the chapter.
10. *The Iliad,* 3.179.
11. It is worth mentioning the theory that the Swiss town of Basle is named after Julian's mother. See Werner Portmann, "Zum Namen 'Basilia,'" *Klio* 75 (1993): 383–86.
12. Libanius, Or. 17.7.
13. The two stories were even occasionally put together. They inspired Lorenzo de Medici's short play in 1489 *La Rappresentazione di San Giovanni e Paolo* (The Play of St. John and Paul), in which John and Paul are martyred and then Mercurius kills Julian.
14. Theodoret, 3.11.
15. Hrotsvitha, *The Plays of Roswitha,* translated by Christopher St. John (London: Chatto & Windus, 1923).
16. Petrarch, *Selected Sonnets, Odes and Letters,* translated by Thomas Bergin (Wheeling, Ill.: Harlan Davidson, 1966), Sonnet 57.
17. At the end of January 1076 the German king Henry IV told Pope Gregory VII to leave God to judge him. "For the wisdom of the holy fathers committed even Julian the Apostate not to themselves, but to God alone, to be judged and to be deposed." *Select Historical Documents of the Middle Ages,* translated by Ernest Henderson (London: George Bell & Sons Ltd., 1910), 372. Julian

appears in the thirteenth-century saga of Norway's patron saint—the history of St. Olav—written as part of the *Heimskringla*. Here, referring to the death of Sven Forkbeard: "That same autumn when King Olav came to England, it happened that King Svein [Forked Beard] died suddenly in his bed in the night; and it is said by Englishmen that St. Edmund killed him, in the same way that holy Mercurius killed the apostate Julian." *St. Olav*, 11. Snorri Sturlason, *Heimskringla or the Lives of the Norse Kings* (Cambridge: W. Heffer & Sons, 1932).

18. Hans Sachs, *Julianus der kayser im badt*, in Hans Sachs, *Werke*, edited by A. von Keller and E. Goetze (Tübingen: University of Tübingen, 1870–1908), vol. 13, 110–41.

19. In his three entries for the play on April 29, May 10, and May 20, Henslowe also calls the play *Julian the Apostata* and *Julian Apostata*. Philip Henslowe, *The Diary of Philip Henslowe*, edited by J. Payne Collier (London: Shakespeare Society, 1845).

20. Michel de Montaigne, 2.19.

21. Julian, *The Caesars*, 307A.

22. Ibid., 316C.

23. This was the last time Julian was dragged into mainstream politics. In 1847 the controversial German Protestant theologian David Friedrich Strauss, in "Der Romantiker auf dem Thron der Cäsaren," drew a satirical parallel between the emperor and Frederick William IV of Prussia. More unpalatably, over dinner with SS leaders Heinrich Himmler and Reinhard Heydrich, Adolf Hitler tried to co-opt Julian in his rants against the Church. "The book that contained the reflections of the Emperor Julian should be circulated in millions. What wonderful intelligence, what discernment, all the wisdom of antiquity! It's extraordinary." October 25, 1941. Hugh Trevor Roper, *Hitler's Table Talk 1941–1944* (London: Weidenfeld & Nicolson, 1953), 87.

24. A curiosity is Henry Fielding's *Journey from this World to the Next,* a satirical account written in 1741–42 about the author's journey to Elysium with other recently departed souls. It is a periodically successful attempt to update Lucian's satires and its charm lies in that it is more whimsical in approach than the satires of either Jonathan Swift or Alexander Pope. The middle section tells of the various transmigrations of Julian's soul. Insofar as it reflects any tradition about the emperor it is in his ambiguity. Each episode shows Julian not quite ready for heaven, but not quite bad enough for hell. Rather than distort the facts of the emperor's reign, Fielding chooses to ignore them.

25. Charles de Secondat, Baron de Montesquieu, *The Spirit of Laws*, translated by Thomas Nugent (London: George Bell & Sons Ltd., 1914), 24.10.

26. Edward Gibbon, *The Letters of Edward Gibbon*, edited by J. E. Norton

(London: Cassell & Co., 1956), letter to Dorothea Gibbon, February 24, 1781.

27. Francoise Waquet, *Latin or the Empire of a Sign* (London: Verso, 2002), 38.

28. Algernon Swinburne, *Letters,* edited by Cecil Lang (New Haven: Yale University Press, 1962), letter to Lady Trevelyan, December 10, 1865.

29. As well as the novels cited, see also Giovanni Giuseppe Franco's *Tigrante* (1867) and Dimitri Merezhkovsky's novel *Julian the Apostate* (1896), the first part of his trilogy of historical novels entitled *Christ and Antichrist.*

30. R. Browning, *The Emperor Julian* (Berkeley: University of California Press, 1976), 232.

31. Julian has inspired few composers. Following the success of several operas with a classical theme—for example, his opera *Genesius* is set in the time of Diocletian—the Austrian conductor and composer Felix Weingartner was inspired in 1925 to write *Der Apostat.* It has never been performed. The only other composer to have addressed the theme is the Russian-born Lazare Saminsky, but similarly his *Defeat of Caesar Julian: Christus vinci: Opera in Three Acts and Six Scenes* published in 1959 (though written in the 1930s) remains unrecorded and unperformed.

32. Julian, *Misopogon,* 357A.

33. The 1962 Italian film *Costantino Il Grande (Constantine the Great)* directed by Lionello de Felice is the only celluloid version of that period of Roman history.

34. Julian, Ep. 42.

35. Prudentius, *The Divinity of Christ/Apotheosis,* vol. 1, translated by H. J. Thomson (Cambridge: Loeb Classical Library, 1949), 449–53.

SELECTED
BIBLIOGRAPHY

PRIMARY SOURCES

Julian

A new edition of Julian's writings is long overdue. The most readily accessible edition of his works in English remains the three volumes in the Loeb Classical Library translated by Wilmer Cave Wright (Cambridge, 1913–23) and I have followed her numbering of letters throughout. A far better edition, for those with French, is the Budé edition, *L'Empereur Julien, œuvres complètes,* translated and edited by J. Bidez (Paris, 1924) continued by G. Rochefort and Chr. Lacombrade (Paris, 1963).

For Julian's laws, the best translation is *The Theodosian Code and Novels and the Sirmondian Constitutions,* translated by Clyde Pharr (Princeton, 1952), although there is a useful online version of the Latin text at www.gmu.edu/departments/fld/CLASSICS/theod.html.

For discussion and the history of the Code, see Jill Harries, *Law and Empire in Late Antiquity* (Cambridge: Cambridge University Press, 1999) and John Matthews, *Laying Down the Law: A Study of the Theodosian Code* (New Haven: Yale University Press, 2000).

Ammianus Marcellinus

The most accessible translation of Ammianus's history is that in the Penguin library, translated by Walter Hamilton, with a useful introduction and notes by Andrew Wallace-Hadrill: Ammianus Marcellinus, *The Later Roman Empire (AD 354–378)* (London: Penguin Books, 1986). I have also used the three-volume Loeb Classical Library version, translated by John Rolfe (Cambridge, 1935–38).

It is also worth mentioning the Ammianus Marcellinus Electronic Project, maintained by J. W. Drijvers: http://odur.let.rug.nl/~drijvers/ammianus/.

Commentaries are provided by Joachim Szidat, *Historischer Kommentar zu Ammianus Marcellinus,* vols. 1–3 (Stuttgart: Franz Steiner, 1977–96) who deals specifically with Julian. The massive work started by de Jonge and finished by his colleagues is more useful to linguists, but is still relevant to the historian: P. de Jonge, *Philological and Historical Commentary on Ammianus Marcellinus,* Books XV–XVII (Groningen: Bouma's Boekhius, 1972–7); J. Den Boeft, D. den Hengst, and H. C. Teitler, *Philological and Historical Commentary on Ammianus Marcellinus,* Books XX–XXIII (Groningen: Bouma's Boekhius, 1987–98).

Ammianus is well served in English. To have any understanding of his life and work, John Matthews' *The Roman Empire of Ammianus* (London: Gerald Duckworth & Co., 1989) is essential. It is also worth looking at E. A. Thompson, *The Historical Work of Ammianus Marcellinus* (Cambridge: Cambridge University Press, 1947), and Gary Crump, *Ammianus Marcellinus as a Military Historian* (Wiesbaden: Franz Steiner, 1975), while current thinking on the historian is examined in *The Late Roman World and its Historian: Interpreting Ammianus Marcellinus,* edited by Jan Willem Drijvers and David Hunt (London: Routledge, 1999).

Libanius

The easiest translations of Libanius's work to get hold of are the two volumes of selected orations (Cambridge, 1969, 1971) and two volumes of selected letters (Cambridge, 1992) all translated by A. F. Norman, in the Loeb Classical Library. Also of relevance is *Antioch as a Center of Hellenic Culture as Observed by Libanius* (Liverpool: Liverpool University Press, 2000), also translated by A. F. Norman, which includes Oration 11, *The Antiochikos.* Another good edition of Libanius's letters is *Lettres aux hommes de son temps,* translated and edited by Bernadette Cabouret (Paris, 2000). For consistency's sake I have followed the numbering of Foerster for the letters, as Loeb prints only a small percentage of Libanius's output (a concordance is in Loeb letters, vol. 2, pp. 465–74).

Church Fathers

The majority of the church fathers to comment on Julian are available in the second series of the *Nicene and Post-Nicene Fathers* published at the end of the nineteenth century in New York. Eusebius is volume 1; Socrates Scholasticus and Sozomen are volume 2; Theodoret is volume 3. For Philostorgius, see Sozomen and Philostorgius, *History of the Church,* translated by Edward Walford (London: H. G. Bohn, 1855) in the Bohn Ecclesiastical Library. In the same series Walford also translated Theodoret and Evagrius (London, 1855) and Socrates Scholasticus

(London, 1853). All the above are available online from the Christian Classics Ethereal Library at www.ccel.org/fathers2/.

Gregory of Nazianzus is rather more difficult. Although many of his writings are contained in vol. 7 of the *Nicene and Post-Nicene Fathers,* the book does not include his two speeches against Julian. The easiest edition to find remains that translated by C. W. King, *Julian the Emperor containing Gregory Nazianzen's Two Invectives and Libanius' Monody with Julian's Extant Theosophical Works* (London: Bohn's Classical Library, 1888).

Eunapius

For biographies of many of Julian's colleagues, see Wilmer Cave Wright's translation of Philstratus and Eunapius, *The Lives of the Sophists* (Cambridge: Harvard University Press, 1921). For fragments of Eunapius's lost histories I have followed the text and numbering in R. C. Blockley, *The Fragmentary Classicising Historians of the Later Roman Empire* (Liverpool: F. Cairns, 1983).

Zosimus

The Byzantine historian is badly served in English. By far the best translation and analysis of his writings is F. Paschoud's parallel French/Greek edition in the Budé collection, *Zosime: Histoire nouvelle* (Paris: Budé, 1971), specifically vols. 1 and 2. In English there is Ronald Ridley's translation, though it is rather difficult to track down: *Zosimus: New History* (Sydney: University of Sydney, 1982). Of immeasurable help, despite its flaws, is the Green and Chaplin 1814 edition (no translator is given) available online at www.ccel.org/p/pearse/morefathers/home.html.

Other Sources

Aurelius Victor. *De Caesaribus.* Translated by H. W. Bird. Liverpool: Liverpool University Press, 1994.

Vegetius. *Epitome of Military Science.* Translated by N. P. Milner. Liverpool: Liverpool University Press, 1996.

Collected Works

Samuel Lieu in his four anthologies collates many of the harder-to-find primary sources on Julian's reign. The translations are modern and the notes are comprehensive. *The Emperor Julian: Panegyric and Polemic,* edited by Samuel Lieu (Liverpool: Liverpool University Press, 1986), contains translations of Claudius Mamertinus's *Speech of Thanks,* John Chrysostom's *Homily on St. Babylas,* and Ephrem Syrus's *Hymns against Julian.* The appendices to part 2 also contain a translation of the relevant parts of Libanius Oration 60 on the temple at Daphne. *The Roman Eastern Frontier and the Persian Wars (AD 226–363), A Documentary*

History, edited by Michael Dodgeon and Samuel Lieu (London: Routledge, 1991), contains a translation and annotation of virtually every source needed to understand the Eastern question. Specifically relevant to Julian, *From Constantine to Julian: Pagan and Byzantine Views,* edited by Samuel Lieu and Domenic Monserrat (London: Routledge, 1996), contains translations of Libanius Oration 59 and the *Ordeal of Artemius.* Finally, chapters 1 and 2 of *The Roman Eastern Frontier and the Persian Wars (AD 363–630), A Narrative Sourcebook,* edited by Geoffrey Greatrex and Samuel Lieu (London: Routledge & Kegan Paul, 2002), gives the sources for Jovian's reign, specifically for the peace signed in the East and the fate of Armenia.

BIOGRAPHIES OF JULIAN

Allard, Paul. *Julien l'apostat.* Paris: Victor Lecoffre, 1900–1903.

Athanassiadi, Polymnia. *Julian: An Intellectual Biography.* London: Routledge, 1992.

Bidez, J. *La Vie de l'empereur Julien.* Paris: Les Belles Lettres, 1930.

Bowersock, G. W. *Julian the Apostate.* London: Gerald Duckworth & Co., 1978.

Browning, Robert. *The Emperor Julian.* Berkeley: University of California Press, 1976.

Gardner, Alice. *Julian, Philosopher and Emperor.* London: G. P. Putnam, 1895.

Geffcken, Johannes. *Kaiser Julianus.* Leipzig: Dieterich, 1914.

Giebel, Marion. *Kaiser Julian Apostata: Die Wiederkehr der alten Götter.* Dusseldorf: Artemis & Winkler, 2002.

Negri, Gaetano. *Julian the Apostate.* Translated by Duchess Litta-Visconti-Arese. London: T. Fisher Unwin, 1905.

Ricciotti, Giuseppe. *Julian the Apostate.* Translated by M. J. Costelloe. Milwaukee: Bruce Publishing, 1960.

Smith, Rowland. *Julian's Gods: Religion in the Thought and Action of Julian the Apostate.* London: Routledge, 1995.

SECONDARY SOURCES OF
SPECIFIC RELEVANCE FOR EACH CHAPTER

Chapter One

Alföldi, Andrew. "Some Portraits of Julianus Apostata." *American Journal of Archaeology* 66 (1962): 403–5.

Aujoulat, Noel. "Eusébie, Hélène et Julien: Le Témoignage de Julien." *Historia* 53 (1983): 78–103.

———. "Eusébie, Hélène and Julien: Le Témoignage des historiens." *Historia* 53 (1983): 421–52.

Baldwin, Barry. "Physical Descriptions of Byzantine Emperors." *Byzantion* 51 (1991): 8–21.

Barnes, Timothy. "Imperial Chronology, AD 337–350." *Phoenix* 34 (1980): 160–66.

———. *Constantine and Eusebius*. Cambridge: Harvard University Press, 1981.

———. "Himerius and the Fourth Century." *Classical Philology* 82 (1987): 206–25.

———. *Athanasius and Constantius*. Cambridge: Harvard University Press, 1993.

Baynes, Norman. "The Early Life of Julian the Apostate." *Journal of Hellenic Studies* 45 (1925): 251–54.

Bleckmann, Bruno. "Constantina, Vetranio und Gallus Caesar." *Chiron* 24 (1994): 29–68.

Blockley, R. C. "Constantius Gallus and Julian as Caesars of Constantius II." *Latomus* 31 (1972): 433–68.

Bowder, Diana. *The Age of Constantine and Julian*. London: Routledge & Kegan Paul, 1978.

Bowersock, G. W. "The Emperor Julian on his Predecessors." *Yale Classical Review* 27 (1982): 159–72.

Bregman, Jay. "The Emperor Julian's View of Classical Athens." *Polis and Polemos: Essays on Politics, War, and History in Ancient Greece in Honor of Donald Kagan,* edited by Charles Hamilton and Peter Krentz, 347–61. Claremont: Regina Books, 1997.

Cameron, Averil. *The Later Roman Empire*. London: Routledge, 1993.

Daly, Lloyd. "Roman Study Abroad." *American Journal of Philology* 71 (1950): 40–58.

Drijvers, Jan Willem. "Flavia Maxima Fausta: Some Remarks." *Historia* 41 (1992): 500–506.

Drinkwater, J. F. "The 'Pagan Underground', Constantius II's 'Secret Service', and the Survival, and the Usurpation of Julian the Apostate." In *Studies in Latin Literature and Roman History* III, edited by Carl Deroux, 348–87. Brussels: Latomus, 1983.

———. "The Revolt and Ethnic Origin of the Usurper Magnentius (350–353), and the Rebellion of Vetranio (350)." *Chiron* 30 (2000): 131–59.

Festugière, A. J. "Julien à Macellum." *Journal of Roman Studies* 47 (1957): 53–58.

Frakes, Robert. "Ammianus Marcellinus and Zonaras on a Late Roman Assassination Plot." *Historia* 46 (1997): 121–28.

Gillard, Frank. "The Birth Date of Julian the Apostate." *California Studies in Classical Antiquity* 4 (1971): 147–51.

Hadjinicolaou, Anne. "Macellum, lieu d'exil de l'empereur Julien." *Byzantion* 21 (1951): 15–22.

Head, Constance. "Physical Descriptions of the Emperors in Byzantine Historical Writing." *Byzantion* 50 (1980): 226–40.

Jonas, R. "A Newly Discovered Portrait of the Emperor Julian." *American Journal of Archaeology* 50 (1946): 277–82.

Juneau, J. "Pietas and Politics: Eusebia and Constantius at Court." *Classical Quarterly* 49 (1999): 641–44.

Leedom, J. W. "Constantius II: Three Revisions." *Byzantion* 48 (1978): 132–45.

Maio, Michael di, and Duane Arnold. "Per Vim, Per Caedem, Per Bellum: A Study of Murder and Ecclesiastical Politics in the Year 337 AD." *Byzantion* 62 (1992): 158–211.

Mooney, Robert. "Gallus Caesar's Last Journey." *Classical Philology* 53 (1958): 175–77.

Pohlsander, Hans. "Crispus: Brilliant Career and Tragic End." *Historia* 33 (1984): 79–106.

Thompson, E. A. "Ammianus' Account of Gallus Caesar." *American Journal of Philology* 64 (1943): 302–15.

Tougher, Shaun. "The Advocacy of an Empress: Julian and Eusebia." *Classical Quarterly* 48 (1998): 595–99.

———. "Ammianus Marcellinus on the Empress Eusebia: A Split Personality." *Greece and Rome* 47 (2000): 94–101.

Tränkle, Hermann. "Der Caesar Gallus bei Ammian." *Museum Helveticum* 33 (1976): 162–79.

Vanderspoel, John. *Themistius and the Imperial Court.* Ann Arbor: University of Michigan Press, 1995.

———. "Correspondence and Correspondents of Julius Julianus." *Byzantion* 69 (1999): 396–478.

Whitby, Michael. "Images of Constantius." In *The Late Roman World and its Historian: Interpreting Ammianus Marcellinus,* edited by Jan Willem Drijvers and David Hunt. London: Routledge, 1999.

Woods, David. "Where did Constantine I Die?" *Journal of Theological Studies* 48 (1997): 531–35.

Chapter Two

Baldwin, Barry. "The Career of Oribasius." *Acta Classica* 18 (1975): 85–97.

Drinkwater, John. "Julian and the Franks and Valentinian and the Alemanni: Ammianus on Romano-German Relations." *Francia* 24, no. 1 (1997): 1–15.

Elton, Hugh. *Warfare in Roman Europe AD 350–425.* Oxford: Oxford University Press, 1996.

Mackie, Gillian. "A New Look at the Patronage of Santa Costanza, Rome." *Byzantion* 67 (1997): 383–406.

Seager, Robin. "Roman Policy on the Rhine and the Danube in Ammianus." *Classical Quarterly* 49 (1999): 579–605.

Woods, David. "The Fate of the magister equitum Marcellus." *Classical Quarterly* 45 (1995): 266–68.

Chapter Three

Blockley, R. C. "Ammianus Marcellinus on the Battle of Strasburg." *Phoenix* 31 (1977): 218–31.

Curta, Florin. "Atticism, Homer, Neoplatonism and Fürstenspiegel: Julian's Second Panegyric on Constantius." *Greek, Roman and Byzantine Studies* 36 (1995): 177–211.

Hatt, J. J., and Schwartz, J. "Das Schlachtfeld von Oberhausbergen." In *Julian Apostata,* edited by Richard Klein, 318–30. Darmstadt: Wiss Buchgesellschaft, 1978.

Woods, David. "On the 'Standard-Bearers' at Strasbourg: Libanius, Or. 18.58–66." *Mnemosyne* 50 (1997): 479–80.

Chapter Four

Buck, David. "Eunapius on Julian's Acclamation as Augustus." *Ancient History Bulletin* 7.2 (1993): 73–80.

Kaegi, W. E. *Army, Society and Religion in Byzantium,* chapter 3. London: Variorum, 1982.

Nixon, C. E. V. "Aurelius Victor and Julian." *Classical Philology* 86 (1991): 113–25.

Painter, K. S. "The Mildenhall Treasure: A Reconsideration." *British Museum Quarterly* 37 (1973): 154–80.

Rosen, Klaus. "Beobachtungen zur Erhebung Iulians 360–61 n, Chr." In *Julian Apostata,* edited by Richard Klein, 409–47. Darmstadt: Wiss. Buchges., 1978.

Chapter Five

Barnes, T. E. "A Law of Julian." *Classical Philology* 69 (1974): 288–91.

Bradbury, Scott. "The Date of Julian's Letter to Themistius." *Greek, Byzantine and Roman Studies* 28 (1987): 235–51.

Dilke, O. A. W. *Greek and Roman Maps.* London: Thames & Hudson, 1985.

Wilson, Peter. *Cataractonium: A Roman Town and its Hinterland.* York: Council for British Archaeology, 2002.

Chapter Six

Downey, Glanville. *Ancient Antioch.* Princeton: Princeton University Press, 1963.

Liebeschuetz, J. H. W. G. *Antioch: City and Imperial Administration in the Later Roman Empire.* Oxford: Oxford University Press, 1972.

Chapter Seven

Adler, Michael. "The Emperor Julian and the Jews." In *The Jews of Palestine: A Political History from the Bar Kokhba War to the Arab Conquest,* by Michael Avi-Yonah. Oxford: Oxford University Press, 1976. First published in *Jewish Quarterly Review* 5 (1893): 591–651.

Avi-Yonah, Michael. "Greek Inscriptions from Ascalon, Jerusalem, Beisan and Hebron." *Quarterly of the Department of Antiquities in Palestine* 10 (1944): 160–69.

Baldwin, Barry. "The Caesares of Julian." *Klio* 60 (1978): 449–66.

Bradbury, Scott. "Julian's Pagan Revival and the Decline of Blood Sacrifice." *Phoenix* 49 (1995): 331–56.

Brock, Sebastian. "The Rebuilding of the Temple under Julian: A New Source." *Palestine Exploration Quarterly* 108 (1976): 103–7.

Downey, Glanville. "The Economic Crisis at Antioch under Julian the Apostate." In *Studies in Roman Economic and Social History in Honor of Allan Chester Johnson,* edited by Coleman-Norton. Princeton: Princeton University Press, 1951.

Gleason, Maud. "Festive Satire: Julian's *Misopogon* and the New Year at Antioch." *Journal of Roman Studies* 76 (1986): 106–19.

Haas, Christopher. "The Alexandrian Riots of 356 and George of Cappadocia." *Greek, Roman and Byzantine Studies* 32 (1991): 281–301.

Hardy, Cameron. "The Emperor Julian and the School Law." *Church History* 37 (1968): 131–43.

Murray, Gilbert. *Five Stages of Greek Religion.* London: Watts & Co., 1935.

Negev, Avraham. "An Inscription of the Emperor Julian at Ma'ayan Barukh." *Israel Exploration Journal* 19 (1969): 170–73.

Nicholson, Oliver. "The Pagan Churches of Maximin Daia and Julian the Apostate." *Journal of Ecclesiastical History* 45 (1994): 1–10.

Pack, Roger. "Notes on the Caesars of Julian." *Transactions of the American Philological Association* 77 (1946): 151–57.

Sivan, Hagith. "Who was Egeria? Piety and Pilgrimage in the Age of Gratian." *Harvard Theological Review* 81 (1980): 59–72.

———. "Holy Land Pilgrimage and Western Audiences: Some Reflections on Egeria and her Circle." *Classical Quarterly* 38 (1988): 528–35.

Vanderspoel, John. "Julian and the Mithraic Bull." *Ancient History Bulletin* 12.4 (1998): 113–19.

Wilkinson, John. *Egeria's Travels*. London: SPCK, 1971.

Woods, David. "Grain Prices at Antioch Again." *Zeitschrift für Papyrologie und Epigraphik* 134 (2001): 233–38.

Chapter Eight

Barnes, T. D. "Constantine and the Christians of Persia." *Journal of Roman Studies* 75 (1985): 126–36.

Baynes, Norman. "Rome and Armenia in the Fourth Century." *English Historical Review* 25 (1910): 625–43.

Blockley, R. C. "Ammianus Marcellinus on the Persian Invasion of AD 359." *Phoenix* 42 (1988): 244–60.

———. "Constantius II and Persia." In *Studies in Latin Literature and Roman History* V. Edited by Carl Deroux. Brussels: Latomus Revue, 1989.

Bowra, C. M. "EIPATE TOI BASILEI." *Hermes* 87 (1959): 426–35.

Burgess, R. W. "The Date of the First Siege of Nisibis and the Death of James of Nisibis." *Byzantion* 69 (1999): 7–17.

Cameron, Averil. "Agathias and Cedrenus on Julian." *Journal of Roman Studies* 53 (1963): 91–94.

Ghirshman, Roman. *Persian Art: 249 BC–AD 651, The Parthian and Sassanian Dynasties*. New York: Golden Press, 1962.

Hewson, R. H. "The Successors of Tiradates the Great: A Contribution to the History of Armenia in the Fourth Century." *Revue des études arméniennes* 13 (1978–9): 99–126.

Lightfoot, C. S. "Facts and Fiction—the Third Siege of Nisibis." *Historia* 37 (1988): 105–25.

MacDermot, B. C. "Roman Emperors in Sassanian Reliefs." *Journal of Roman Studies* 44 (1954): 76–80.

Sykes, Percy. *A History of Persia*. London: Macmillian, 1930. This book is old-fashioned but provides a useful narrative.

Thompson, E. A. "The Last Delphic Oracle." *Classical Quarterly* 40 (1946): 35–37.

Yarshater, Ehsan, ed. *The Cambridge History of Iran: Volume 3 (1). The Seleucid, Parthian and Sassanian Periods*. Cambridge: Cambridge University Press, 1983.

Chapter Nine

Chalmers, Walter. "Eunapius, Ammianus Marcellinus and Zosimus on Julian's Persian Expedition." *Classical Quarterly* 54 (1960): 152–60.

Dillemann, L. "Ammien Marcellin et les pays de l'Euphrate et du Tigre." *Syria* 38 (1961): 87–157.

Fornara, Charles. "Julian's Persian Expedition in Ammianus and Zosimus." *Journal of Hellenic Studies* 111 (1991): 1–15.

Kaegi, Walter. "Challenges to Late Roman and Byzantine Military Operations in Iraq." *Klio* 73 (1991): 586–94.

Kennedy, D. L. "Ana on the Euphrates in the Roman Period." *Iraq* 48 (1986): 103–4.

Killick, R., and M. Roaf. "Excavations in Iraq 1981–82." *Iraq* 45 (1983): 202–3.

Musil, Alois. *The Middle Euphrates: A Topographical Itinerary.* New York: American Geography Society, 1927.

Ridley, R. T. "Three Notes on Julian's Persian Expedition." *Historia* 22 (1973): 317–30.

Woods, David. "The Role of the Comes Lucillianus during Julian's Persian Expedition." *Antiquité Classique* 67 (1998): 243–48.

Wylie, Graham. "How did Trajan Succeed in Subduing Parthia where Mark Antony Failed?" *Ancient History Bulletin* 4.2 (1990): 37–43.

Chapter Ten

Azarnoush, Massoud. "Le Mort de Julien l'Apostat selon les sources iraniennes." *Byzantion* 61 (1991): 322–29.

Baynes, Norman. "The Death of Julian the Apostate in a Christian Legend." *Journal of Roman Studies* 27 (1937): 22–29.

Büttner-Wobst, Theodor. "Der Tod des Kaisers Julian." *Philologus* 51 (1892): 561–80.

Hahn, Istvan. "Der ideologische Kampf um den Tod Julians des Abtrünnigen." *Klio* 38 (1960): 225–32.

Lascaratos, John, and Dionysios Voros. "Fatal Wounding of the Byzantine Emperor Julian the Apostate (361–363 A.D.): Approach to the Contribution of Ancient Surgery." *World Journal of Surgery* 24 (2000): 615–19.

Salazar, Christine. *The Treatment of War Wounds in Graeco-Roman Antiquity.* Leiden: Brill Press, 2000.

Epilogue

Allen, Walter. "The Last Pagan, *Julian* by Gore Vidal," *New York Review of Books* (July 30, 1964): 20–21.

Ball, W. "Soundings at Seh Qubba, a Roman frontier station on the Tigris in Iraq." In *The Eastern Frontier of the Roman Empire,* edited by D. H. French and C. S. Lightfoot, 7–18. Oxford: *British Archaeological Reports,* 1989.

Blockley, R. C. "The Romano-Persian Peace Treaties of AD 299 and 363." *Florilegium* 6 (1984): 28–49.

Downey, Glanville. "The Tombs of the Byzantine Emperors at the Church of the Holy Apostles in Constantinople." *Journal of Hellenic Studies* 79 (1959): 27–51.

Ehling, Kay. "Der Ausgang des Perserfeldzuges in der Münzpropaganda des Jovian." *Klio* 78 (1996): 186–91.

Findlay, L. M. "The Art of Apostasy: Swinburne and the Emperor Julian." *Victorian Poetry* 28 (1990): 69–78.

Greatrex, Geoffrey. "The Background and Aftermath of the Partition of Armenia in AD 387." *Ancient History Bulletin* 14.1–2 (2000): 35–48.

Grierson, Philip. "The Tombs and Obits of the Byzantine Emperors (337–1042)." *Dumbarton Oaks Papers* 16 (1962): 1–63.

Heather, Peter. "Ammianus on Jovian." In *The Late Roman World and its Historian,* edited by J. W. Drijvers and D. Hunt. London: Routledge, 1999.

Lascaratos, John, and Spyros Marketos. "The Carbon Monoxide Poisoning of Two Byzantine Emperors." *Clinical Toxicology* 36 (1998): 103–7.

Lenski, Noel. "The Election of Jovian and the Role of the Late Imperial Guards." *Klio* 82 (2000): 492–515.

Maio, Michael di. "Transfer of the Remains of the Emperor Julian from Tarsus to Constantinople." *Byzantion* 48 (1978): 43–50.

Mango, Cyril. "Three Imperial Byzantine Sarcophagi Discovered in 1751." *Dumbarton Oaks Papers* 16 (1962): 397–404.

Nicholson, Oliver. "The Corbridge Lanx and the Emperor Julian." *Britannia* 26 (1995): 312–15.

Portmann, Werner. "Zum Namen 'Basilia.'" *Klio* 75 (1993): 383–86.

Seager, Robin. "Ammianus and the Status of Armenia in the Peace of 363." *Chiron* 26 (1996): 275–84.

Wind, Edgar. "Julian the Apostate at Hampton Court." *Journal of the Warburg and Courtauld Institutes* 3 (1939–40): 127–37.

Wirth, Gerhard. "Jovian. Kaiser und Karikatur." In *Vivarium: Festschrift für Theodor Klauser zum 90. Geburtstag,* 353–84. Munster: Aschendorff, 1984.

INDEX

Note: *Italic* page numbers refer to maps. Numbers in brackets preceded by *n* are note numbers, followed by chapter numbers (*ch*) where necessary. All writings are by Julian, except where indicated. Some entries are in chronological order, where appropriate.

249